U. S. SENATORS AND THEIR WORLD

By

DONALD R. MATTHEWS

With a new Introduction

The Norton Library

W·W·NORTON & COMPANY·INC·

NEW YORK

To Maggie, Molly and Jonathan

Copyright © 1973 by W. W. Norton & Company, Inc.
Copyright © 1960 by The University of North Carolina Press

First published in the Norton Library 1973
by arrangement with The University of North Carolina Press

Books That Live
The Norton imprint on a book means that in the publisher's
estimation it is a book not for a single season but for the years.
W. W. Norton & Company, Inc.

Library of Congress Cataloging in Publication Data
Matthews, Donald R.
    U.S. Senators and their world.
    (The Norton library)
    Reprint of the 1960 ed. published by University
of North Carolina Press, Chapel Hill.
    Includes bibliographical references.
    1. United States. Congress. Senate.
I. Title.
[JK1161.M35   1973]   328.73′07′1   73-9805
ISBN 0-393-00679-4

PRINTED IN THE UNITED STATES OF AMERICA
1 2 3 4 5 6 7 8 9 0

Introduction
to the Norton Library Edition

CERTAINLY, if I were to write or even revise *U.S. Senators and Their World* today, it would be a very different book—even if the Senate had not changed at all. The Senate it describes was the Senate of Robert Taft, William Knowland, and Eugene Millikin; of Walter George, Richard Russell, Carl Hayden and Lyndon Johnson. Harry Truman and then Dwight Eisenhower occupied the White House. As my personal observation of the Senate and senators came to an end, John Kennedy was quietly gearing-up his bid for the presidency; Vice-President Richard Nixon was busily trying to become Ike's heir-apparent. The big issues of the time were labor-management relations (The Taft-Hartley Act and its revision), the alleged threat to internal security from communist agents and "subversives," the Cold War and Korea, corruption and "chroney-ism."

U.S. Senators and Their World is a product of the 1950's in still another way. At the time it was written, the "behavioral revolution" in political science was in its early stages. Behavioralists were dedicated to a more scientific, value-free and quantitative study of politics than their elders. Many, certainly I was among them, had been heavily influenced by recent developments in structural-functional sociology and anthropology. Only a small handful of behaviorally-oriented political scientists had set foot on Capitol Hill before I began my research there: most of their work was published too late to have any influence on *U.S. Senators and Their World*. The strengths and weaknesses of this book are best understood when set within this intellectual climate and the primitive state of research on Congress at that time.

The late E. E. Scattschneider used to say that most academicians spend the bulk of their careers defending their first book. I have sought to avoid this trap in the past and do not intend to fall into it now. Nevertheless, those who read this book in the 1970's deserve some guidance in sorting-out what is now history from what remains Senate reality.

While I have not conducted the substantial research required to answer this question definitively, I believe this book is much less dated, generally speaking, than the wholesale change in names, faces and issues since the late 1950's seems to imply. Like other institutions, the Senate resists change. The sociological-anthropological orientation I adopted in trying to make some sense of what I saw and heard there led me to focus on informal but persistent patterns of behavior, unwritten rules and expectations, which are less amenable to rapid change than formal and legal arrangements. The book proposes a way of looking at the Senate which was then quite new; it is not the only way, or necessarily the best way to study legislatures, but this implicit methodological message is timeless.

Nonetheless, several potentially significant changes in the Senate seem to be underway. First of all, the Senate has become the most advantageous position (save the office of Vice-President) from which to launch a bid for the presidency. All the major party nominees since 1960, and most of their less successful competitors, have been senators or former senators. If this trend persists, and there are good reasons for believing that it will, it should have profound effects on the recruitment of new members to the Senate, the internal life of the chamber, and presidential-congressional relationships. Contemporary senators not only become presidential candidates, they also play an appreciable role in the creation and popularization of new issues and policies. The impact of reform proposals first suggested by Senate liberals in the 1950's on President Johnson's Great Society programs and the importance of a few senators in spreading and legitimizing opposition to the Viet Nam War are examples of what I have in mind. This aspect of the Senate is scarcely touched upon in *U.S. Senators and Their World,* largely, I suspect, because my intellectual orientation at that time directed attention elsewhere. The maintenance needs of the institution received more, and the policy and decision-making roles of senators received a great deal less, emphasis that I would give them today. Finally today's Senate is less dominated by southern patriarchs then when I studied it. The growing strength of southern Republicanism, the emergence of a significant black vote in the region, and the grim facts of the mortality tables have taken their toll of the men who once set the style and controlled legislative power in the chamber. Today's younger senators from below the Potomac—less senior and secure, by no means all Democrats—are unlikely to run the show as their predecessors did.

Thus the Senate changes, as do intellectual fashions in studying it. So far *U.S. Senators and Their World* has survived both developments pretty well. At some point, it will be superseded by more contemporary analysis. But even when that time arrives, I shall remain proud of *U.S. Senators and Their World* and pleased that it was still read almost fifteen years after its original publication.

D. R. M.
Washington, D.C.
February, 1973

Preface

THIS IS A BOOK about present-day United States senators, who they are, how they behave, and why they behave the way they do. It is not an "inside story" of the Senate, at least not in the lurid, "now it can be told" tradition. It is neither an attack nor a defense of the chamber and its ways. It is merely a description and an explanation.

This is a very large undertaking. I have worked on this book—at first without realizing it and then with many interruptions—since 1950. And yet, even after all these years, this book is often impressionistic, and always tentative and exploratory. It will take a generation or more of intensive and systematic work by many students of legislative behavior before the questions with which this book deals can be answered in a reasonably scientific fashion. In the meantime, imprecise and provisional findings are better than none.

While the purpose of this book is serious and scholarly, I hope that it is not dull. The Senate is an exciting place, full of drama, conflict, and history. No description of the senators' world is complete which does not capture at least some of this atmosphere. Moreover, since the scientific study of legislative behavior is so new, a book on the behavior of United States senators provides a rare opportunity for the social scientist to communicate directly to interested laymen. Specialized vocabularies and highly technical research techniques serve, in more highly developed areas of social and political research, as barriers to such communication at the same time that they contribute to greater rigor and precision in analysis. These aides to analysis but impediments to communication scarcely exist for students of legislative behavior. I have therefore sought to take advantage of this disadvantage and to write a book that would be of interest to laymen as well as my fellow scholars.

This book is based largely upon interviews with United States senators, Senate staff members, lobbyists, and Washington journalists. I have learned most of what I know from them, and I wish to take this opportunity publicly to thank them for giving so freely of their time and insight. I am not at liberty to list their names here; I merely hope that they realize that my respect, affection, and gratitude are no less deep for having to be expressed in this manner.

I would like to thank the Social Science Research Council, the Elizabeth Edwards Chase Fund of Smith College, the University Research Council, and the Political Behavior Committee of the University of North Carolina for their financial support of this study. I wish also to acknowledge my indebtedness to the Ford Foundation for a grant under its program for assisting American university presses in the publication of works in the humanities and the social sciences.

A number of colleagues were kind enough to give me advice and encouragement at various times during the course of my research. My greatest debts are to Richard C. Snyder, Melvin M. Tumin, and David B. Truman who were extraordinarily helpful during the initial stages of my work. Others who served, sometimes quite unwittingly, as sounding-boards, critics, and advisors were Earl Latham, Robert K. Merton, Herbert Hyman, Richard Neustadt, Pendleton Herring, Stephen K. Bailey, John Eberhardt, James W. Prothro, Frederic Cleaveland, Alexander Heard, Andrew Scott, Benjamin Walter, Roy Pierce, John Chapman, and the late Michael Olmsted. Lewis A. Dexter, Charles Gilbert, Duncan MacRae, Jr., and H. Douglas Price kindly permitted me to read their unpublished manuscripts on Congressional behavior. None of these men, of course, are in any way responsible for the errors of fact and judgment which I have made.

Barbara Harding, Burton Onstine, and Lewis Bowman were careful yet imaginative research assistants; Margaret Taylor gave me sorely needed editorial advice; Mary Scroggs translated my rough sketches into finished drawings; Dorothy Templeton and Pat Rodgers typed innumerable drafts of the manuscript with unusual efficiency. The staff of the University of North Carolina Press contributed to the manuscript in many ways. Thank you each and every one.

I am also indebted to the following for permission to quote at length from copyrighted material:

Harper and Brothers, Publishers: "Personal and Otherwise," *Harper's Magazine*, February, 1955.

The Johns Hopkins Press: Stanley Kelley, *Professional Public Relations and Political Power* (1956).

The New York Times: March 18, 1957, issue.

Drew Pearson: "Confessions of 'an S.O.B.,'" *Saturday Evening Post*, November 24, 1956.

The World Publishing Company: F. Crissey, *Theodore E. Burton: American Statesman* (1956).

Portions of this work originally appeared in the *Public Opinion Quarterly*, Vol. XVIII (1954), and the *American Political Science Review*, Vol. LIII (1959) and are used here with their permission. Congressional Quarterly, Inc. has kindly permitted me to make extensive use of the invaluable data contained in their *Congressional Quarterly Almanac* and *Weekly Report*.

This is hardly the time, place, or manner fully to express my gratitude to my wife and children who have lived through the prolonged pangs of authorship with admirable tolerance and understanding. The dedication of this book to them is more than a token of affection, it is also a recognition of their partnership in its creation.

D. R. M.
Chapel Hill, North Carolina
March, 1960

Contents

Tables

Figures

U. S. Senators and Their World

No man is allowed to be judge in his own cause, because his interest would certainly bias his judgment, and, not improbably, corrupt his integrity. With equal, nay with greater reason, a body of men are unfit to be both judges and parties at the same time; yet what are many of the most important acts of legislation, but so many judicial determinations, not indeed concerning the rights of single persons, but concerning the rights of large bodies of citizens? And what are the different classes of legislators but advocates and parties to the causes which they determine?

James Madison, *The Federalist,* No. 10

It is said to be necessary, that all classes of citizens should have some of their own number in the representative body, in order that their feelings and interests may be the better understood and attended to. But we have seen that this will never happen under any arrangement that leaves the votes of the people free. Where this is the case, the representative body, with too few exceptions to have any influence on the spirit of the government, will be composed of landholders, merchants, and men of the learned professions. But where is the danger that the interests and feelings of the different classes of citizens will not be understood or attended to by these three descriptions of men?

Alexander Hamilton, *The Federalist,* No. 35

CHAPTER I

Introduction

THE KLIEG LIGHTS are on in the crowded caucus room. At one end of the large marble room, a handful of middle-aged men sit behind a mahogany table cluttered with microphones, electrical wires, and water glasses. Some are shuffling through stacks of papers, others are shaking hands, laughing and talking with one another. One whispers seriously into the ear of an assistant. Reporters drift into the room, pick up some mimeographed handouts and yellow paper near the door, then find seats at the crowded press tables flanking the witness chair. Finally, the chairman, a short, muscular man, brings some order with his gavel. A witness is called, sworn, and seated in the witness chair. The TV cameras swing, relentlessly bringing him into focus. Newspaper photographers crowd around. The glare is punctuated by the bright pop of flash bulbs. The witness begins to perspire.

The hearing drones into action. Some of the audience leaves. Suddenly the tone changes. The chairman asks a question; the witness refuses to answer, claiming constitutional privilege. The chairman orders the witness to answer. The witness tensely refuses. The chairman glowers and, with an air of exasperated patience, begins to lecture the witness. He is a "fifth-amendment Communist," a "dupe," a "tool of traitors," an "unwitting handmaid of the Communist conspiracy." Before he is through, the chairman is shouting.

The newsmen rush from the room to write their stories—as usual the story broke just in time to make the afternoon edition. Messengers dressed in black leather jackets, boots, and goggles leave for their motorcycles carrying the films of the episode. That evening millions of Americans see the ugly incident on their television screens. Is this the Senate of the United States?

Every year thousands come to see for themselves. Most of the tourists pour into the gallery shortly after noon. The chamber is as it should be—the neat semicircle of Victorian desks, the red carpet, the snuff boxes, the gawky page boys. But everything else is wrong. One man, evidently a senator, reads from a typescript with all the feeling of a man who has never seen it before. Only two or three other members are in attendance and none of them appears to be listening. At the dais, where the tourists know the vice-president should be sitting, is an unfamiliar man reading his mail. The lone newsman in the large press gallery yawns conspicuously. Finally the speaker finishes his sing-song recital, picks up his papers, and hurries out of the chamber. Another man begins to read another speech on an entirely different subject. Is this "the greatest deliberative body in the world"?

It is near the close of a long, hot session. The solons have long since decided to adjourn and go home. Then one of them begins to talk. As night approaches, his voice becomes an inaudible croak. He begins to totter for he is not permitted to sit down or lean upon his desk and he is not young. If too many of the other men leave the room, the speaker demands a quorum. Bells ring throughout the Capitol and the absent members slowly return to the chamber. The call permits him to rest his rasping voice for half an hour. So some members remain in the chamber while others stretch out on the couches in the cloakrooms or sleep on folding cots set up nearby. And the man keeps on talking. Finally, after interminable hours of mumbled words, the one man talkathon ends. Is this the most powerful democratic legislature in the world?

Almost all the members are there. A dozen or so assistants tensely line the rear walls of the chamber. The press and visitors' galleries are jammed in anticipation. A white-haired man rises from a seat near the front and begins to speak. Everyone listens. As he talks—the style is old-fashioned, the accent clearly Southern—his voice, at first tentative, grows until it booms forth loud and rich with emotion. The closing of the speech is once again pianissimo. For a moment there is silence, and then a brief flurry of forbidden applause. Is *this* the United States Senate?

The answer is yes. All of these are the United States Senate: a legislative chamber of imposing power which sometimes finds it impossible to act; an institution heavy with tradition whose members occasionally act like school boys on a spree; a group of men with far more than their share of wisdom who sometimes act like knaves and fools; an organization with an unequaled opportunity to educate and lead the people which, at times, has served as an awesome engine of oppression. Yes, this is the Senate of the United States, the legislative body which proudly calls itself the greatest deliberative body in the world. And, yes, this probably is the most powerful and independent legislative chamber in the world.

THE POWER OF THE SENATE

The United States Senate came into existence as a result of a political deal. The constitutional convention of 1787 was deadlocked by conflict between the small and the large states. The small states demanded equal representation in the Congress as the price of union. The larger states argued, just as cogently, that the states should be represented according to population. The Founding Fathers settled for both, the political log jam was broken, and the Senate came into being as a result of the bargain.

At first, the role of this inelegantly conceived upper house of Congress was not at all clear. Some of the framers expected it to become an advisory council to the president; others thought it would serve primarily as a protector of the states; still others, as a guardian of the "rich and well born." For a time, the Senate was clearly overshadowed, both in power and prestige, by the more popular House of Representatives.

As the nation increased in size, so, proportionally, did the House, while the Senate remains to this day an intimate legislative body. The development of a democratic party system, which needed patronage for the indirect compensation of party workers, magnified the import of the Senate and senators, for they were to "advise and consent" to the presidents on federal appointments. As America emerged from its adolescent isolation to play a major part in world politics, the Senate's power over treaty making took on new importance. The long six-year terms and the leisureliness and informality of the smaller body made responsible debate easier in the Senate than in the House. All these things served as powerful attractions to able and ambitious politicians. The Senate became the dominant chamber in the American Congress.

Of course, the Senate does not possess a monopoly of political power in America. The framers of the American system of government feared the concentration of political power and designed a government of "separation of powers" and "checks and balances" in which neither the president, the Congress, nor the courts could rule without the co-operation or consent of the others. The political balance among these agencies of government is far from stable: at some times a strong president is able to dominate the Congress and at others the Congress is able to reduce the presidency to little more than a servant of its will. The long-run trend has been toward greater executive power. A modern urban-industrial society like that in America "has required [political] decisions that in their sheer number, detail, prerequisite knowledge, and dispatch cannot be made by legislatures."[1] But even so, the Senate of the United States has been able to maintain a position of great power and prestige compared to that of other democratic legislative bodies.

Americans have never been entirely happy about the Senate's unusual power. Its almost incredible system of representation, the filibuster, the chamber's fondness for seniority, its sometimes controversial role in making presidential appointments and ratifying treaties, its ability to launch and sustain investigations with brutal consequences, its tolerance of demagoguery—all of these things have concerned thoughtful Americans for a long time.[2]

THE SENATE IN THE POSTWAR ERA

Americans were never more critical of the United States Senate than in the years which followed the close of World War II. These were trying years, as everyone who lived through them knows. After a generation of never-ending crises, the people were anxious to return

1. R. A. Dahl and C. E. Lindblom, *Politics, Economics and Welfare* (New York: Harper and Brothers, 1953), p. 320.

2. On the equal representation of the states in the Senate see G. E. Baker, *Rural versus Urban Political Power* (Garden City: Doubleday and Company, Inc., 1955), Ch. 5. The filibuster is analyzed in F. L. Burdette, *Filibustering in the Senate* (Princeton: Princeton University Press, 1940). The seniority system of selecting committee chairmen is almost universally deplored in the literature. See, for example, James M. Burns, *Congress on Trial* (New York: Harper and Brothers, 1949). The Senate's role in making federal appointments is critically analyzed by J. P. Harris in his *The Advice and Consent of the Senate* (Berkeley: University of California Press, 1953). The Senate's investigatory power, its use and abuse, is thoroughly dissected in T. Taylor, *Grand Inquest* (New York: Simon and Shuster, 1955). H. H. Wilson, *Congress: Corruption and Compromise* (New York: Rinehart and Company, 1951), critically discusses the Senate's ethical code and failure to discipline its own members. The best existing defense of the Senate is in Lindsay Rogers, *The American Senate* (New York: Alfred A. Knopf, 1926).

to "normalcy," but "normalcy" stubbornly refused to return. The perennial bread-and-butter problems—who should pay for government, who should benefit from its services, the relations between labor and management, the husbanding of our natural resources, and so on— were still with us, accentuated by the strains of war, inflation, and years of temporizing. In the cities, the nation's minority groups were moving up the social ladder, seeping into the suburbs. America faced a crisis in racial and ethnic toleration that common adversity, depression, and war previously had managed to blur. In a world in which millions starved, Americans faced an ironic crisis of agricultural abundance. A more or less permanent inflation threatened to erode the old, tried and true values of thrift and financial responsibility. Abroad, things were even more unsettling. The "Cold War"—a state of semi-violent competition between the Soviet Union and the West so novel that a new phrase had to be coined to describe it—demanded heavy sacrifices in money and peace of mind. The Korean War took a heavy toll of American lives, and for what end? Then, too, there was the threat of internal communism. Who would have thought that an Alger Hiss or a Judith Coplan might be a spy? Lurking always in the wings was the possibility of nuclear war and the obliteration of civilization. America was ripe for leadership or demagoguery in the postwar years. The Senate provided more than its share of both.

This book is about the Senate during the postwar years. It is not a history, nor is it an analysis of the chamber's formal organization and procedures. Rather this book is about the people who served in the Senate during the critical years between 1947 and 1957 and how they behaved.[3]

This approach is a departure from the traditional ways of studying the Senate or, for that matter, any other legislative chamber. Historians have brilliantly described the Senate's evolution and development;[4] political scientists have studied the chamber's formal organization and procedure in painstaking detail.[5] Neither type of study, however, is particularly concerned with "human factors" in the Senate; in both, "the standard procedure is to take the legal formalities as the theme and treat everything else as variation."[6] Biographers and

3. The membership of the Senate between 1947 and 1957 is listed in Appendix A.
4. See especially G. H. Haynes, *The Senate of the United States* (2 vols.; Boston: Houghton Mifflin Company, 1938).
5. For a first-rate, recent example of this kind of analysis, see G. B. Galloway, *The Legislative Process in Congress* (New York: Thomas Y. Crowell Company, 1953).
6. D. B. Truman, *The Governmental Process* (New York: Alfred A. Knopf, 1951), p. 262.

journalists, who are acutely aware that "Congressmen are people with all that that banality implies,"[7] usually deny that it is possible to generalize meaningfully concerning the characteristics and behavior of groups and are therefore content to describe unique individuals and events. Pushed to extremes—and many biographers and journalists do just that—this point of view is absurd: if human behavior was unpredictable and without pattern, life as we know it would be impossible.

Our behavioral perspective[8] leads us to ask somewhat different questions than did the earlier scholars. Who are the United States senators? How did they get there? Why do some men become senators while others do not? Do a senator's personal background and pre-Senate experiences make any difference in how he behaves in office? How do senators define their role? What are their patterns of work? Are there unwritten "rules of the game" in the Senate? If so, do they affect senatorial behavior? Officially, all senators are equal. Yet if the Senate is similar to other groups, some have far more influence than others. What are the patterns of influence in the Senate? Who is influential and why? Senators, of necessity, are thrown into close contact with lobbyists, journalists, constituents, administrators. Can their relations with these "significant others" be described? How much influence do they have on the senators? Why do senators vote the way they do? How do they make up their minds? This list could be very greatly expanded. For when you begin to look at the Senate, not as an institution entombed in an impressive marble building, but as a group of people—with unique features, to be sure, but also with characteristics common to other groups—the number of significant questions to ask becomes almost infinite.

Perhaps one reason these questions have not been asked before is that they are extremely difficult to answer. For the most part, the answers are not to be found in books. The official records of the Senate—the *Congressional Record,* committee hearings and reports, the chamber's rules and precedents—are often not helpful. When the requisite information can be obtained from published sources, it is often at a heavy cost of time and tedium.

7. S. K. Bailey, *Congress Makes a Law* (New York: Columbia University Press, 1950), pp. 189-90.

8. "Behavioral" is a much abused adjective in social science literature. For the contemporary meaning of the word in political science, see the Social Science Research Council's Interuniversity Summer Seminar on Political Behavior, "Research in Political Behavior," pp. 64-82, in H. Eulau, S. J. Eldersveld, and M. Janowitz (eds.), *Political Behavior* (Glencoe, Illinois: Free Press, 1956). This book also contains excellent examples of "behavioral" research by political scientists.

For example, in order to answer a single one of the questions above—who are the senators?—it was necessary to collect biographical materials on 180 men. To do this with the rich detail of the traditional biography would, of course, take a platoon of researchers several generations. Even when one decides to sacrifice depth for generality of understanding, the task of gathering limited biographical information on almost two hundred subjects is an arduous one. Thousands of books, biographical directories, newspaper articles, and magazine stories were consulted, and extensive correspondence proved necessary before a collective portrait of the postwar senators could be drawn.[9]

The questions concerning the internal and informal operations of the Senate are even more difficult to answer. The only way to explore them is through personal observation and interviews. Yet, the Senate is so complex an organization that it can remain largely incomprehensible to some who have spent the better part of a lifetime in and about it.[10] The author spent, all told, about ten months on Capitol Hill watching the senators in operation. During this period, the author sought, in the manner of the anthropologist studying an unfamiliar tribe, totally to immerse himself in the daily life of the Senate. Interviews were held with senators and their staffs. Lobbyists and journalists, whose work brings them into regular contact with the Senate and senators, were also interviewed.[11] While the author did have the considerable advantage of training for this kind of inquiry, it must be recognized that the personal observations, impressions, and interviews which form the main foundation of this book are necessarily limited.

For all these reasons, the picture of the postwar senators' world which appears on these pages is a snapshot rather than a studio portrait. We hope that the reader will find the snapshot, with all its blemishes, better than no picture at all.

A word about the construction of this book. No notes were taken during the Capitol Hill interviews lest their spontaneity be destroyed. The essence of these conversations—captured in extensive notes taken immediately afterwards—are presented in the text as direct quotations. They are, of course, only approximately verbatim. But they do catch much of the flavor of the Senate and Capitol Hill. The reader is asked to indulge the literary license thus taken.

9. For fuller bibliographical details see Appendix B.
10. On the other hand, almost everyone who has spent more than a few days on the Hill *thinks* he knows how the Senate *really* works and is highly articulate about it.
11. More details on the interviewing program are presented in Appendix C.

This book has been written so that it may be read—hopefully with profit and enjoyment—both by general readers and professional students of politics. The layman, whose interest in this book is solely that of learning more about United States senators and how they behave, can safely restrict his attention to the text. Moreover, the major conclusions to be drawn from all tables and figures are summarized in the body of the text and may be skipped as well. But scholars, who must be interested not only in conclusions but how they were arrived at and the evidence upon which they are based, will find an examination of the tables, figures, footnotes, and appendices to be profitable.

CHAPTER II

The Men

"EVER SINCE Webster and Calhoun," one perceptive observer of the American scene has recently observed, "the style in senators has been as rigid, classic and widely recognized as the Washington Monument. Everybody knew what a proper senator was supposed to look like; the mane of white hair sweeping down over his collar, the dignified paunch, the black string tie knotted like a Mississippi gambler's, the frock coat, the broad-brimmed Stetson, the mottled jowls, the countenance of a slightly apprehensive Roman emperor. He had been born in a log cabin; his voice sounded like a church organ with the *vox humana* pulled out; he walked as if he were leading a parade."[1] There is one trouble with this mental image—the classic senator is "gone, wind and all."

The first aim of this book is to create a more accurate and revealing picture of today's United States senators. If we are to understand their behavior we must know who they are; the kinds of experiences they have had; the skills, group loyalties, and prejudices they bring with them into the Senate chamber. "You've got to approach them within the context of their own experience," one Washington lobbyist, himself a former senator, said. "A man doesn't change a whole lot just because he has been elected to the Senate. If he's been a small-town lawyer, or a banker, or a businessman he is going to think and act like one when he gets to the Senate." Actually, things are not quite that simple. Not all small-town lawyers, or bankers, or businessmen think or act the same way, either in or out of the Senate. And, as we

1. "Personal and Otherwise," *Harper's*, CCX (February, 1955), 18.

shall see, a man *is* changed by service in the Senate. Nonetheless, as we shall demonstrate in subsequent chapters, a senator's behavior pattern is set to some degree long before he comes to Washington. Thus in this chapter and the next we shall present a group portrait, a collective biography, of the men and women who served in the postwar Senate. We shall not be entirely content to describe. We shall also try to explain why the senators are the kinds of people they are.

Our story begins on July 7, 1865, when Arthur Capper was born in Garnett, Kansas, a hamlet of about one thousand souls. Capper, the first born of the postwar senators, grew up according to the grand old "log-cabin-to-Capitol-Hill" ideal of American politics. The son of an immigrant, his career included turns as a printer, reporter, editor, farm-journal publisher, governor of Kansas, United States senator, and organizer of the farm bloc. As the Eightieth Congress began, and it was to be his last, he presided over the important Agriculture Committee—a very old man, prosperous, experienced, and more than a little senile.

The years of Capper's career were a period of great national expansion. Arizona, Colorado, Idaho, Montana, Nebraska, Nevada, New Mexico, North Dakota, Oklahoma, South Dakota, Utah, Washington, and Wyoming were admitted to the Union.[2] The population of the United States increased from under 35,000,000 to more than 150,000,000: for every American at Capper's birth there were now four. The country changed from one in which eight out of every ten persons lived in rural areas to one in which most Americans lived in metropolitan areas. The first transcontinental railroad was completed, and the automobile, airplane, radio, and television were invented and came into common use. The nation fought several wars—the last ending with the advent of nuclear weapons and the very real possibility of human self-destruction. The United States changed from an economically underdeveloped nation, standing in the wings of the world political stage, to the most powerful and prosperous nation on earth.

These were the years in which the post-World War II senators grew up. These were the years during which the people of the United States were sifted and sorted until only a relative handful were left to serve in "the greatest deliberative body in the world," the United States Senate.

2. Perhaps this is the time to remind the reader that this book is written as of the 1947-57 period. The admission of Alaska and Hawaii to the Union had not occurred at that time.

Much of this selection took place years before the future senators cast their first ballots or entered their first campaigns or made their first political speeches. During these early decades the opportunity for service in the Senate was substantially reduced for most Americans while the chances of a few were greatly enhanced. And during these same years, the future senators were to gain some of the attitudes and skills so important in determining how later in life they were to face the stark fact of responsibility and power.

AGE AND SEX

Originally, a Senate was an assembly of old men. The description is less apt but not too inappropriate when applied to the upper house of the American Congress today. Article I, Section 3 of the Constitution requires that United States senators be at least thirty years of age. On the whole, during the postwar period, the senators met this age requirement with quite a few years to spare. The "average" senator is in his mid-fifties and was in his late forties or early fifties when first elected or appointed to the chamber (Figure 1). True, a handful became senators while still in their thirties, and a few were over seventy-five before they were elected. We shall try to explain these differences later. For now it is enough to note that a far smaller proportion of the senators are in their thirties than is true for the population, and about the same proportion of senators as ordinary citizens are over sixty-five. It is the late forties and fifties that are "overrepresented"[3] in the "most exclusive gentlemen's club in Washington."

The Senate is indeed a gentlemen's organization: of the 180 persons who served in the United States Senate between January, 1947, and January, 1957, only three were women. Two of these, Eva Bowring and Hazel Abel, served for only a few weeks each. The almost simultaneous deaths of Senators Butler and Wherry, two dominant figures in Nebraska's Republican party, touched off a factional fight during which the Nebraska ladies, both prominent party workers and heavy campaign contributors, were called upon to serve as temporary, compromise senators. No doubt their lack of office-holding experience and political ambitions were among their major qualifications for the job.

Only one woman, Margaret Chase Smith of Maine, served in the Senate for a significant period during the postwar years. The widow

3. The word "overrepresentation" is used here and on the following pages of this book in a statistical sense to mean merely that there is a larger proportion of senators possessing a given attribute than of the American people as a whole. The term should not be taken to imply that members of the Senate *ought* to be exactly like the people they represent.

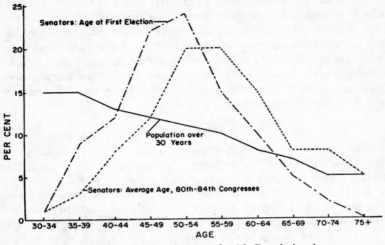

FIG. 1. Age Distribution Compared with Population in 1950

of a state politician and congressman, she was elected to her first public office when she filled the House vacancy caused by her husband's death. After serving four terms in "the other body," she was e'ected to the Senate in 1948—the first, and still the only, woman to have served in both houses of Congress. Her success in the Senate constitutes a major exception to the hoary rule that politics is a man's game, but in another sense, her career underlines the past and present male domination of the Senate. She, like almost all the other women who have served in the Congress, is a widow of a congressman. Few others have been able or willing—as has Mrs. Smith—to launch what amounts to an independent career.[4]

MAINSTREET, MIDDLETOWN, U.S.A.

America was a rural country when most of the postwar senators were born. It is not surprising, then, that a majority of them were born in rural areas. Places like Centerville, South Dakota; Isabel, Illinois; Ten Mile, Pennsylvania; Rising Sun, Delaware; and Honea Path, South Carolina, nurtured more senators than all the cities of the United States combined. While the rural-born are in a clear majority, there are fewer of them than might reasonably be expected. In 1900,

4. See the annual study by the Women's Division, Republican National Committee, entitled "Women in the Public Service" (mimeographed) for the careers of other women congressmen.

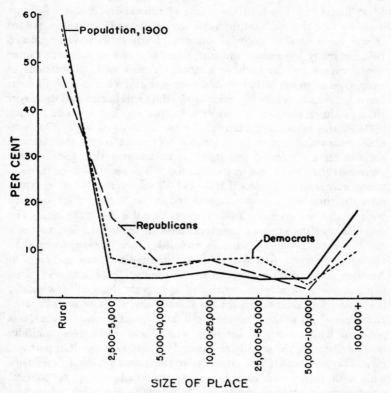

Fig. 2. Size of Birthplaces Compared with Population Distribution in 1900

which is the census year closest to the median birth date of the senators, 60 per cent of the American people lived in rural areas, yet only 52 per cent of the senators were rural-born. While in a minority, the urban-born actually won more than their statistical share of the Senate seats in the period from 1947 to 1957.[5] But there are many varieties of urban places. There is New York and there is Fayetteville, North Carolina; there is Chicago and there is Moorhead, Minnesota. The difference is that between Broadway or Lake Shore Drive and Main Street, Middletown, U.S.A. Our statistical picture indicates that it is

5. This conclusion is based on the assumption that the 1900 urban and rural dwellers had similar birthrates. Since the rural dwellers actually produced more than their share of subsequent generations, the statistical underrepresentation of the rural-born in the Senate is actually larger than the figures in the text indicate.

Main Street that has been the cradle of urban-born senators. Figure 2 shows that the most consistently overrepresented birthplaces ranged in size from 2,500 to 5,000 inhabitants. These small towns produced twice as many Democrats and four times as many Republicans as one might expect on the basis of chance. Towns with populations of from 5,000 to 50,000 in 1900 reared from one and a half to two times as many senators as might be anticipated, while rural areas and the larger cities produced considerably fewer senators than chance would predict.

Why this apparent preference for the small-town boy? One possible explanation might be the equal representation of the states in the Senate, a system of legislative apportionment that greatly overrepresents the rural states in the chamber. The senators born in small towns may tend to be elected from today's relatively rural states; then, since the rural states are overrepresented in the Senate, so are the men with small-town origins. Table 1 shows that this is not the case. The proportion of the senators who were born in small cities and towns is actually greater among senators from the more urban states than among those from rural states. Thus, the smaller towns and cities in America seem peculiarly fecund in the production of senators.[6] Perhaps, as some sociologists argue, this is because the small-town child is exposed to a cross-section of the community, to those both "above" and "below" his position on the social ladder. As a consequence, he is provided with models of behavior which neither the geographically isolated farm nor the socially segmented big city provides. Or, perhaps, men with small-town backgrounds—having some personal familiarity with both urban and rural life—are particularly attractive political representatives of large constituencies which include both urban and rural areas.

No matter what the explanation, the same overrepresentation of the nation's small towns and cities is true for the senators' present-day residences. By 1950, 64 per cent of the American people lived in urban

6. Another way of demonstrating that the overrepresentation of small- and medium-sized towns and cities among the birthplaces of the senators is not merely a reflection of the equal representation of the states in the Senate is to divide the states into groups according to their urban-rural character in 1950 (under 40 per cent, 40-50, 50-60, 60-70, and over 70 per cent urban) and then to determine the population distribution by size of place, within each of these groups of states, for 1900. When the distribution of the senators' birthplaces is compared to the population distribution within each of the five groups of states, it is found that the small- to medium-sized cities and towns are consistently overrepresented among the senators' birthplaces.

The opposite tendency has been found among today's business leaders; they were born in disproportionate numbers in the nation's larger cities. W. L. Warner and Associates, *Big Business Leaders in America* (New York: Harper and Brothers, 1955), pp. 185-87.

Table 1

PERCENTAGE OF HOME STATE POPULATION WHICH WAS URBAN IN 1950
AND SIZE OF BIRTHPLACES

Percentage State Population Urban in 1950	Size of Senators' Birthplaces			
	Rural Areas	Small Cities and Towns	Large Cities	
Under 40%	70%	30%	0	100% (37)
40%–50%	61%	26%	13%	100% (34)
50%–60%	56%	39%	5%	100% (41)
60%–70%	44%	38%	18%	100% (26)
70% plus	26%	45%	29%	100% (40)

NOTE: Rural areas defined as all those places with less than 2,500 population at the census date nearest the senator's birth date; small cities and towns as those with 2,500 to 100,000 populations; and large cities as those with populations over 100,000. The figures in parentheses following 100% in this and all subsequent tables are the number of cases upon which the percentages are based.

areas and 56 per cent in metropolitan areas.[7] The present-day residences of the senators reflect this shift: 86 per cent of the senators have their official residences in urban areas, 41 per cent in metropolitan areas; but most of the urban senators live in the small- and medium-sized cities of the United States (Figure 3). The rural areas and large cities remain underrepresented, and further statistical evidence indicates that this is not merely the consequence of the overrepresentation of rural states in the Senate.[8] Main Street has changed since the turn of the century, but it still supplies far more than its share of United States senators.

CLASS ORIGINS

Despite a widespread preference not to talk about such matters, few observant Americans would deny that individuals in the United States

7. The 1950 census definition of "urban" included all places of 2,500 or more incorporated as cities, boroughs, villages, and towns (except New England), unincorporated places of 2,500, and the densely settled urban fringe (incorporated and unincorporated) around cities of 50,000 or more. A "Standard Metropolitan Area," of which there were 168 in 1950, contains at least one city of 50,000 or more and includes the entire county containing the core city and other contiguous counties considered to be closely integrated economically with that city.

8. The same procedure outlined in footnote 6 was employed to control the effects of the equal representation of the states on the size of the places of residence of the senators. The states were divided into five groups, according to the percentage of their 1950 population residing in urban places. The average 1950 population distribution, by size of place, was then figured for each group and compared to the distribution of residences of the senators from the same group of states. The small- and medium-sized cities and towns were found to be consistently overrepresented among the senators' residences.

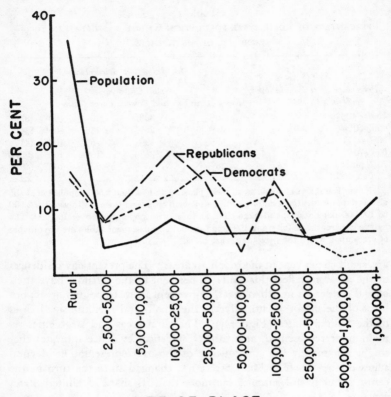

FIG. 3. Size of Residences Compared with Population Distribution in 1950

are ranked or "stratified" on generally accepted scales of social inferiority and superiority. Moreover, most would agree that individuals sharing roughly equal positions in this system of invidious distinctions tend to group into "classes."

But there is still much legitimate confusion about the American class system.[9] Many different criteria of ranking are used—family reputation, occupation, race and ethnic origins, income, religious affiliation, education, power and authority, group and association memberships, style of life, and so on—and an individual may rank high on

9. For a good survey of the literature see R. M. Williams, Jr., *American Society* (New York: Alfred A. Knopf, 1951), Ch. 4.

some and relatively low on others. The relative significance of the various criteria, the number of classes and their boundaries are uncertain, vague, and changeful. Upward and downward mobility are so common that class consciousness and identification are relatively weak. As a result, there is not a very close correspondence between the classes people think they and others belong to (subjective class) and the classes in which an impartial observer would place them on the basis of objective criteria (objective class). Yet despite all these ambiguities and difficulties of analysis, the evidence is overwhelming that classes of some sort exist and have substantial impact on how Americans behave and think and on what their opportunities are. Where do American senators fit into this unsystematic system? What influence has the class system had upon their recruitment? What are the senators' class origins?

The most important single criterion of ranking in the United States seems to be occupation. While it is by no means a certain index to social standing, it is the closest approach to such an infallible guide. Thus information on the occupations of the senators' fathers should provide a reasonably accurate picture of the senators' class origins. Table 2 shows the senators were sons, with only a handful of exceptions, of men possessing upper- and middle-class occupations.[10] The children of low-salaried workers, wage earners, servants, and farm laborers, which together comprised 66 per cent of the gainfully employed in 1900, contributed only 7 per cent of the postwar senators.[11] Only two of the 180 men, Senators Wagner and O'Daniel, were the sons of unskilled, urban wage earners. Wagner's father was a janitor in a New York City tenement; O'Daniel's father was a construction worker.[12] Senator Purtell was the son of a cigarmaker; McNamara, of a shipfitter; Daniel (S.C.), of a millwright; Welker, of a carpenter; Pastore, of a tailor; Cordon and Dirksen, of painters; Payne and Dworshak, of printers; Anderson, of a salesman; Myers, of a bookkeeper; Lennon, of a clerk; Margaret Chase Smith was the daughter of a barber. The remaining senators from urban backgrounds were

10. The occupational-class categories used in this study were first developed by A. H. Hansen, "Industrial Class Alignments in the United States," *Journal of the American Statistical Association*, XVII (December, 1920), 416-25. The criteria of inclusion and exclusion from these categories are presented in this article.

11. The validity of this comparison assumes, of course, that the birthrates of the different occupational classes are the same. Since, as a general rule, the lower the occupational class the higher the birthrate, the disparity in political life-chances was actually greater than these figures indicate.

12. O'Daniel's father was killed in an accident while the future senator was still a small child. His stepfather was a farmer.

sons of professional men, proprietors, or officials. Among the sons of farmers, some were born in relative poverty, yet it is virtually impossible to ascertain this in specific cases. It is still possible to conclude that very few senators were born in working-class and lower-class families. Moreover, the differences in occupational-class origins of Democrats and Republicans are small. Fifty-eight per cent of each party were the sons of either professionals, proprietors, or officials; the remainder, sons of farmers, low-salaried workers, or wage earners.

Table 2

OCCUPATIONAL CLASS DISTRIBUTION OF FATHERS COMPARED
WITH LABOR FORCE IN 1900

Occupational Class	Fathers of Senators	Labor Force in 1900	Index of Over-representation*
Professional	24%	6%	4.0
Proprietors & Officials	35	7	5.0
Farmers	32	22	1.5
Low-salaried Workers	2	5	0.4
Industrial Wage Earners	5	39	0.1
Servants	0	5	0.0
Farm Laborers	0	17	0.0
Unknown	2	0	
	100% (180)	100%	

SOURCE: T. M. Sogge, "Industrial Classes in the United States in 1930," *Journal of the American Statistical Association*, XXVIII (June, 1933), 199-203.

* The "index of overrepresentation" is a way of expressing numerically the relationship between an actual and an expected proportion. If the senators' fathers' occupations had been represented in perfect proportion to their percentages of the 1900 labor force, the index for each occupation would be 1.0. Where the index is greater than 1.0, the occupation is overrepresented; where less than 1.0, underrepresented. See Appendix D.

Within these necessarily broad categories, important differences exist in the occupational origins of the members of the two parties (Table 3). The Democrats were more often the sons of lawyers, doctors, professors, and journalists than were the Republicans; the GOP senators were more often the sons of ministers. Among the sons of proprietors and officials, the Democrats mostly came from families headed by merchants, insurance and real estate agents, construction contractors, and bankers. All the sons of manufacturing executives

Table 3

OCCUPATIONS OF FATHERS, BY PARTY AND "CLASS"

Fathers' Occupations, by "Class"	Democrats	Republicans
Professional	(28%)	(19%)
Lawyer	16%	7%
MD	5	2
Minister	1	6
Professor	1	0
Engineer	1	1
Journalist	1	0
Teacher	1	1
Poet	0	1
Government official	0	1
Proprietor and Official	(30%)	(39%)
Manufacturing executive	0%	3%
Publisher	0	6
Merchant	14	17
Banker	3	3
Insurance—Real estate agent	7	3
Construction contractor	3	1
Railroad official	1	2
Other	1	2
Farmers	(33%)	(31%)
Low Salaried Workers	(3%)	(0%)
Salesman	1%	0%
Clerk	2	0
Industrial Wage Earners	(5%)	(7%)
Printer	0%	2%
Carpenter	0	1
Painter	0	2
Barber	0	1
Cigar Maker	0	1
Tailor	1	0
Shipfitter	1	0
Millwright	1	0
Janitor	1	0
Construction laborer	1	0
Unknown	(0%)	(3%)
TOTALS	100%	100%
	(92)	(88)

and publishers were Republicans. Finally, among the group of senators born to industrial wage earners, the Republicans tended to be sons of men with quasi-middle-class occupations—printers, carpenters, barbers, and painters—while the Democratic sons of industrial wage earners were born to fathers of somewhat lower status.

RACE, NATIONALITY, CREED

America is a land of many peoples—white, black, yellow, red, and all shades between. We are all immigrants and sons of immigrants, but we came to America from different lands and at different times, bringing different religious faiths. The American attitude toward this diversity has varied at different times in our history. At first, people—any people—were needed to work the land and build the factories, but about the time our story begins, this attitude changed to a less welcoming one. The "melting pot" ideology was still lauded in Fourth of July oratory. And, officially, Americans still believed in the words at the base of the Statue of Liberty, "Give me your tired, your poor, your huddled masses yearning to be free . . . ." But the facts of everyday living were different, very different.

As a result, the happy diversity of the American people is dimly reflected in the racial, national, and religious backgrounds of the senators. One out of every ten Americans is a Negro. Negroes may have been amply represented in the Senate in other ways but not, during the period following World War II, by a member of their own race.[13] Immigrants and second-generation whites suffer from a milder discrimination. A substantially smaller proportion of senators than of the white population were first- or second-generation Americans (Table 4). Moreover, this preference for Anglo-Saxon origins is clearly demonstrated by the fact that all three immigrants who served in the postwar Senate came from Great Britain, Canada, and Germany. Furthermore, virtually all the second-generation Americans in the Senate were from Northwestern and Central Europe, while the many new Americans from other parts of the world were almost unrepresented in the chamber (Table 5).

Table 4

PERCENTAGE OF FIRST- AND SECOND-GENERATION AMERICANS
COMPARED WITH WHITE POPULATION IN 1950

	Democrats	Republicans	All	White Population 1950	Index of Over-representation
Immigrants	2%	1%	2%	7%	0.3
Second generation	15%	11%	13%	16%	0.8

13. Only two Negroes have ever served in the United States Senate. Both represented the state of Mississippi during the Reconstruction. Legislative Reference Service, Library of Congress, "List of Negro Members of the House of Representatives," undated, typewritten MS.

Table 5

ORIGINS OF SECOND-GENERATION SENATORS COMPARED WITH
ALL SECOND-GENERATION AMERICANS IN 1950

Region	Senators	All Second-Generation Americans, 1950	Index of Over-representation
Northwestern Europe	75%	28%	3.7
Central Europe	17	32	1.9
Eastern Europe	0	11	0.0
Southern Europe	6	14	0.4
Other Europe	0	1	0.0
Asia	0	1	0.0
America	0	12	0.0
All Other	0	1	0.0
	100%	100%	

NOTE: Northwestern Europe includes the British Isles, Scandanavia except Finland, the Low countries, France, and Switzerland. Central Europe includes Germany, Poland, Czechoslovakia, Austria, Hungary, Yugoslavia. Eastern Europe includes the USSR, Baltic states, Finland, Rumania, and European Turkey. Southern Europe includes Greece, Italy, Spain, Portugal. Asia includes Palestine, Syria, Asian Turkey, and the other Asiatic countries. America includes all the American continent with the exception of the West Indies. All others includes Australia.

This preference for senators with "Yankee" backgrounds—or, failing that, for those with origins that approach as closely as possible the Anglo-Saxon ideal—is also reflected in the religious affiliations of the senators. Protestants are substantially overrepresented, Roman Catholics and Jews underrepresented in the Senate (Table 6). The same preference for those with high-prestige religious affiliations is found among the Protestants (Table 7). There are about three times the number of Episcopalians and twice the number of Presbyterians among the Protestant senators as would be found in a randomly selected group of Protestants. The Methodists and Congregationalists have about their fair share of the Senate seats, while the Baptists and Lutherans are considerably underrepresented.[14]

The seriousness of this bias against members of America's minority groups is mitigated, however, by several factors. First of all, the Demo-

14. For prestige rating of Protestant denominations, see W. and B. Allinsmith, "Religious Affiliation and Politico-Economic Attitude: A Study of Eight Major U.S. Religious Groups," *Public Opinion Quarterly,* XII (Fall, 1948), 377-89. For the effects of a congressman's religious affiliation on his electoral chances, see M. M. McKinney, "Religion and Elections," *Public Opinion Quarterly* VIII (Spring, 1944), 110-14.

Table 6

RELIGIOUS AFFILIATION COMPARED WITH U.S. POPULATION

	Senators Democratic	Senators Republican	All	Population, Self Identification	Claimed Church Membership	Index of Overrepresentation
Protestant	81%	95%	88%	72%	59%	1.2
Roman Catholic	15	5	11	21	34	0.5
Jewish	4	0	1	3	6	0.3
Other	0	0	0	3	1	0.0
	100%	100%	100%	100%	100%	

NOTE: Religious self-identification was computed from a sample of the national electorate in A. Campbell, G. Gurin, and W. Miller, *The Voter Decides* (Evanston, Ill.: Row, Peterson and Company, 1954), p. 214. The figures on claimed church membership are from *The World Almanac*, 1951, p. 481. The index of overrepresentation was computed using self-identification as the criterion of church membership.

Table 7

DENOMINATIONS OF PROTESTANTS COMPARED WITH
CHURCH MEMBERSHIP IN 1950

Denomination	Protestant Democrats	Protestant Republicans	All Protestant Senators	Claimed Protestant Membership	Index of Overrepresentation
Methodist	21%	17%	19%	22%	0.9
Baptist	23	5	13	34	0.4
Presbyterian	15	17	16	7	2.3
Episcopal	8	20	14	5	2.8
Congregational	5	12	9	10	1.1
Disciples of Christ	3	0	1	3	0.3
Lutheran	3	2	3	10	0.3
Mormon	3	2	3	2	1.5
Quaker	1	1	1	*	
Christian Science	0	1	1	**	
Unitarian	0	4	1	*	
Christian	5	2	4	*	
Unspecified, Other	13	16	14	5	
	100%	100%	100%	100%	
	(75)	(84)	(159)		

SOURCE: *The World Almanac*, 1951, p. 481.

* Less than 1%.

** Membership figures not published.

cratic party is far more open to minority group political talent than is the Republican party. (See Tables 4 and 6.) Moreover, a minority group member's chances of becoming a senator depended upon the constituency he sought to represent. Generally speaking, the heavier the concentration of minority group members in his state, the better were his chances (Tables 8 and 9), but notice that this tendency holds true *only* when the senators are Democrats. In those parts of the country with heavy immigrant or Catholic concentrations, the parties appear to divide sharply along majority-minority or Protestant-Catholic lines with the Democratic party becoming the almost exclusive means of political ascent for the underdog groups. In states with few minority group members, although neither party sends many of them to the Senate, the Republicans do so as often as the Democrats.[15]

Table 8

FOREIGN BORN IN CONSTITUENCY AND FOREIGN-NATIVE BACKGROUNDS
(in percentage of all senators first- and second-generation)

Percentage of White Population Foreign Born in 1950	*Democrats*	*Republicans*	*Percentage Point Difference between Democrats and Republicans*	*All*
States with:				
10% plus	56%	0%	+56	21%
5%-10%	39%	16%	+23	25%
Less than 5%	6%	15%	− 9	9%

EDUCATION

It would be a mistake to assume that senators are "born," not "made." In the race for senatorial office most of the senators began with a considerable headstart. Yet American society is a *relatively* open and competitive society, both in fact and in ideology, and the senators had to display considerable ability, ambition, and achievement to get where they are.

Senators are among the most educated—in the formal sense of the word—of all occupational groups in the United States.[16] Almost 85

15. The second-generation American senators were born to families in the upper reaches of immigrant society. Of the second-generation Democrats, 7 per cent were sons of professional men, 43 per cent were sons of proprietors and officials, and 29 per cent were sons of farmers. The corresponding percentages for second-generation Republicans were, 10, 35, and 40. Cf. S. Lubell, *The Future of American Politics* (New York: Harper and Brothers, 1952), Ch. 4.

16. See J. R. Shannon and M. Shaw, "Education of Business and Professional Leaders," *American Sociological Review*, V (June, 1940), 381-83.

Table 9
ROMAN CATHOLICS IN CONSTITUENCY AND CATHOLIC AFFILIATION
(in percentage of all senators Catholic)

Percentage of States' Population Roman Catholic, 1950	Democrats	Republicans	Percentage Point Difference between Democrats and Republicans	All
Over 30%	50%	7%	+43	28%
20%-30%	38%	4%	+34	16%
10%-20%	22%	5%	+17	10%
0%-10%	0%	0%	0	0%

SOURCE: Bureau of Research and Survey, National Council of Churches, *Churches and Church Membership in the United States*, Series A, Number 3, 1956.

per cent of them attended college, a level of education achieved by only 14 per cent of the adult population in 1950 (Table 10). The educational gap between the people and the members of the Senate is actually much wider than these figures indicate: 45 per cent of the senators attended both undergraduate college and law school, and 8 per cent of them performed some other form of postgraduate work.

Table 10
EDUCATIONAL ATTAINMENT COMPARED WITH WHITE POPULATION
TWENTY-FIVE YEARS OR OVER IN 1950

Highest Level of Schooling	Democrats	Republicans	All Senators	White Population over 25 (1950)	Index of Overrepresentation
Grade School	1%	1%	1%	48%*	0.2
High School	7	22	14	38	0.4
College	91	77	84	14	6.0
Law School	(10)	(7)	(8)		
College	(22)	(25)	(23)		
College & Law	(48)	(41)	(45)		
Postgraduate	(11)	(5)	(8)		
Unknown	1	0	1	0	
	100%	100%	100%	100%	
	(93)	(88)	(180)		

SOURCE: *Statistical Abstract of the United States*, 1954, p. 121, Table 135.
* Includes those with no formal education.

This high level of education can be accounted for, in part, by the senators' relatively high class origins. Numerous studies show that while the American educational system is one of the most equalitarian in the world, substantial differences in educational opportunities exist between social classes. Financial pressure, lack of motivation for academic success, the unconscious preference of middle-class teachers for middle-class children, and so on, place the child from working- or lower-class families at a distinct disadvantage even when his intelligence is the same as that of the middle-class child.[17] This is far from a total explanation of the superior educational attainments of the senators, for, regardless of their class origins, more senators attended college than the other members of the white adult population (Table 11). Thus the high educational level of senators is not just the result of their greater opportunities but also reflects exceptional academic interest, ability, and achievement.

Table 11

PERCENTAGE ATTENDING COLLEGE, BY OCCUPATIONAL LEVELS OF FATHERS

Occupational Class of Father	Democrats	Republicans	All Senators
Professional	93%	100%	96% (43)
Proprietors and Officials	96%	82%	84% (61)
Farmers	87%	74%	81% (51)
All Lower Occupations	75%	24%	53% (15)

There are interesting party-line differences in educational levels, too. The Democrats are more educated than the Republicans (Table 10). Again, this is not the result of different class origins, for, when the level of education of Democratic and Republican senators with roughly the same class origins are compared (Table 11), the Democrats come out well ahead, especially among the senators with the lower-class origins. This evidence of the Democrats' greater concern with, or ability for, formal study is supported by several other pieces

17. E. Sibley, "Some Demographic Clues to Stratification" in L. Wilson and W. Kolb (eds.), *Sociological Analysis* (New York: Harcourt, Brace and Co., 1949), pp. 642-50; W. L. Warner, R. J. Havighurst, and M. B. Loeb, *Who Shall Be Educated?* (New York: Harper and Brothers, 1940); C. A. Anderson, "Social Class Differentials in the Schooling of Youth Within the Region and Community Sized Groups of the United States," in K. Davis, M. Levy, and H. C. Bredemeier, *Modern American Society* (New York: Rinehart and Company, 1949), pp. 421-31; R. A. Mulligan, "Socio-Economic Background and College Enrollment," *American Sociological Review*, XVI (April, 1951), 188-96; A. B. Hollingshead, *Elmtown's Youth* (New York: John Wiley and Sons, 1949).

Table 12

TYPES OF COLLEGES ATTENDED COMPARED WITH MALE
COLLEGE GRADUATES IN 1940

Type of Undergraduate College	Democrats	Republicans	All College Graduate Senators	All Male College Graduates 1940	Index of Overrepresentation
Harvard-Yale-Princeton	5%	19%	10%	5%	2.0
Other Ivy League*	2	2	2	6	0.3
20 Outstanding Eastern Schools**	9	14	11	5	2.2
Big Ten***	4	12	6	12	0.5
All Other	81	52	69	72	1.0
	100%	100%	100%	100%	
	(54)	(42)	(96)		

SOURCE: F. C. Babcock, *The U.S. College Graduate* (New York: The Macmillan Company, 1941), p. 42, Table DD.

* Dartmouth, Cornell, Pennsylvania, Columbia.

** Amherst, Bates, Bowdoin, Brown, Clark (Maine), Colby, Franklin and Marshall, Hamilton, Haverford, Hobart, Lafayette, Lehigh, Middlebury, Rutgers, Swarthmore, Trinity (Conn.), Tufts, Union (N.Y.), Wesleyan, Williams.

*** Chicago, Illinois, Indiana, Iowa, Michigan, Minnesota, Northwestern, Ohio State, Purdue, Wisconsin.

of evidence. Seventy-two per cent of the Democrats, but only 65 per cent of the Republicans, who entered undergraduate colleges graduated. Of those who did graduate, 24 per cent of the Democrats, but only 14 per cent of the Republicans, were elected to Phi Beta Kappa, the national scholastic honorary society.[18]

What kinds of schools did the senators attend? As undergraduates, the senators studied in 104 different educational institutions. State universities were the most popular type of undergraduate institution—about half of the senators attending undergraduate schools went to a state university at one time or another—but a very large share of all college graduates in the United States attended these uniquely American institutions. What type of college graduated the largest share of senators, taking into account the size of its alumni body? The answer —as clearly as we are able to supply one—is to be found in Table 12.

18. The magnitude of this achievement is underscored by the fact that a large number of senators attended undergraduate colleges not accredited by Phi Beta Kappa and not more than 10 per cent of a graduating class is elected to the society.

Harvard, Yale, Princeton, and the smaller but well-known Eastern colleges graduated more than their share of the senators. The other Ivy League universities and the Big Ten universities can claim only one-third the number of senators among their alumni one would expect on the basis of chance. The less well-known colleges and universities graduated just about their proportional share of future senators.

Again, we find some significant differences between Democrats and Republicans. Four times as many Republicans as Democrats graduated from "The Big Three" and half again as many from the smaller (but still expensive and prestige-laden) Eastern colleges. The senators from Big Ten universities—concentrated in the heavily Republican Midwest—were Republicans three to one, and a great many more Democrats than Republicans attended the less well-known institutions of the South and West. While the Democrats are more highly educated and seem to have done better work in undergraduate college, they did not as often attend the nationally known, expensive institutions of the Northeast.

A similar picture emerges from a close look at the fifty-one law schools the senators attended. On the basis of a thorough survey of legal education in 1920 (about the time most senators went to law school), A. Z. Reed found four levels of excellence in the nation's law schools.[19] These were:

1. High-entrance-requirement, full-time law schools which were parts of recognized colleges and universities and which required at least two years of undergraduate work before admission plus a three-year course of study for the LL.B.

2. Low-entrance-requirement schools which offered a full-time course of standard length but required only one year of study, or none at all, for admission.

3. Part-time law schools, often not connected with any university, which offered their courses at night or late afternoon. Often the instruction was indifferent and preoccupied with local law, and the students were exhausted from the strain of combining their legal studies with a full-time job.

4. Short-course law schools which were little more than glorified cram schools whose sole purpose was to prepare their students within a year or two for the bar examination. In 1920 these schools were concentrated in the South, Indiana, and the District of Columbia, where bar entrance requirements were low.

19. A. Z. Reed, *Training for the Public Profession of Law* (New York: Carnegie Foundations for the Advancement of Teaching), Bulletin #15 (1921).

Almost half the law schools attended by the senators were high-entrance requirement schools (at a time when only one-fifth of all American law schools belonged to that category) and another 30 per cent attended the second-ranking type (Table 13). Note also the considerably greater percentage of Republicans than Democrats attending the first ranking schools. This may be explained in part by the fact that the best law schools were located in the strongly Republican areas of New England and the Middle West. The Democratic South simply had fewer first-rate law schools for her young men to attend.

Table 13

TYPES OF LAW SCHOOLS ATTENDED COMPARED WITH ALL LAW SCHOOLS IN 1920
(in percentage of all schools attended)

Type of School	Democrats	Republicans	All Legally Trained Senators	Percentage of all Law Schools in Category, 1920	Index of Overrepresentation
High Entrance, Full-Time	31%	68%	47%	21%	2.2
Low Entrance, Full-Time Standard Length	38	20	30	29	1.0
Part-Time	23	12	18	39	0.5
Short Course	8	0	5	11	1.5
	100% (61)	100% (49)	100% (109)	100% (142)	

SOURCE: A. Z. Reed, *Training for the Public Profession of Law* (N.Y.: Carnegie Foundation for the Advancement of Teaching, Bulletin No. 15, 1921), pp. 414-44.

OCCUPATION

As might be expected from a group of highly educated men, most of the senators started work near the top of America's occupational hierarchy.[20] Eighty-eight—almost exactly one-half—of the senators began working as lawyers, thirteen as teachers, twelve as journalists, six as professors, six as merchants, five as executives in manufacturing

20. Part-time employment while in school is not included in this analysis. The senator's "first job" has been defined as his first full-time job after completion of schooling. If a senator's education was interrupted for more than one year, the employment followed during this hiatus is counted as his "first job."

concerns. On the other hand, a few of the senators began work in
less desirable jobs. Eight senators, for example, started out as farmers,
another eight as clerks, four as salesmen, two as common laborers, three
as printers, one each as an electrician, machinist, pipefitter, factory
worker, and farm laborer. When all the senators' first occupations
are lumped into occupational classes, it is clear that the "log-cabin-to-
Capitol-Hill" myth of American politics needs considerable revision.
Eighty-one per cent of the senators *started work* in the two highest
classes.[21]

By the time the senators settled into their main nonpolitical occupations, a good deal of job shifting had occurred (Figure 4).[22] All save
one of the teachers had abandoned their original jobs for more reward-
ing endeavors—mostly law (four Southern Democrats) and business
(six Republicans). All the men who started out as low-salaried em-
ployees, industrial wage earners, or farm laborers had moved up the
status ladder. The number of lawyers, farmers, merchants, manufacturing executives, publishers, insurance and real estate agents, contractors, and oil-gas producers had noticeably increased. The net result of
these occupational changes was a considerable increase in the class
positions of the senators. By this stage of their careers, all the senators
are to be found in the top quarter of the labor force.

By the time our subjects became senators, they had bettered their
lot even more. Almost 60 per cent of them were serving in political

21. Those senators—about one in five—who started work in relatively menial occupations tended to have relatively low class origins and to have obtained relatively little
formal education. As the table below indicates, their lack of education was by far the
more important of these two reasons for their relatively slow start.

Percentage Starting Work Either as Low-Salaried Workers, Industrial Wage Earners,
  Servants, or Farm Laborers, by Father's Occupation and Level of Education

Father's Occupational Class	Attended College	Did not Attend College	Totals
Professional	0%	0%	0% (43)
Proprietors and Officials	9%	33%	12% (60)
Farmers	7%	60%	16% (56)
All lower	0%	43%	20% (15)
Totals	5% (149)	44% (25)	

22. The determination of a senator's principal, nonpolitical occupation is not without
its arbitrary aspects for those senators who have followed numerous callings or who have
had more than one occupation at a time. In making the relatively few difficult decisions required, the following rules have been followed: If a senator had pursued a
number of occupations either the last or the one followed for the longest period of time
was selected. The choice here was made in favor of the more time-consuming occupation. For example, if a senator had been a lawyer and a farm owner or a corporation
director, he is defined as a lawyer. When two or more occupations were followed
simultaneously the same criteria were considered controlling. For a complete list of
the senators' occupations, see Appendix E, Table 1.

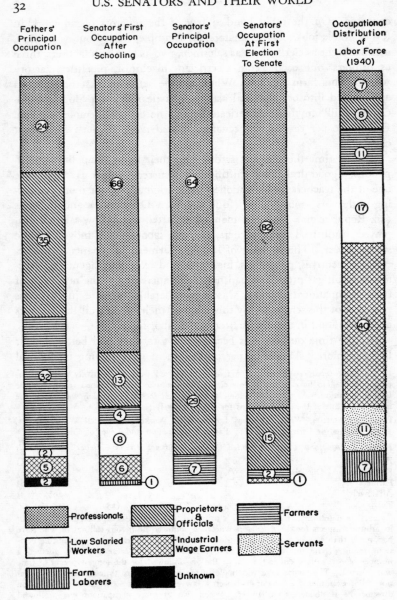

FIG. 4. Occupational Class Distribution, by Stage of Career

office at the time of their election or appointment to the Senate.[23] Of those elected to the upper house from "civilian" occupations, the lawyers were most numerous (38), followed at a considerable distance by merchants (6), publishers (3), and manufacturing executives (3). All told, 82 per cent of the prospective senators were professionals (including public officials) and 15 per cent proprietors and officials at the time of their election. Only four of the 180 men were full-time farmers[24] and one was a factory worker when elected to the Senate. Senators, quite obviously, are elected from, or near, the top of the nation's occupational class system. In getting there, a head start helps.

The Lawyers

The second most striking feature of the occupational histories of the senators is the number of them who at one time or another were lawyers. The legal profession comprises about 0.1 per cent of the American labor force, and yet about half of the senators were lawyers. No other occupational group even approaches the lawyers' record. Why this predominance of lawyers? Obviously they meet what seems to be one test of top-level leadership—they are a high prestige profession. But why are not other equally highly esteemed occupations equally represented among the senators?

A partial answer to these questions can be found in the skills of the lawyer and in the nature of the legal profession in America. The skills of the lawyer in America tend to give him an advantage in the race for office if not actual training for filling the office once it is achieved. With the erosion of the historic view that a lawyer is an officer of the court, the modern American conception developed that the lawyer is a paid servant of his client, justified in using any weapon that the law supplies in his client's interest.[25] His job is primarily one of making the best possible case from the point of view of his clients. In filling this new role, the lawyer has become "a mediator of forces," a "specialist in human relations."[26] The lawyer, in his everyday occupational role, develops not only ability in interpersonal mediation and conciliation but also skill in verbal manipulation. Lasswell and

23. Occupation at the time of election or appointment to office was defined as the last occupation held within one year of election or appointment.

24. A large number of senators owned farm land, however. This merely strengthens the conclusion of this section, for the ownership of farm land is a mark of upper-middle- and upper-class standing in much of America.

25. A. A. Berle, Jr., "Modern Legal Profession," *Encyclopedia of the Social Sciences* (New York: The Macmillan Company, 1930), IX, 343.

26. J. W. Hurst, *The Growth of American Law* (Boston: Little, Brown and Company, 1950), p. 335.

McDougal do not exaggerate when they say: ". . . the lawyer is today . . . the one indispensable advisor of every responsible policy-maker of our society—whether we speak of the head of a government department or agency, of the executive of a corporation or labour union, of the secretary of a trade or other private association, or even of the humble independent enterpriser or professional man. As such an advisor the lawyer, when informing his policy-maker of what he can or cannot legally do, is in an unassailably strategic position to influence, if not create, policy. . . . For better or worse our decision-makers and our lawyers are bound together in a relation of dependence or identity."[27] With the development of these skills in the normal course of a legal career, the lawyer has a substantial advantage over the average layman who decides to enter politics.

The professional skills developed by lawyers do not alone explain their dominance in the political leadership groups of America. Unlike many European countries, the United States has never had a landed aristocracy with a tradition of political participation. Relatively few senators are the possessors of inherited wealth. In a highly competitive society, where occupational success is the most highly valued goal for the ambitious, who can, with the least danger, leave their jobs for the tremendous risks of a political career? Among the high-prestige occupations it seems to be the lawyers. Certainly, other professional men find the neglect of their careers for political activity extremely hazardous. To those in professions where the subject matter is rapidly changing, a few years of neglect of their vocations and their skills would be either lost or outmoded.[28] The active businessman, be he an individual entrepreneur or a member of a corporate bureaucracy,[29] would find the neglect of his vocation for politics no asset to his primary occupational interest. Politics demands more and more time from its practitioners: the farmer, under these conditions, finds it difficult to indulge a taste for politics while still keeping the farm going. These barriers to political participation either do not exist or are decreased in significance for the lawyer. The law changes relatively slowly, and a politician is in a position to keep up with many of the changes in the

27. H. D. Lasswell and M. S. McDougal, "Legal Education and Public Policy," in Lasswell, *Analysis of Political Behavior* (London: Routledge and Paul, 1948), p. 27.

28. B. Barber, " 'Mass Apathy' and Voluntary Social Participation in the United States" (Ph.D. dissertation, Harvard University, 1948), p. 118.

29. The rise of a salaried "new middle class" seems likely to place even greater restrictions on the political activities of middle-class Americans. See C. W. Mills and M. J. Ulmer, *Small Business and Civic Welfare,* Report of the Smaller War Plants Corporation to the Special Committee to Study Problems of American Small Business, Senate Document 135, 79th Congress, 2nd Session, Part IV, p. 27.

law while active in politics. The lawyer, either in individual practice or in a law firm of a few members, is "dispensable."[30] He can most easily combine his occupation, on a part-time basis, with political activity. Moreover, this activity can be a positive advantage to his occupational advancement—free and professionally legitimate advertising, contacts, and an opportunity to meet important lawyers of his region result from his political activities. The politician must be prepared for at least an occasional defeat at the polls: the lawyer has an insurance policy against this inescapable risk in his professional skill, reputation, and practice.

Finally, lawyers possess a monopoly of public offices relating to the administration of law and the court system.[31] Since in America "every political question tends to become a legal question," the offices of judge and prosecuting attorney provide lawyers (and lawyers alone) relatively easy entry into the political world and important springboards to higher offices. Almost half of the lawyers in the Senate (and therefore about one-quarter of all the senators) began their political careers by serving in law-enforcement offices open only to the legally trained. Twenty-five per cent of the senators held such offices at the time of their election to the Senate.[32]

Party, Constituency, and Occupational Careers

So far nothing has been said about the occupational differences between Democrats and Republicans. As Table 14 indicates, these dif-

30. M. Weber, "Politics as a Vocation," in H. Gerth and C. W. Mills (eds. and trans.), *From Max Weber: Essays in Sociology* (New York: Oxford University Press, 1946), p. 84 ff. for the classic analysis.

31. J. A. Schlesinger, "Lawyers and Politics: A Clarified View," *Midwest Journal of Political Science*, I, (May, 1957), 26-39.

32. The legal profession is a large and heterogeneous one. To discover that most senators are lawyers and to point out some of the reasons why this is so does not advance our understanding as far as we might like. What kind of lawyers are the senators? A few bits and pieces of information provide some insight on this subject.

The lawyers in the Senate have practiced law mostly in the nation's small towns and medium-sized cities while the profession as a whole is heavily concentrated in a few metropolitan areas. W. Weinfeld, "Incomes of Lawyers," *Survey of Current Business*, XXIX (August, 1949), 22, Table 8, reports that 46 per cent of all nonsalaried lawyers in 1947 practiced in cities of a quarter of a million or more in population. Only 20 per cent of the senator-lawyers practiced in cities that large. The most successful lawyers are members of the larger firms. *Ibid.*, Table 7, reports that 88 per cent of all nonsalaried lawyers were in practice alone in 1947, 11 per cent in firms with from two to five members, and 1 per cent belonged to firms of five or more. The corresponding figures for the lawyer-senators are 40, 47, and 13 per cent—with the Republican lawyers coming in far greater numbers than the Democrats from the larger firms. One reason the lawyer-senators—and again especially the Republicans—came in disproportionate numbers from the larger and presumably more prosperous law firms is their exceptionally good legal training. The better the law school the lawyer-senator attended, the more likely he was to belong to a sizeable firm.

ferences are substantial. Half again as many Democrats as Republicans, for example, are lawyers. Republican businessmen outnumber their Democratic counterparts by more than two to one. All the college professors in the Senate were Democrats save one (Wayne Morse of Oregon, and he bolted the GOP for the Democratic party after the 1952 election).

Table 14

PRINCIPAL OCCUPATIONS, BY PARTY

Occupation	Democrats	Republicans
Lawyer	63%	45%
Businessman	17	40
Farmer	7	8
Professor	7	1
Other Professional	5	5
	100%	100%
	(92)	(83)

At first blush, these occupational differences seem easily explicable in terms of the different policies and electoral followings of the parties. The Republican party is, on the whole, more friendly with, and sensitive to the needs of, the American business community: hence a far larger proportion of its senators are former businessmen. The Democratic party (outside the South) draws a disproportionate share of its support from the lower reaches of the economic hierarchy and from members of minority groups. Leadership selection in such a party is more difficult than in the Republican case. Fewer Democratic voters have the status, education, skills, or opportunity to be active office seekers. By necessity the "underdog" must turn to men and women of relatively high status for political leadership. Yet the upper reaches of American society are mostly Republican. The politically oriented professional man—especially the lawyer—seems to fill this need for "underdog" political leaders.

In the North, this interpretation is supported by the data. The Northern Democrats started life with considerably fewer advantages than the other senators. Sixty per cent of them were born into some kind of religious or nationality minority group, while only 4 per cent of the Southern and Border Democrats and 14 per cent of the Republicans were (Table 15). Moreover, the Northern Democrats have been far more mobile occupationally than the others (Table 16). In the North, then, the Democrats tend to have "underdog" origins; they were once "of" the people whose interests they serve in the national legislature. Among Senate Democrats from the North and West, minority group members are far more often professional men than are Yankee-Protestants (Table 17). Thus the indications are that this "underdog effect" accounts for a large number of Northern Democratic lawyers.

Table 15
SOCIAL ORIGINS, BY PARTY AND SECTION

Type of Origin	Northern and Western Democrats	Southern and Border Democrats	Republicans
Non-Protestant, 1st or 2nd Generation	28%	0%	2%
Non-Protestant, 3rd plus Generation	17	4	2
Protestant, 1st or 2nd Generation	17	0	10
Protestant, 3rd plus Generation	39	96%	86
	100%	100%	100%
	(36)	(55)	(88)

Table 16
OCCUPATIONAL MOBILITY, BY PARTY AND SECTION

	Relation between Senator's Principal Occupational Class and That of His Father			
	Higher	Same	Lower	
Northern & Western Democrats	80%	17%	3%	100% (35)
Southern & Border Democrats	47%	49%	5%	100% (55)
Republicans	49%	51%	1%	100% (88)

Table 17
SOCIAL ORIGINS OF NORTHERN AND WESTERN DEMOCRATS
AND PRINCIPAL OCCUPATIONS

	Non-Protestant 1st & 2nd Generation (n-10)	Non-Protestant 3rd plus Generation (n-6)	Protestant 1st & 2nd Generation (n-6)	Protestant 3rd plus Generation (n-15)
Percentage with Professional Occupation	80%	100%	67%	71%
Percentage Lawyers	70%	80%	33%	50%

This, by itself, does not account for the fact that there are more lawyer-senators in the Democratic than in the Republican party. For the South—where the Democrats claim the allegiance of almost all the electorate and are hardly an "underdog" party—sends a larger proportion of lawyers to the upper house of Congress than does the North (Table 18). How can this be explained?

Table 18

DEMOCRATS' OCCUPATIONAL DISTRIBUTION, BY SECTION

	South	Border	North & West
Lawyers	74%	53%	56%
Businessmen	13	29	19
Farmers	8	12	3
Professors	5	0	11
Other Professionals	0	6	11
	100%	100%	100%
	(39)	(17)	(36)

Perhaps differences in political opportunities in Northern and Southern states has something to do with it. In the predominantly one-party South the inevitable risks of a political career are considerably lessened and politicans may, therefore, spend a larger share of their lives in public office than in the more competitive North and West. This may place a premium on following the occupation most compatible with sustained political endeavor—law. Seventy per cent of the Democrats from one-party states were lawyers, and only 62 per cent of those from states which lean Democratic and 65 per cent of those from two-party states followed the law as their principal occupation. None of the three Democrats elected from states leaning Republican were lawyers.[33] While the differences are small they are generally in the right direction: where a career in politics is most possible the number of lawyers is highest; where political possibilities are least promising the number of lawyers is smallest.

Another possible key to the large numbers of lawyers from the South is the rural nature of that region. A business class and business values have been largely absent from the region until recent years. While farming has been a major industry, farmers are a relatively un-

[33]. The typology of state party systems used throughout this book is from A. Ranney and W. Kendall, "The American Party Systems," *American Political Science Review*, XXXXVIII (June, 1954), 477-85.

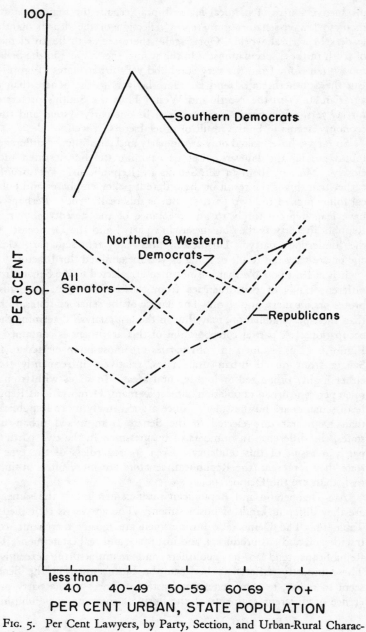

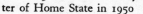

FIG. 5. Per Cent Lawyers, by Party, Section, and Urban-Rural Character of Home State in 1950

productive source of political leadership. Perhaps the region's attachment to lawyer-senators is merely a reflection of the dearth of other leaders in a rural world. Once again, there seems to be an element of truth in these speculations. On the whole, the lawyers in the Senate most often come from the very rural and very urban states (Figure 5). But the Southern states send far more lawyers to the Senate than do agrarian states in the North and West. Thus the South's preference for lawyers, while partly a reflection of its one-party system and rural economy, seems to be the result of other factors as well.

So far we have looked only at the party and constituency differences found among the lawyers. Let us examine the businessmen more closely. Most of them in the Senate are Republicans. We assumed earlier that this is the result of the different policy emphases and political followings of the two parties. But is this really true? Perhaps we have leaped prematurely to an acceptance of the stereotype that the Republican party is the "businessman's party" and the Democrats are the "underdog's party." Do these figures really represent party cleavage or are they the result of some as yet unexamined third factor?

It is at least possible that businessmen are elected to the Senate from different kinds of constituencies from those of lawyers, journalists, professors, farmers, and so on. The nature of the senators' states, rather than their party affiliation, may thus in the last analysis determine their occupations. A partial corroboration of this argument is contained in Figure 6. Businessmen in both parties are most often elected to the Senate from mixed urban-rural states, relatively infrequently from either highly urbanized or highly rural areas. In states with from 50 to 60 per cent urban population, almost as many Democratic as Republican senators are businessmen. Since a good many more Republicans than Democrats are elected to the Senate from mixed urban-rural states, the difference in numbers of businessmen in the two parties is partly a result of this tendency. Even so, regardless of the type of state they represent, the Republican senators are more often businessmen than are the Democrats.

Are Democratic and Republican businessmen much the same, or are they different kinds of businessmen? The answer is contained in Table 19. The Democratic businessmen are mostly merchants, contractors, oil and gas producers, and insurance and real estate men. The Republicans tend to be publishers and manufacturing executives. These industry differences between the businessmen in the Senate seem to reflect, to some extent at least, differences in the party preference of different segments of the business community. Publishing

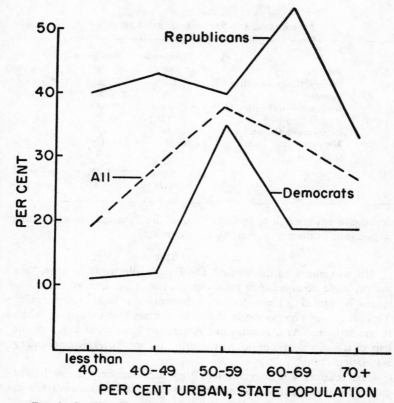

Fig. 6. Per Cent Businessmen, by Party and Urban-Rural Character of Home State in 1950

and manufacturing are heavily Republican in their sympathies; finance and insurance less clearly so. Oil and gas producers, perhaps because of their concentration in the Southern states, have been a major source of campaign funds for the Democratic party. Contractors, who normally do a large share of their business with the government, may prefer the Democrats' free-spending policies to Republican "economy." Retail merchants, dependent as they are on mass demand, are also likely to be sympathetic to the party which promises to pump spending power out to the masses of the people. Even if these differences between Democratic and Republican businessmen do not reflect significant party cleavages within the business world, they are big enough

Table 19

DEMOCRATIC AND REPUBLICAN BUSINESSMEN

	Democrats	Republicans
Publisher	6%	25%
Manufacturing Executive	6	22
Banker	6	8
Insurance—Real Estate Man	12	14
Oil-Gas Producer	12	8
Construction Contractor	12	3
Merchant	29	17
Other	18	3
	100%	100%
	(17)	(36)

and consistent enough to indicate that, in the Senate, Democratic and Republican businessmen tend to be different.[34]

ASSOCIATIONAL LIFE

"In no country in the world," De Tocqueville wrote in 1835, "has the principle of association been more successfully used, or more unsparingly applied to a multitude of different objects than in America."[35] This oft-quoted observation is, if anything, more true today than when it was written. As a result, most Americans have spent a significant part of their lives in joining, participating in, and governing voluntary associations.

The senators are no exception; they are extremely active in the nation's private groups. The average senator claims membership in about ten voluntary associations (Table 20). By way of contrast, Warner and Lunt found that the average "Yankee City" resident belonged to two voluntary associations; in midwestern "Jonesville," Warner found that the average person belonged to only 1.3 asso-

34. A number of other differences between the Democratic and Republican businessmen might be pointed out. Over half of the Republican businessmen in the Senate were *sons* of businessmen. About one quarter of them were sons of either publishers or manufacturing executives. Only about one quarter of the Democratic businessmen, on the other hand, were sons of businessmen and not one Democrat was the son of a publisher or manufacturer. As is the case for the Democrats as a whole, the Democratic businessmen were far more often "non-Yankees." Twenty-nine per cent of the Northern Democratic businessmen were first- or second-generation non-Protestants; only 3 per cent of the Republican businessmen were.

35. A. de Tocqueville, *Democracy in America*, trans., H. Reeve (2 vols.; New York: Alfred A. Knopf, 1946), I, 191.

36. W. L. Warner and P. S. Lunt, *The Social Life of a Modern Community* (New Haven: Yale University Press, 1941), p. 303; W. L. Warner and Associates, *Democracy in Jonesville* (New York: Harper and Brothers, 1949), p. 131.

ciations.[36] Moreover, the senators' joining activities are not typically confined to one or a few types of associations. The most popular associations are lodges, followed closely by college fraternities, professional associations, veterans' and patriotic groups, and social clubs. The variety of associations to which the senators belong is so vast that probably most Americans share a common membership in some sort of private group with at least one senator.

Table 20

MEMBERSHIPS IN NONPOLITICAL ASSOCIATIONS

Number of Memberships	Democrats	Republicans	All
None, Unknown	12%	3%	8%
1- 4	27	22	24
5- 9	22	30	26
10-14	20	23	21
15-19	8	15	12
20-24	4	6	5
25 and over	7	2	4
	100%	100%	100%
	(92)	(88)	(180)

There are a number of reasons for the senators' hyperactivity in the associational life of the country. First of all, this participation seems, in part, to be a reflection of the senators' class position. Numerous studies have shown that the higher an individual's social status, the larger the number of associations he is likely to join.[37] Moreover, it appears that highly mobile members of a community are active in a large number of different types of associations, whereas the stable members of the community belong to a narrower range of groups. The membership pattern of the senators thus may result from their high status and their upward mobility.

A second, and by no means mutually exclusive, interpretation of the senators' heavy participation in voluntary associations is political. It may be that persons who are extremely active in associations possess the type of personality to which the political career appeals. One must like people to be a politician (or at least appear to), and a record as a "joiner" may indicate the possession of this attitude, as well as the

37. Warner and Lunt, *Social Life of a Modern Community*, p. 329; M. Komarovsky, "The Voluntary Associations of Urban Dwellers," *American Sociological Review*, XI (December, 1946), 686-98; W. Mather, "Income and Social Participation," *American Sociological Review*, VI (June, 1941), 380-93; Williams, *American Society*, p. 148.

ability to get along with others. It is a well-known fact that persons already in politics consciously seek out associations to join as an aid to electoral success. In politics, the more "brothers" you have, the better.

The new look in senators can be quickly summarized. The "typical" senator during the postwar years was a late-middle-aged or elderly, white, Protestant, native-born man with rural or small-town and upper-middle-class origins, a college-educated lawyer, and a "joiner." This collective portrait is probably what most informed observers would have guessed without charts, graphs, and statistics, but the analysis performed in this chapter tells us much which even the best guesswork will not.

1. We have been able to see how far the "typical" senator differs from the "typical" American. Probably less than 5 per cent of the American people have any significant chance of ever serving in the Senate as long as the present informal "requirements" for the office hold. While these barriers seem rapidly to be weakening, huge blocs of Americans still have little chance for service in the Senate. Many of the factors which so heavily influence the political life-chances of Americans seem to have little if any relationship to political ability.

2. We have been able to see why the typical senator is such an atypical American. One reason, certainly, is the constitutional requirements for Senate membership. The constitution requires that senators be at least thirty years of age, that they be citizens of at least nine years' standing, and that they be residents of the states they represent. The first of these legal requirements explains why the senators are older than the average American, but it does not tell us why they are so much older than they are required to be. The nine-year citizenship requirement may account for the fact that few immigrants are senators, but it does not tell us why some groups of second-generation Americans are discriminated against. The requirement that senators live in the states they represent, when combined with the equal representation of the large and small states, may help explain the bias in favor of Americans from the nation's smaller towns and cities, although we saw that this was not a total explanation of this bias. If we are to understand the "typical" senator, we must look well beyond the legal formalities to the structure of American society.

The senators were selected, with only rare exceptions, from near the top of the society's class system. While many more studies of this nature are necessary before conclusions can be definite, this study and others like it indicate that governmental offices are class ranked—the more important the office, the higher the social status of its normal incumbent.[38] While this conclusion rings harsh in many an American democrat's ear, it should not be a particularly surprising conclusion. A stratified society places different evaluation on various social positions, and the prestige of the office or position tends to be transferred to the person who fills it. Thus the bank president or lawyer is a "better" man than the janitor or policeman. As long as the system of stratification in a society is generally accepted, one must expect people to look for political leadership toward those who have met the current definition of success and hence are considered worthy individuals. Voters seem to prefer candidates who are not like themselves but are what they would like to be.[39]

Of course, the existence of this class bias in the recruitment of senators may not be solely the result of popular consent. Those with high status positions in American society tend to have more money (and easier access to still more) than the ordinary American, and as we shall see, it takes a good deal of money to become a senator. They tend to have more leisure and more flexible work schedules, too. Members of the upper and upper-middle classes in America are more politically aware than the average American and may be more prone to enter politics.[40] As a general rule, they are likely to possess the relevant skills—verbal ability, ability at inter-personal conciliation and manipulation, "functional" and "substantial" rationality[41]—for politics in a democratic land.

3. We have been able to account for many of the differences in background found among the senators. The collective portrait of the United States senator presented in this chapter is a useful fiction, but

38. See D. R. Matthews, *The Social Background of Political Decision-Makers* (Garden City: Doubleday and Company, Inc., 1954).

39. Ironically enough, in a society with a relatively rigid class system like that of Great Britain the class bias in the recruitment of top-level public officials is less than in the United States. Evidently, in class systems with substantial mobility, such as America's, individuals tend to identify with higher strata and accept it as their standard of value. In a less open society, this identification does not exist, and there is a tendency to look to one's own class for political leadership.

40. That the upper classes are more concerned with politics is clear. See J. L. Woodward and E. Roper, "Political Activity of American Citizens," *American Political Science Review*, XLIV (December, 1950), 872-85. But the higher status groups in American society are also the most biased against a political career (See H. Cantril, ed., *Public Opinion: 1935-46* (Princeton: Princeton University Press, 1951), p. 534.) and have the best opportunities in other lines of endeavor.

41. The distinction between functional and substantial rationality was originated by Karl Mannheim. In his terminology, functional rationality is the ability to coordinate means so as to obtain most efficiently a given end, while substantial rationality is made up of individual insight and understanding of complex situations.

like other fictions it has its limitations. While most of the senators studied fit the picture, a minority does not. The analysis in this chapter helps explain why.

The two major parties, for instance, recruit somewhat different types of men for the Senate. The Democrats were elected at an earlier age and were born and live in larger towns and cities than the Republicans. Their fathers, as a group, possessed somewhat higher occupational class positions but were also more often immigrants, Catholics, Jews, and members of relatively low prestige Protestant denominations. The Democrats obtained more education than the Republicans, but less often at the well-known schools. They were more often lawyers, but they practiced in smaller towns and as members of smaller law firms than the Republicans. The Republicans were more often businessmen and came from industries different from those of the Democratic businessmen in the Senate.

Party is not the only factor, however, which helps account for differences in the senators' careers. Different constituencies tend to elect different types of men to the Senate. Rural states incline toward senators with rural origins; states with large concentrations of foreign-born or Roman Catholic voters more often elect members to the Senate with these social characteristics; the more competitive a state's party system, the less often lawyers are chosen as senators; and businessmen tend to be elected from mixed urban-rural states. As we shall see, these differences among senators are just as significant as their similarities.

CHAPTER III

The Politicians

In the Middletown of 1925 the Lynds found that politics and politicians were suspect. One businessman told them, "Our politics smell to heaven, elections are dirty and unscrupulous, and our better citizens mostly don't mix in them." Another said, "No good man will go into politics here. Why should he? Politics is dirty. I wouldn't mix in it here. Maybe if I was rich and independent I would, but I'd think twice about it even then."[1] Upon their return to Middletown ten years later the Lynds were greeted with the remark, "Whatever changes you may find elsewhere in Middletown, you will find that our politics and government are the same crooked shell game."[2]

Much the same attitudes are prevalent today. Recently a representative sample of the nation's electorate was asked, "If you had a son would you like to see him go into politics as a life's work when he gets out of school?" Sixty-eight per cent of the sample answered no, 21 per cent answered yes, and 11 per cent had no opinion. Even more significant are the reasons given by the respondents in support of their answers. Those who opposed a political career did so on the grounds that politics was crooked, unethical, and that the temptations of a political career were too great; that there were better opportunities in other lines of endeavor; and that a political career was too insecure. The principal reason given for favoring a political career by the 21 per

1. R. S. and H. M. Lynd, *Middletown* (New York: Harcourt, Brace and Company, 1929), p. 421.
2. R. S. and H. M. Lynd, *Middletown in Transition* (New York: Harcourt, Brace and Company, 1937), p. 319.

cent of the sample who indicated such approval was the need for clean-minded men in politics to supplant the people that are in it now! All told, about half the American electorate, if this poll is to be trusted, believe that it is difficult to be an honest politician.[3]

Despite these public attitudes, the subjects of this study became politicians. Why? What incentives were strong enough to attract this group of generally able men and women into politics? Neither our understanding of human motivation (the psychologists working in contrived laboratory situations have not made much progress; how can we hope to do better?) nor our data permit a definitive answer to this question. We can, however, hazard a few more or less informed guesses.

POLITICAL INCENTIVES

One incentive to political activity is the desire for prestige and power. This seems paradoxical when contrasted with the lurid public image of "politics" and "politicians" sketched in above, but the American public's picture of politicians has another side. The Gallup poll, for example, often asks a cross section of the voting population whom they most admire. Time and again, the most admired Americans include prominent politicians. High public office also possesses great prestige in the United States. One recent survey, which sought to discover the public's prestige-ranking of occupations, found that United States Supreme Court justices, state governors, cabinet members, diplomats, mayors of large cities, and United States representatives were rated among the top ten occupations in the country.[4] The normal incumbents of these offices are "politicians." While politicians as a class may not enjoy great prestige, many successful politicians do. The people often think that their politicians are different, that they are "good politicians," or not politicians at all.

Of course, politics is not the only way one can achieve power and prestige, but it is a particularly attractive one to some groups within the American population. Look, for example, at the position of a successful business or professional man in one of the nation's smaller cities and towns. Suppose that he is not content to be a big fish in a little pond; where can he turn? The upper reaches of the nation's corporate businesses are not open to him; the prominent law firms in the

3. H. Cantril (ed.), *Public Opinion: 1935-46* (Princeton: Princeton University Press, 1951), p. 534.

4. "Jobs and Occupations: A Popular Evaluation," *Opinion News*, IX (September 1, 1947), 3-13. United States senator was not among the occupations the sample was asked to rate.

larger cities are not likely to bring him in as a partner. His opportunity to enter either of these worlds came at his graduation from college or law school. He did not take that option then. Where does he turn to assuage his lofty ambitions? Politics is always a possibility. Or take a member of an American ethnic group. The United States, he has been told, is the land of opportunity. One should strive to "get ahead." As a practical matter, his chances of getting ahead are not good. But in politics—especially, of course, if he lives in an area containing a concentration of voters with similar nationality or religious backgrounds—his foreign name, ancestry, and religion are a positive advantage. In this way politics furnishes an avenue of upward mobility for those groups whose opportunities in other lines of endeavor are poor.[5]

Another incentive to political activity is love of the game. Politics provides, even to the neophyte, a sense of power, excitement, camaraderie, a sense of being "in on things," a sense of importance. The strength of these psychic lures should not be underestimated. They may attract some people more than others—Harold Lasswell, for example, has suggested that politicians have a special need for such satisfactions because of an unusually low esteem of the self[6]—but they appeal to most people more than they are willing to admit.

Most politicians say that they are in politics to be of "public service." Much, perhaps most, of this can be dismissed as rationalization, but not all of it. Some men have such a clear-cut image of "the public interest" and such a strong emotional commitment to it that they decide to do something about it themselves.

Finally, there is the family influence. The evidence that our political attitudes are shaped early in life is impressive.[7] At least one-third of the senators came from politically oriented families. No less than 15 per cent of them were sons of politicians, and at least another 15 per cent had one or more members of their families active in politics during their formative years. A child born into such an environment is likely to be instilled with more favorable attitudes towards politics and politicians than the average American. Moreover, the right contacts and a familiar name can give him a considerable head-start in politics.

5. Cf., S. Lubell, *The Future of American Politics* (New York: Harper and Brothers, 1951), Ch. 4.

6. H. D. Lasswell, *Power and Personality* (New York: W. W. Norton, 1948).

7. H. Hyman, *Political Socialization* (Glencoe, Illinois: The Free Press, 1959). On the subject of this entire section see also H. Eulau, W. Buchanan, L. Ferguson, and J. C. Wahlke, "The Political Socialization of American State Legislators," *Midwest Journal of Political Science*, III (May, 1959), 188-206.

But *why* our subjects became politicians must remain an open question. More is known about *how* they became senators—although again not as much as we would like. Complete and reliable information is available only on the public offices the senators held. The data on the senators' activities in political parties and campaigns, the political situation in their states at the time of their nomination and election, and the senators' unsuccessful bids for elective office is too fragmentary to merit analysis. This means, unfortunately, that we are unable to deal with some of the most interesting and significant questions concerning the senators' political careers. It means that we are able to describe only the open political activity of the senators and only a part of that. Given these strict limitations on our data, what can be said about how these men became senators?

GETTING STARTED IN POLITICS

Most of the men who served as senators after World War II began their political careers early in life. Almost half of them held their first public offices before their thirtieth birthdays; a full three-quarters of them were public officials before they were forty years old (Table 21). Of course, these figures exaggerate the age at which the senators became politically active, for few persons achieve public office without prior years of work for a political party. We can assume, therefore, that the "average" senator probably became immersed in politics shortly after the completion of his education.

Nonetheless, a few politically precocious senators began their office-holding careers before they were old enough to vote; others did not start out until they were over sixty. Those who held their first public offices early in life tended to be sons of politicians; to have been born

Table 21

AGE AT ACHIEVING FIRST PUBLIC OFFICE

| | Age Group | | | | |
	20-29	30-39	40-49	50 plus	Totals
All Senators	46%	30%	15%	9%	100% (177)
Northern and Western Democrats	47%	30%	22%	0%	100% (36)
Southern and Border Democrats	64%	22%	11%	4%	100% (55)
Republicans	35%	35%	14%	16%	100% (86)

NOTE: The age at achieving first public office of three senators is unknown. They have been omitted from this analysis.

in families of relatively high occupational standing; to be minority group members rather than Yankee-Protestants; and to be farmers or lawyers rather than businessmen or professors. The Democrats, especially those from the one-party Southern and Border states, held their first public offices earlier in life than the Republicans.[8]

The senators' first public offices varied widely in their character and importance (Table 22). Almost exactly half of the senators began either as law-enforcement officers (prosecuting attorneys, judges, or marshals) or by serving in their state legislatures. While no other offices were nearly so popular at this stage in their careers, a sizeable minority also started out by being elected to local office or appointed to some kind of administrative position.[9]

Table 22
FIRST PUBLIC OFFICE ACHIEVED

Type of Office	Number	Percentage
U.S. Senator	17	9%
State Governor	4	2
United States Representative	7	4
State Legislator	38	21
State-wide Elective Official	8	4
Local Elective Official	25	14
Law Enforcement	50	28
Administrative Official	26	14
Congressional Staff	5	3
	180	100%

8. To say that so many factors are associated with an early start in politics is to beg the question: Which ones are the most important? It is possible, by a process of cross tabulation too lengthy and tedious to report fully here, to approximate an answer to this question.

First of all, the earlier age at which Democrats launched office-holding careers was not the result of a larger proportion of them coming from one-party and modified one-party states. The Democrats from one-party states tended to be younger at their first public office than the one-party state Republicans, while the Democrats from two-party states were younger than Republicans from two-party states, and so on. Second, a senator's party affiliation is more closely and consistently related to his age at first public office than the type of party system in his state. Finally the Southern and Border Democrats were younger than the Northern and Western Democrats who in turn were younger than the Republicans, even when they all possessed similar personal backgrounds. Party and sectional affiliations, therefore, appear to be more important in influencing the age at which the senators launched office-holding careers than either the type of party system in their state or their personal backgrounds.

9. This classification of offices has been adapted from J. A. Schlesinger, *How They Became Governor* (East Lansing: Michigan State University Press, 1957). The criteria of inclusion in and exclusion from the categories may be found in *ibid.*, p. 10.

The ages of future senators had a great deal to do with the kinds of offices they first achieved. Those who entered politics as relatively young men usually began by serving as state legislators, in law-enforcement or in statewide or local elective offices, or as Congressional staff members. The older men tended to begin as senators, governors, United States representatives, or as some kind of administrator.[10]

The senators' occupations were also related to their first public offices. Half of the lawyers began as law-enforcement officers, a quarter of them as state legislators. No other offices came close to rivaling these two as the place for the Senate lawyers to begin. The other senators started out their political careers in a wider variety of public offices. Twenty-five per cent of the businessmen began as local elective officials, jobs which businessmen can combine with their regular occupations with relative ease. Nineteen per cent of the businessmen began as senators, another 19 per cent as state legislators, and 17 per cent as administrators. The farmers usually started out as state legislators (33 per cent), as local officials (25 per cent), as administrators or as senators (17 per cent each). The professors most often began in appointive administrative positions (43 per cent).

LEVELS OF POLITICAL ACTIVITY

Once started, most senators stayed in politics. By the time they were elected to the Senate, they had held no fewer than 495 public offices, not counting re-elections to the same office.[11] The mythical "average senator" had held about three public offices and had devoted about ten years or approximately half his adult life to officeholding before arriving at the upper chamber (Table 23). But again we find vast departures from these norms. Some of the senators had served in seven, eight, or nine offices for more than twenty-five years, virtually their entire adulthood. Others were completely without officeholding experience before their election or appointment to the Senate.

What kinds of men tended to be most politically active before their election to the Senate? What kinds of men were elected or appointed to the Senate with little previous experience?

10. Ninety-four per cent of the senators whose first public office was state legislator achieved this office before they were forty years of age. Eighty-nine per cent of those who began as law enforcement officers, 88 per cent beginning as state-wide elective officials, 80 per cent beginning as Congressional staff members, 71 per cent beginning as administrators, 50 per cent beginning as U.S. representatives, 33 per cent beginning as governors, and 6 per cent beginning as U.S. senators held their first public offices before their fortieth birthdays.

11. See Appendix E, Table 2.

Table 23
LEVELS OF POLITICAL ACTIVITY BEFORE REACHING SENATE

Number of Years in Public Office before Entering Senate	Percentage of Adult Life in Public Office				
	0%-19%	20%-39%	40%-59%	60%+	Totals
0	10%	0%	0%	0%	10%
1- 4	10	1	0	0	11
5- 9	7	15	3	0	25
10-14	0	7	12	2	21
25-19	0	2	9	7	18
10-24	0	0	2	9	11
25+	0	0	1	4	5
TOTALS	27%	25%	27%	22%	100% (179)

There appear to be two major differences between the most and the least politically experienced senators. The first of these is occupational: the farmers and lawyers were the most politically active and experienced before their election to the Senate; the businessmen and professors were least politically experienced (Table 24).[12] The second difference is partisan: the Democrats, especially those from the Southern and Border states, were more active than the Republicans.

It would be hazardous to conclude, on the basis of this alone, that the senators' occupations and party affiliations caused these differences in levels of political activity. A larger number of Democrats than

Table 24
PERCENTAGE OF ADULT LIFE IN PUBLIC OFFICE, BY OCCUPATION

Senators' Principal Occupation	0-19	20-39	40-59	60-79	80 plus	
Lawyers	19%	26%	25%	23%	7%	100% (96)
Businessmen	42%	25%	25%	8%	0%	100% (53)
Farmers	15%	15%	46%	8%	15%	100% (13)
Professors	50%	50%	0%	0%	0%	100% (8)

NOTE: The "other professionals" have been omitted from this and all subsequent tables in this chapter. As a residual category, it contains such a diverse group of occupations that further analysis of it is inadvisable.

12. There were some differences within these necessarily broad categories. The lawyers who attended the poorer law schools and belonged to the smaller law firms were more politically active than their professional colleagues, and the real estate and insurance men were far more politically involved than the other businessmen.

Republicans, for example, come from one-party states, where holding public office is less hazardous than in areas of vigorous partisan competition. Perhaps the difference between Democrats and Republicans is the result of this factor. But if one compares the Democrats with the Republicans from the same kinds of states as has been done in Table 25, one sees that the Southern Democrats tend to have been the most politically active; the non-Southern Democrats, the next most active; and the Republicans, the least active regardless of the party system in their states. A partisan and regional difference in level of political activity exists independent of the different numbers of Democrats and Republicans from one- and two-party areas. This raises a further point: does the difference in occupational makeup of the two parties explain the difference in political involvement of Democrats and Republicans? The answer is contained in Table 26. The farmers, lawyers, businessmen, and professors tend to have been politically active in that order within each party and section. Thus occupation does make a difference, even when the effects of party and section are controlled. But the Democrats also tend to be more active than the Republicans with the same occupations. Therefore, both a senator's party affiliation and his occupation affect the level of his political activity before becoming a senator.

CHANNELS TO THE SENATE

By the time they became senators, our 180 subjects had held almost every conceivable kind of public office. From this it might be inferred

Table 25

PERCENTAGE SPENDING MORE THAN 40 PER CENT OF PRE-SENATE ADULT YEARS
IN PUBLIC OFFICE, BY TYPE OF STATE PARTY SYSTEM

Type of State Party System	Northern and Western Democrats	Southern and Border Democrats	Republicans	All Senators
Two-Party System	50% (32)	71% (7)	33% (58)	41% (97)
Modified One-Party System: Senator from Strong Party		57% (21)	50% (26)	53% (47)
One-Party System		63% (27)	50% (2)	62% (29)
All States	47% (36)	52% (55)	39% (88)	

NOTE: Senators from the weaker party in modified one-party states were omitted because of too few cases.

Table 26

PERCENTAGE SPENDING MORE THAN 40 PER CENT OF PRE-SENATE ADULT YEARS
IN PUBLIC OFFICE, BY OCCUPATION

Occupation	Northern and Western Democrats	Southern and Border Democrats	Republicans	All Senators
Lawyers	60% (20)	68% (37)	41% (39)	55% (96)
Businessmen	43% (7)	40% (10)	30% (36)	34% (53)
Farmers	0% (1)	80% (5)	71% (7)	69% (13)
Professors	0% (4)	0% (2)	0% (1)	0% (8)

that almost any public office can serve as a likely steppingstone to the power and prestige of the Senate chamber. Such, however, is not the case.

Look, for instance, at Table 27, in which the distribution of the senators' last public offices before election or appointment to the Senate is presented. About 30 per cent of the senators were elected from the House; 20 per cent after serving as governors; 17 per cent, administrators; 15 per cent, law-enforcement officers; and 10 per cent, as state legislators. Very few senators were elected from any other kind of office. When one stops to think that there were only 48 state governorships and 435 seats in the House, while there were many thousands of these other positions, it is clear that a far larger proportion of governors and congressmen were "promoted" to the Senate than is true of

Table 27

LAST PUBLIC OFFICE BEFORE ACHIEVING SENATE

Last Public Office	Northern and Western Democrats	Southern and Border Democrats	Republicans	All Senators
State Governor	17%	21%	25%	22%
U.S. Representative	25	39	23	28
State Legislator	3	10	15	10
Statewide Elective Office	0	0	3	2
Local Elective Office	11	0	7	6
Law-Enforcement Office	19	13	11	15
Administrative Office	25	17	17	17
Congressional Staff	0	0	1	1
	100% (36)	100% (52)	100% (75)	100% (164)

other officeholders. In this sense, the governorships and the House are the two major channels to the Senate.

The senators' occupations were definitely related to the channels they followed to the Senate (Table 28). The lawyers most often came up via the House of Representatives, with law-enforcement offices and governorships running a close second and third. Businessmen were usually elected to the Senate from administrative positions, with the governorships, the House, and "civilian" jobs tied for second place. Farmers were most often elected from governorships, with state legislatures running a poor second. All the professors with political experience came from administrative posts, local elective office, or the House.

Table 28
PRINCIPAL OCCUPATION AND LAST PUBLIC OFFICE

Last Public Office	Lawyer	Businessman	Farmer	Professor
None	2%	19%	15%	14%
Governor	21	19	38	0
U.S. Representative	30	19	15	29
State Legislator	7	9	23	0
Statewide Elected Office	2	0	0	0
Local Elected Office	1	11	0	29
Law Enforcement Office	22	2	0	0
Administrative Office	15	21	8	29
Congressional Staff	1	0	0	0
	100%	100%	100%	100%
	(97)	(53)	(13)	(7)

The party system in the senator's state also seems to have had a great deal to do with the channel he followed to the Senate (Table 29). Those from one-party states, of either the "pure" or "modified" variety, arrived via the two usual gateways far more often than did the men from two-party states. Sixty per cent of those from one-party, and 70 per cent of those from modified one-party states, were elected from either a governorship or a seat in the House; this was true of only 30 per cent of those from two-party states. The senators from two-party states were elected from a far wider range of less important offices or with no officeholding experience at all.[13]

13. This is true in both political parties. The proportion of the senators whose last public office was either governor or U.S. representative is as follows for each party and

Table 29

LAST PUBLIC OFFICE, BY STATE PARTY SYSTEM

Last Public Office	Two-Party	Modified One-Party	One-Party
None	14%	2%	3%
Governor	12	34	28
U.S. Representative	18	36	31
State Legislator	9	9	10
Statewide Elective Office	2	0	0
Local Elective Office	8	0	0
Law Enforcement Office	14	6	14
Administrative Office	21	13	14
Congressional Staff	1	0	0
	100%	100%	100%
	(98)	(47)	(29)

AGE AT ELECTION

The Senate of the United States is organized, in large part, on the basis of seniority. Given this principle of organization and the hard facts of the mortality tables, the age at which a man becomes a United States senator is of considerable importance. What factors influence the age at which these men are elected?

First of all, while there is a great deal of overlapping, the Democrats as a group became senators five or so years before the Republicans (Figure 7). It is conceivable that this difference is a reflection of a basic difference between the two major parties. On the other hand this association between political party and age of election to the Senate may be the result of some other factor. For instance, more Democrats than Republicans are elected to the Senate from one-party states; can the differences in ages of newly elected Democrats and Republicans be accounted for on the basis of the fact that members of the two parties tend to come from different kinds of state party systems? Figure 8 says no. The Democrats tend to be younger at their original election than the Republicans no matter what kind of state party system they came from.

type of party system:

	Two-Party States	Modified One-Party States	One-Party States
Democrats	25%	67%	59%
Republicans	27%	73%	50%

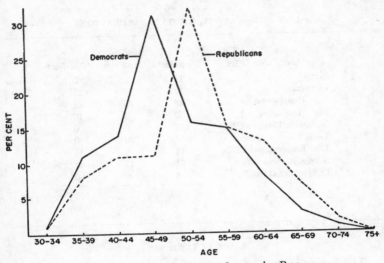

FIG. 7.   Age at Election to Senate, by Party

Certain features of the senators' lives and careers also affected the stage in life at which they became senator. Those elected to the Senate especially early in life most often were born in families of relatively high social status (Table 30). Professional men became senators at an earlier age than farmers or businessmen (Table 31). And, as one might expect, the earlier in life the senators entered politics, the younger they were when elected to the Senate (Table 32).

TYPES OF CAREERS

So far we have found that the senators were, as a group, very politically active before their election or appointment to the Senate and that, as a group, these same men possessed unusually high social status. But not all senators possessed both of these characteristics. Logically, therefore, there are four possible combinations of social status and political activity to be found among the senators:

	Social Status	*Political Activity*
1.	High	High
2.	High	Low
3.	Low	High
4.	Low	Low

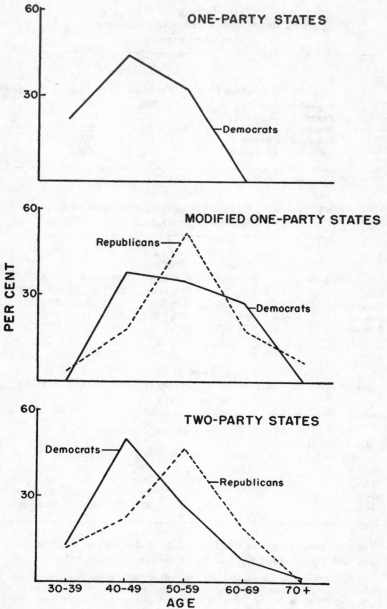

Fig. 8. Age at Election to Senate, by Party and Home-State Party System

Table 30
PERCENTAGE ACHIEVING SENATE UNDER FORTY YEARS OF AGE,
BY CLASS OF FATHER

	Party	
Father's Occupational Class	Democratic	Republican
Professional	23%	12%
Proprietor and Official	12%	12%
Farmer	3%	6%
Low-Salaried Worker	0%	0%
Industrial Wage Earner	0%	0%

Table 31
PERCENTAGE ACHIEVING SENATE BEFORE FIFTY YEARS OF AGE,
BY PRINCIPAL OCCUPATION

Occupation	Northern and Western Democrats	Southern and Border Democrats	Republicans	All
Lawyer	67% (21)	63% (38)	30% (40)	50% (99)
Businessman	43% (7)	30% (10)	28% (36)	30% (53)
Farmer	0% (1)	60% (5)	43% (7)	46% (13)
Professor	33% (3)	59% (2)	100% (1)	50% (6)

Table 32
AGE AT ACHIEVING FIRST PUBLIC OFFICE AND AT ELECTION/APPOINTMENT
TO THE SENATE

Age at Achieving First Public Office	Age at Election/Appointment to Senate				
	30-39	40-49	50-59	60 plus	
20-29	12%	44%	33%	11%	100% (82)
30-39	15%	28%	45%	11%	100% (53)
40-49		38%	42%	19%	100% (26)
50 plus			37%	63%	100% (16)

When the senators are classified according to this scheme and examined with care, four distinct types of senatorial careers emerge.[14]

14. This typology of careers, as is the case with so many others like it, is not particularly easy to "operationalize." Clear-cut examples of each type came quickly to mind, but when 180 senators must be assigned to one or the other category, some

Patrician Politicians

About 7 per cent of the senators possessed both relatively high social status and relatively high political accomplishment before becoming senators. We shall call them Patrician Politicians.

The Patricians come from America's "old families," with the assured social positions, wealth, and security that this connection provides. They are also highly experienced politicians. "Public service," as political activity is known in these circles, tends to run in the family. More than half of the Patricians' fathers were in politics before them. All of them had numerous ancestors and relatives prominent in state or national politics before their time. Usually, they entered politics by running for a relatively minor elective office (about half of them for state legislatures and a quarter for law-enforcement offices) shortly after graduating from college or law school. Eighty-five per cent were officeholders while still in their twenties, and all of them were in public office before they were forty years old. Their rise to the Senate was steady and fairly rapid. A third were in their thirties when elected or appointed to the chamber; three-quarters of them were senators before they were fifty.

Senators Saltonstall and Lodge, both from Massachusetts, are good examples. They were born into the leading families of the Commonwealth. Both attended private schools and then Harvard University. Saltonstall practiced law for a few years in Boston before beginning (at the age of twenty-eight) an almost uninterrupted political career as alderman, assistant district attorney, state representative, speaker of the

agonizing decisions have to be made. The following operational definitions were used:

Patrician Politicians are senators who came from "old families" and had served ten or more years in public office, or had been in office more than 30 per cent of their adult lives. (This alternative criterion was added so as not to introduce an age bias into the categories.)

Amateur Politicians are defined as those senators who had served less than ten years and less than 30 per cent of their adult years in public office.

Professional Politicians are senators who meet the public-service requirements of the Patricians but did not come from "old families."

Agitators have served less than ten years and less than 30 per cent of their adult lives in public office *and* have displayed little occupational attainment.

Distinguishing between Professionals and Patricians and between Amateurs and Agitators requires the exercise of subjective judgment concerning the senators' social origins and occupational attainments. In making these decisions, the author assigned a senator to the Patrician or Agitator category only if the evidence was overwhelmingly in favor of doing so. A more liberal interpretation of the definitions would have resulted in a larger number of Patricians and Agitators, a highly desirable consequence for purposes of statistical analysis. It would also have resulted, however, in a more heterogeneous group of senators in the Patrician and Agitator categories.

The statistical tabulations upon which the text descriptions of Patricians, Professionals, Amateurs, and Agitators are based are presented in Appendix E, Tables 3 to 5.

House, governor, and senator. Lodge, a government major at Harvard, began work as a reporter, correspondent, and editorial writer for the *New York Herald Tribune*. Then, moving back to Massachusetts, he began his political career by running for a seat in the state legislature when he was thirty-one years old. Only four years later he was a United States senator.

The Patricians tend to come from the Northeast and the South, portions of the country which most clearly contain "old family" strata. They are just as often Democrats as Republicans.

Amateur Politicians

Thirty-four per cent of the postwar senators were Amateur Politicians. They are distinguished from the Patricians by their far lower degree of political involvement and accomplishment before they became senators.

Most of the Amateurs came from middle-class families, although a few of them were from very well-to-do or working-class homes. They were quite successful businessmen (45 per cent), lawyers (33 per cent), and professors (10 per cent). More often than not, they were prosperous. As a group, they started political careers later in life than the other senators, about 60 per cent of them being over forty when they achieved their first public offices. Usually, they began their political careers by being appointed to an important executive position or being elected to a major public office. Indeed, a quarter of the Amateurs had held no previous public office when they became senators. Often they won their Senate seats via appointment to a vacancy rather than by election. They were the oldest group of senators at their entry into the chamber; almost a third of them were over sixty when they began their Senate careers.

An example is Homer E. Capehart. The son of an Algiers, Indiana, tenant farmer, Capehart went to work as a salesman immediately upon his graduation from high school. He was an almost immediate success. By the time he was in his early thirties, he was already president of the Capehart Corporation, manufacturers of radio, phonograph, and television equipment. Then, a rich man by the time he was forty, Capehart held a huge Republican rally at his large farm in Washington, Indiana. Seven years later, still with no officeholding experience, Capehart was elected to the Senate. Senator Kerr is another example. He made a fortune in oil and then entered active politics in his fifties by successfully running for governor of Oklahoma. Senator Murray was also a wealthy lawyer and businessman in his fifties before a job as chairman of the Montana Advisory Board for the WPA launched him

on a political career. William Benton was a nationally known advertising executive before he was forty years old. Resigning from his firm
of Benton and Bowles, he tried his hand at education (vice-president
of the University of Chicago) and diplomacy (assistant secretary of
state, United States delegate to numerous international conferences)
before being appointed to the Senate to fill a vacancy.

All told, about 43 per cent of the Republicans were Amateurs; only
a quarter of the Democrats followed this career line to the Senate.
Paradoxically, the politically inexperienced Amateurs were most apt to
become senators from two-party states, where politics is most competitive and the risks of a political career most severe. At the same time,
the cost of a Senate campaign is also greater in these states, and the
Amateurs are usually in a position to pay for a large share of their
own campaigns. Moreover, in two-party states, the nomination process
is more likely to be controlled by the party leadership than in one-party
areas. Apparently, Amateurs fare better in such a situation than in
a wide-open, every-man-for-himself primary contest in which a wide
personal following is needed to secure a Senate nomination.

Professional Politicians

The most common type of senator is the Professional Politician—
55 per cent of the postwar senators fall into this category. The Professionals were as politically involved and experienced as the Patricians
but did not possess "old family" backgrounds. The majority of them
trained as lawyers (64 per cent), the Professionals entered politics very
early in life—usually as law-enforcement officers or state legislators.
Their rise to the Senate was relatively slow but steady; most of them
came up via the House of Representatives or state governorships. As a
group, they were a little younger than the Amateurs and considerably
older than the Patricians upon their first election to the Senate.

Alben Barkley's career is a fairly typical one. Born near Lowes,
Kentucky, the son of a tenant farmer, the irrepressible "Veep" attended
Marvin College in nearby Clinton and Virginia Law School. After
only five years of private law practice, Barkley was elected prosecuting
attorney of his county, then county judge, and then congressman.
After more than two decades of officeholding experience, he was elected
United States senator.

John Bricker of Ohio is another example. The son of a Mount
Sterling, Ohio, farmer, Bricker attended college and law school at
Ohio State University and then immediately plunged into politics as
a city solicitor, assistant attorney general of Ohio, public utilities com-

missioner, attorney general of Ohio, and governor. By the time he was first elected to the Senate in 1947, Bricker had spent a total of twenty-five years in public office. Not all the other Professional Politicians in the Senate have had as extensive pre-Senate careers, but most of them at least approximate this pattern.

The Professional Politicians are the most numerous in both parties and in all types of states. However, 60 per cent of the Democrats were Professionals while only 45 per cent of the Republicans were so classified. They also tend to be elected from one-party areas more frequently than from two-party states.

Agitators

Occasionally, a senator is elected to the Senate without the inherited position of the Patricians, the solid record of business or professional accomplishment of the Amateurs, or the political accomplishments of the Professional Politicians. These men, the exceptions to the general rule that substantial prestige is requisite for Senate membership, may be called Agitators. They constituted 4 per cent of the senators during the postwar years.

The Agitators tend to have relatively low social origins. Usually lawyers, they started political careers early in life and were elected to the Senate while still relatively young; only the Patricians were younger than they at their election to the chamber. On the other hand, their nonpolitical careers were hardly distinguished, nor did they have much of a political record to show before they became senators. Usually, they rocketed into the chamber from relatively minor state or local public offices.

An excellent example is Glen Taylor of Idaho. After completing an eighth-grade education, Taylor went to work as a hired manager of motion-picture theaters, joined a dramatic stock company, and then struck out on his own as the guitar-playing leader of a second-rate hillbilly band. Inspired by the incongruous notion that he should be a congressman, the singing cowboy campaigned—hillbilly band and all—unsuccessfully for a seat in Congress in 1938 and in the Senate in 1940 and 1942. Badly beaten in politics, out of the good graces of the party leaders, unsuccessful as an entertainer, Taylor then got a job as a sheet-metal worker, which he held until the beginning of his successful 1945 campaign for the Senate.

A somewhat different case is presented by Sheridan Downey of California. Born in the Wyoming Territory—his father was the territory's Republican congressman for a while—Downey followed family tradition and became a lawyer. At first in Laramie and then in Sacramento, Downey was reasonably successful. But in 1928 his extensive real estate speculations caught up with him and he was financially ruined. Then the impoverished California lawyer suddenly experienced flashes of economic insight. Books and pamphlets (*Why I Believe in the Townsend Plan, Pensions or Penury*) followed, and Downey became active in the panacea fringe of California politics. Several unsuccessful campaigns as an EPIC and Townsendite candidate followed until his advocacy of wholesale pension plans as a Democrat overcame his lack of political experience and he was elected to the Senate in 1939.

The most famous young-man-in-a-hurry to be elected to the Senate in recent years was Joseph R. McCarthy of Wisconsin. Born into an Irish Catholic farming family, McCarthy left school at the age of fourteen to work as a hand on his father's farm. Subsequent stints as a self-employed chicken farmer and as a grocery clerk failed to satisfy his ambitions. Then at nineteen he returned to school. It must have been an ordeal for the man-sized Joe McCarthy to squeeze into the child-sized desks and to be forced into the company of fourteen-year-olds. The future senator not only bore this, but, with considerable help from a sympathetic school superintendent, he completed the regular four-year high school course in one. Then, piecing together a living from night work in restaurants and gas stations with some financial aid from home, McCarthy went to Marquette University.

After graduating with an LL.B., McCarthy began legal practice in the small town of Waupaca, Wisconsin. His practice was so anemic that, according to his (unfriendly) biographers, he largely supported himself from his poker winnings. Politics, for which he had shown some flair at Marquette, seemed like a possible solution to his financial problems, but McCarthy was a Democrat in a normally Republican state. A losing campaign for district attorney on the Democratic ticket showed that the party was a blind alley, so when the struggling young lawyer was offered a job by a prosperous and respected Republican lawyer in nearby Shawano, he took it—and became a Republican. Several years later McCarthy was elected a circuit judge, the youngest man ever to be so honored in his state. Thus began one of the most rapid, and most ruthless, political careers in modern American politics. Seven years later—thirty months of which were spent in the United States Marines—McCarthy was a United States senator at the extraordinarily early age of thirty-seven. Few senators have gone so far so fast.

Normally, becoming a senator is a time-consuming and difficult task. The merits of those who aspire to the office are pretested in a rough and ready (and not entirely equitable) way by the necessity for a fairly distinguished career, either in or out of politics. The election of men to the Senate who have not distinguished themselves in either respect may well be a symptom of a breakdown in the regularized methods of senatorial recruitment in the United States. These men have "beaten the game." Sometimes this may have been because of fantastic good luck, but more often it would seem to have been the result of a willingness to resort to demagoguery and unscrupulous methods, to ignore "the rules of the game."

The Agitators are most frequently elected from the Western states. The reason for this is not at all clear, but perhaps this is because the social structure of the West is more "open," less stratified, than in the East and South. Moreover, in the Western states, the party leadership is relatively powerless to influence nominations. Agitators are not the kind of candidates likely to appeal to responsible party leaders. In the Southern one-party states, where party leaders have even less influence on the nomination process than in the West, the social structure is more highly stratified. The combination of a relatively fluid social structure with almost leaderless political parties seems to provide the conditions from which Agitators are most likely to emerge.

We have attempted to describe and analyze the senators' political careers up to the time of their election or appointment to the chamber. We have found that the "typical" senator started a political career shortly after graduating from college by being elected state legislator or becoming a prosecuting attorney or some other kind of law-enforcement officer. By the time he was elected to the Senate he had held three previous public offices and had spent about ten years or half of his adult life in public office. The chances are that he was elected to the Senate while, or shortly after, serving as a state governor or member of the House of Representatives.

But this "typical" picture is overly simple. For one thing, it may lead us to overlook the significant role of happenstance, drift, and just plain luck in senatorial careers, and it tells us very little about the politics of the senators' careers. In part, this is the result of inadequate information, but also it is an inherent weakness of studies such as this one which concentrates on career patterns. The reader should be warned that this chapter does not, because it can not, tell the whole story.

In the second place, the picture of the "typical" senator's political career, presented above, obscures the fact that the senators followed a wide variety of paths to the Senate. We have sought to overcome this limitation by describing and analyzing the *differences* in senatorial careers. The result has been not one "typical" senator but four—Patricians, Amateurs, Professionals, and Agitators.

In subsequent chapters we shall see that these different types of men often behave differently as United States senators.

CHAPTER IV

The Senators' Way of Life

MOST PROFESSIONS impose a way of living upon a man. A lawyer's life, for instance, is quite different from that of a physician; both differ from that of a professor. Each group has its own distinctive problems, shared experiences, special language, and patterns of work. These create an emotional tie to the group which survives the most vigorous intraprofessional rivalry.

Much the same is true of United States senators. Even bitter political enemies in the Senate have had many common experiences and face many similar problems, they "speak the same language," they identify with each other. Within limits, they lead similar lives. Let us look at the senators' way of life to discover how its patterns affect the men and women who follow it.

CAMPAIGNING

Perhaps the most important thing to know about United States senators is the most obvious—they are elected officials. It is difficult really to understand the senators, how they act and why, without considering what happens to them while they are running for office.

Months "on the road"—traveling from city to city, town to town, hamlet to hamlet, meeting and talking and listening to all kinds of people—leave a permanent imprint upon a man. A ten o'clock "coffee hour" populated by middle-class housewives; a noontime visit to a factory gate for a speech delivered perched atop a sound truck, followed by a rushed appearance at a Kiwanis Club luncheon; a visit to the livestock barn at a county fair; handshaking at the Italian, Polish, or Lithuanian Club as the men drift in for a beer and a game of pool on the way home from work; a formal address to the party faithful—all this and often more an aspiring senator may do in a single day. Political campaigning forces a man out of the comfortable cocoon of self-imposed uniformity within which most of us live. It results in an acute awareness of the vast differences in the conditions, interests, opinions, and styles of life of the American people and a detached tolerance toward this diversity.

Campaigning also engenders an almost infinite faith in the personal touch: the surprised but pleased look of the total stranger accosted on the street corner; the city fathers' jockeying to stand next to the candidate while a photograph is taken or to sit near him at "the head table"; the endless handshaking, the everlasting "Hello, Jim, you don't remember me, do you?";[1] the proprietary air of his hosts and hostesses at the inescapable parties which rob the candidate of much-needed sleep; the warm response to almost any reference to local celebrities or landmarks—all point to a single moral: the voters love those who seem to love them.

The moral tone of American political campaigns is not so high as it might be. "From the beginning of the Republic, candidates have at times been falsely accused of bribery, perjury, graft, fraud, treason, sexual irregularities, pro-Toryism, communism, fascism, anti-Semitism, anti-Catholicism, and of racial prejudices or the lack of them."[2] The fashion in "smears" has varied with popular mores, prejudices, and fears. Today, open attacks on the personal and private lives of candidates are considered risky. "The people," according to one well-known campaign manager, "don't like anything that smacks of 'dirty politics,' and personal attacks usually do." Besides, some of the old standbys no longer work: "Nowadays, if you accuse an opposing candidate of getting drunk it doesn't work. Even plain fornication doesn't seem to outrage the people—unless it's complicated by a deserted wife and

1. The senators find this greeting particularly irritating. There's an old Capitol Hill joke about some congressmen hanging around the cloakrooms. One of them asked the others what each would do if he suddenly inherited a million dollars. The first couple of congressmen gave rather ordinary answers—new homes, foreign travel, and so on. But the last one said, "I'd go to Detroit and buy me the biggest and longest Cadillac made. I'd drive it to the center of my district's biggest town. When I got out and a constituent came up to me and said, 'You don't remember my name, do you, Congressman,' I'd say, 'No, I don't, you son-of-a-bitch, and I don't give a damn either!' "

2. S. Kelly, Jr., "Some Hazards of Candidacy," paper presented to the American Political Science Association, September 5-7, 1957, (mimeographed), p. 1.

kids or something. Just trying to 'make' the hired girl doesn't pack a political wallop anymore—plain old fornication is too popular, I guess."

However, unfair and misleading attacks on opposition candidates were common during the postwar years. In the South, these charges usually played on racial prejudices—Willis Smith's defeat of Frank Graham in North Carolina, for example, seems clearly attributable to charges that Graham favored the "mixing" of the races.[3] Elsewhere, the monomania was different but the campaign tactics were much the same.

"In New York, John Foster Dulles found that the Communists were in Herbert Lehman's corner. In Florida, George Smathers distributed a booklet entitled 'Red Pepper' and each day named a new 'subversive' or 'Communist' group which Senator Claude Pepper had at some time addressed. In California, Richard Nixon and his manager, Murray Chotiner, made the Communist issue the basis of their campaign against Helen Gahagan Douglas. In Ohio, Senator Robert Taft said that the entire campaign against him had been blueprinted by convicted Communist Gus Hall. In Utah, Republican workers distributed a tabloid detailing the allegedly Communist record of Senator Elbert Thomas. In Colorado, Senator Eugene Millikin charged that Americans were dying in Korea because of Communist infiltration into the United States Department of State."[4] In Colorado, Gordon Allott asked "How Red is John Carroll?" while in Montana a campaign pamphlet entitled "Senator Murray and the Red Web Over Congress" enjoyed a wide circulation.[5] In Wyoming, Senator Joseph O'Mahoney was confronted with

> They took our boys, they took our land,
> They wasted our money, backed Truman's last stand.
> They talked with the Commies, we toss 'em out.
> Joe forgot Wyoming
> Without any doubt.[6]

In Maryland, a four-page tabloid, circulated in the closing days of the John Marshall Butler campaign, displayed a composite picture of his opponent, Senator Millard Tydings, in conversation with the Com-

---

3. S. Lubell, *The Future of American Politics* (New York: Harper and Brothers, 1951), pp. 100-8.

4. S. Kelly, Jr., *Professional Public Relations and Political Power* (Baltimore: The Johns Hopkins Press, 1956), p. 107.

5. *Washington Post and Times Herald*, July 12, 1956.

6. *New York Times*, January 14, 1955.

munist leader Earl Browder.[7] One radio spot announcement used in a number of campaigns began with the roar of printing presses that, an announcer revealed, were "the printing presses of the Communist party . . . turning out the official Communist line." Another voice with a fake Russian accent then began to read the "line": "Defeat the Republican Congressional candidates in 1954! That is our order from Moscow! Return America to a New Deal type Administration!"[8] In Ohio, the labor unions widely circulated a vicious comic book depicting Robert Taft as the tool of "J. Phineas Moneybags," and similar comic books, with their crude appeals to class prejudices, played a prominent role in many other Democratic campaigns.

These tactics were employed because, in the judgment of the campaigners and their managers, they "worked." Speaking to an audience of politicians, Mr. Murray Chotiner explained why: "I say to you in all sincerity that if you do not deflate the opposition candidate before your own campaign gets started, the odds are that you are going to be doomed to defeat . . . . The American people . . . vote against a candidate, against a party, or against an issue, rather than for a candidate or an issue or a party."[9]

When confronted with such tactics a candidate can do very little even if the charges are clearly untrue.[10] The courts move so slowly and the laws of libel and slander are such that a "smeared" politician can seldom gain anything from initiating legal proceedings save a reputation as a "sorehead." To answer the charges in detail merely publicizes them further and forces the attacked candidate to accept his opponent's definition of the relevant issues in the campaign. Perhaps the most effective thing a candidate can do is to retaliate in kind in an effort to destroy his attacker's credibility. This type of campaigning tends to feed on itself, and the campaign becomes (at least in the eyes of the average voter) a "contest of rascals"[11] carried on in an atmosphere of moral squalor.

Most men who run for the Senate are experienced politicans and, as one of them has said, "You get pretty callous in this business." Even those who have developed "a hide like an elephant"[12] can be shocked and bitter with this kind of campaigning—shortly after his defeat one Professional Politician confided that "campaigns these days are no

7. Kelly, *Public Relations*, Ch. 4.
8. *New York Times*, January 14, 1955.
9. Quoted in Kelly, "Hazards of Candidacy," pp. 2-3.
10. See *ibid.*, *passim*.
11. *Ibid.*, p. 7.
12. R. E. Baldwin, *Let's Go Into Politics* (New York: Macmillan, 1952), p. 100.

place for common honesty." At the same time, our politicians are expected to be "good sports." "While you may have taken a solemn oath that after the campaign was over you were going to knock all that fellow's teeth out, when the campaign *is* over and he comes to shake your hand, you have to be able to shake his hand and smile."[13]

Senate campaigns are expensive. Despite the Corrupt Practices Act of 1925, which limits the amount a candidate for the Senate can spend in general elections to $25,000, most political experts place the absolute minimum cost of a Senate campaign at around $100,000. Perhaps the "normal" expenditures, to strike a rough average of the varying reports of experts, is in the neighborhood of $500,000 and closely contested battles in large two-party states often cost over a million dollars. "The people are funny about this. If a candidate went out and said, 'I'm going to spend a half-million dollars in an effort to become your senator,' he would be soundly defeated. They would think that he was trying to buy a seat. But that's what he probably has to spend."

Obviously, the spirit, if not the letter, of the law is broken in every campaign. "Under existing law," a campaign manager explained, "a candidate cannot 'know' about most of the money spent in his behalf. He may be surrounded by billboards and deluged with spot announcements boosting his candidacy but as long as he doesn't 'know' about how they are paid for, it's O.K." A senator was more cryptic: "I don't know how much it costs to run for the Senate. *I wasn't supposed to know.*"

Where does the money come from? If the candidate is wealthy, a portion of it is likely to come from his own pocket. Some is "emotional money,"[14] donated by personal friends and admirers without thought of return. The bulk of his campaign fund, however, is likely to be made up of a few large contributions from individuals and groups with a vital interest in his behavior in office. Explicit *quid pro quo*'s are seldom attached to these donations, lurid popular mythology notwithstanding: "Sure, we are all dependent upon contributions from our friends and supporters—people who like what we stand for. If, after we are elected, we vote in a way that pleases our financial backers, is that graft?"

Nonetheless, it must be admitted, as another member of the upper chamber has written, that "The twilight zone between huge campaign

13. *Ibid.*

14. The phrase is Senator Benton's. Subcommittee to Study Senate Concurrent Resolution 21 of the Senate Committee on Labor and Public Welfare, 82nd Congress, 1st Session, *Hearings: Establishment of a Commission on Ethics in Government,* pp. 43-44.

contributions and outright bribes . . . [is] . . . murky."[15] A successful candidate for a Senate seat is understandably grateful to those individuals and interests who have supplied him with the sinews of battle. While, most of the time, he would be in general sympathy with their political goals in any event, he is likely to be especially sensitive to their wants and needs. Their expressions of opinion are bound to be given more weight, their requests for favors, more attention, than those of people to whom the senator is not beholden. The contributor thus gains access, and the senator loses freedom of maneuver. The influence is latent, but it is still there.[16] The senators know this, of course: "Many a candidate, including this one, has rationalized campaign contributions on the theory that they were offered merely to assist a 'good' senator—but it doesn't necessarily follow that the contributor feels the same way."[17] In the heat of political battle, it seems a relatively small price to pay for victory.

A campaign for the Senate is not only a moral crisis but a physical ordeal. Campaigns, especially when both a primary and a general election are contested, drag on month after month. The atmosphere is tense, the pace hectic, the crises almost without end, and the distances traveled reckoned in the tens of thousands of miles. Adequate sleep, regular meals, and relaxation are rare luxuries in this driving quest for power. Toward the end, exhaustion sets in. One senator tells how he used to say to himself, "Only eight more speeches—seven more speeches—six more speeches—."[18] Then the day arrives, and there is nothing to do but await the election returns, "nonchalantly chewing my nails."[19] Those who end up on the long end of the tally go to Washington as United States senators.

But they are not the same men that they were before the campaign began. A Senate campaign is a unique educational experience for the candidate, if for no one else. Those who have gone through the experience learn much about their future constituents, their conflicting interests, opinions, and biases, in the process. A candidate learns, too, that most of his constituents expect contradictory behavior from him: he should be above petty politics but he should bring home the bacon;

15. R. L. Neuberger, "Who Should Pay for Political Campaigns?" *New York Times Magazine*, June 3, 1956, p. 65.

16. Cf. A. Heard, *Money in Politics* (New York: Public Affairs Pamphlet No. 242, 1956), p. 14.

17. Senator Gore, quoted in W. S. White, "Realistic Reformer from Tennessee," *New York Times Magazine*, March 4, 1956, p. 34.

18. Baldwin, *Let's Go Into Politics*, p. 92.

19. Tom Connally [at told to Alfred Steinberg], *My Name is Tom Connally* (New York: Thomas Y. Crowell Company, 1954, p. 125.

he should run a clean and dignified campaign but he should be a fighter; he should bring his campaign to the voter but he should not spend money doing so; he should frankly state and act on his convictions but represent his constituents. The candidate has become accustomed to the evasiveness, minor deception, and hypocrisy required to satisfy these conflicting expectations. Candidates learn, too, about themselves and the insidious appeal, when the chips are down, of the doctrine that the end justifies the means. After the glow of victory passes, cynicism and feelings of guilt often linger on. "When I first ran for the Senate, —— told me that I would do and say things during the campaign that I would not recognize a year later. 'You are going to be ashamed of yourself,' he warned. And he was right."

WASHINGTON: THE CONTEXT AND ITS CONSEQUENCES

It is commonplace to observe that Washington is an "artificial" city. For one thing, it is a handsome place, and most Americans equate large cities with ugliness. Its geometric pattern, impressive monuments, spacious parks and avenues, and ponderous white marble buildings testify to the fact that Washington did not grow, it was made—and made to be a capital city. Moreover, it has almost no industry, no large group of employers, no factory workers, no financial nerve centers, no agricultural hinterland.[20] Its only significant industry is politics, and, unlike the other major capitals of the world, Washington is not a major center of art, literature, music, or the theater.

It is a city of people who do not think of themselves as permanent residents; "its important inhabitants identify themselves as 'coming from' some place or expecting to 'return' to another."[21] A constant flow of visitors—tourists, governors, mayors, convention-goers, lobbyists, job seekers—helps give the city "some of the character of a hotel lobby."[22] This is the city in which United States senators live and work during most of the year. Its character and way of life affect them profoundly.

There is no escape from politics in Washington. Political "inside-dope" stories, rumors, tips, reports of personal feuds, and party intrigue are its favorite topics of conversation. The Washington "party" is not so much a social as a political occasion, an opportunity to make contacts,

20. L. C. Rosten, *The Washington Correspondents* (New York: Harcourt, Brace and Company, 1937), p. 11.
21. *Ibid.*, p. 16.
22. *Ibid.*, p. 17. Washington "is a vast rooming house for politicians, civil servants, diplomats and lobbyists." [Washingtonians] "are transients in mind and spirit. . . ." J. Reston, in an address to the National Cathedral Association, reported in the *Washington Post and Times Herald*, April 18, 1956.

to swap gossip, to "find out what's really going on." The senators, be they country politicians, millionaires turned statesmen, products of urban political machines, or Patrician Politicians, are automatically members of this "Society."[23]

Life in this environment has a brittle brilliance about it; most senators find it powerfully attractive. "Glamour, limelight, exaltation, prominence, distinction, position, prestige, influence, power, delightful associations—" one oldtime senator has written of his life in Washington. "It is all most entrancing."[24] Few senators retire voluntarily,[25] and not many of those who retire or are defeated return home. "It's not easy," one defeated senator explains, "to buy a ticket for Podunk after being at the center of things."[26] Moreover, such a humiliating course is seldom necessary. If his party controls the executive branch, a defeated or retiring senator can generally count on an honorific executive appointment. Even if his party is out of power, the former senator's contacts, know-how, and political prestige have great value to a Washington law, lobbying, or public relations firm. Thus defeated or retiring senators and congressmen in Washington "are like a constantly growing deposit of coral. Accumulating with the years, they form a sort of barrier reef around the palm-fringed islands of power. . . ."[27]

While the attractions of the senator's life cannot be denied, some of its features are clearly unfortunate from their point of view. The world in which senators move is almost entirely dominated by politics; everything is viewed in narrowly political terms. Washington, with its preoccupation with influence, rivalry, ambition, suspicion, and frus-

23. On Washington social life, see A. Drury, "Politics is the Be-All and End-All of Society in the Nation's Capital," *New York Times*, January 21, 1957; Rosten, *Washington Correspondents*, p. 13 ff.; R. H. Rovere, " 'Hick Town' or World Capital?" *New York Times Magazine*, April 17, 1955, p. 13 ff.

24. H. L. Myers, *The United States Senate: What Kind of Body?* (Philadelphia: Dorrance and Company, 1939), pp. 102-3.

25. Myers, for example, explains his retirement in this way: "At the end of my second senatorial term I retired voluntarily. I did so for two reasons, each sufficient of itself, *i.e.*, I did not desire another term, and I believed that I could not get it had I desired it." *Ibid.*, p. 7.

26. This is a paraphrase of a remark made by the late Senator McNary of Oregon reported in R. L. Neuberger, *Adventures in Politics* (New York: Oxford University Press, 1954), p. 160. Senator Neuberger's analysis of why men in national politics seldom return to their home states begins at page 153.

27. Marquis Childs in Subcommittee to Study Senate Concurrent Resolution 21 of the Senate Committee on Labor and Public Welfare, 82nd Congress, 1st Session, *Hearings*, p. 152. "Cactus Jack" Garner, a long-time Speaker of the House and Vice President under Franklin Roosevelt, has made the same point less kindly. "Some people," he said, "would stay in Washington if they had to live in trees." B. N. Timmons, *Garner of Texas: A Personal History* (New York: Harper and Brothers, 1948), p. 281.

tration, provides no respite from the extreme tensions and anxieties of the senator's job.[28]   Men in this environment are likely to become as distorted in their perspectives as the psychiatrist who, upon being greeted by a colleague with a cheery, "Good morning," asked himself, "I wonder what he *really* means by that?"   Washington is, in the eyes of the senators, the world's worst place from which to judge the political "temperature of the American people."[29]

At the same time that the senators' lives in Washington overdevelop their political sensitivity and thereby reduce their ability accurately to assess the wants and needs of their constituents, the senators' legislative responsibilities force them to spend a large majority of their time away from home.   During these absences, rivals both within and outside the party chip away at their following unopposed.   "Senators," one literarily inclined member says, "come to feel much like the chief of the Alban tribe, whom Frazer described in his *Golden Bough* as pacing at midnight in the grove by the Lake of Nemi, waiting for the rival who would slay him with a sword and then succeed to his chieftanship."[30]   Moreover, the Senate is, among other things, an educational institution.   "Men learn more, faster, in the Senate than any other time in their lives after the age of five," and what they learn does not necessarily make them more popular back home.   Senators, as a necessary consequence of their jobs, learn a good deal about the complexities of national problems and are exposed to points of view which conflict with the interests and assumptions of their constituents.   They can and sometimes do grow away from their supporters.

Whether the senators grow in office or, as Woodrow Wilson once put it, "just swell" is sometimes hard to tell.   Certainly, "at first blush, most senators are all ego."   Some of the typical senators' egocentrism, selfassertiveness, and vanity appears to antedate their election to "the greatest deliberative body in the world," but much of it appears to result from their experiences as senators.   You can catch more flies with sugar than with vinegar, as the old saying goes, and the hordes of people who want favors from members of the Senate universally

28. E. A. Shils, "The Legislator and His Environment," *Chicago Law Review*, XVIII (1951), 575.   This entire section has been greatly influenced by this brilliant article.

29. The quote is from Senator Hubert Humphrey, Subcommittee to Study Senate Concurrent Resolution 21 of the Senate Committee on Labor and Public Welfare, 82nd Congress, 1st Session, *Hearings*, p. 73.   See also the exchange between Senators Douglas and Aiken and Professor Greene on page 68 in the same *Hearings;* P. H. Douglas, "The Gap Between Congress and Main Street," *New York Times Magazine*, September 16, 1951, p. 13; D. P. Griswold, "A Freshman Senator Makes a Report," *New York Times Magazine*, March 8, 1953, p. 55.

30. Douglas, "The Gap Between Congress and Main Street," *NYT Mag.*, p. 56.

adhere to the maxim. People seldom miss an opportunity to make a senator feel important: his state issues him a special license plate for his car; at Washington dinners and banquets, he is the object of much bowing and scraping; even a routine phone call from a senator can create a panic in an executive department; and on Capitol Hill, he is fed a heady diet of flattery by his colleagues and subservience by his staff. "Take an ordinary unassuming small businessman and put him into this atmosphere," one Senate staff member remarked, "and he'll be a prima donna in no time."

The senator's air of self-importance may sometimes serve him well in Washington. "Before I came here," one freshman explained, "I had always believed that the senators I had known were aloof, hard to reach, perhaps a little stuck up. Now that I have been a senator for a year and one-half, I realize that this is merely their way of *insulating* themselves. The number of requests I get is amazing. You can't escape these eternal 'Give-me's.' Why, I can't go to one of these Washington cocktail parties and be there more than a few minutes before someone starts twisting my arm. Back home if I walked down the street and didn't speak to everybody I passed they'd think I was sick. Here, I find myself trying to avoid people because I know that they will try to get something from me."

Back home, unfortunately, this mode of behavior seems to mean that he has become a "big shot" and "statesman" who has forgotten the plain people at home and sold out to the flesh-pots of the effete East. "What happens to a representative or senator when he is elected to the Congress?" one senator asks, reflecting in his questioning the whole complex of popular fears about Washington. "What happens to a cabinet officer when he is appointed to a cabinet job and comes to Washington, and finds these soft cushions, air-conditioning, and so forth? It is a very good setup. What happens to make him seem to vote with a wet finger, and makes him think that the sentiment of the country is formed in Washington? There is no public sentiment in Washington. The only city that approaches Washington in its danger to the welfare of the country is the city of New York. It is a close second."[31]

These attitudes can be, and are, played upon by the senators' adversaries in re-election compaigns. For example, it was once alleged in a bitter primary battle that Senator Bilbo, whose strength among Mississippi's backwoods red-necks was amazing, had "learned how to

31. Senator Malone of Nevada in *Congressional Record* (Daily Edition), July 18, 1956, p. 12079.

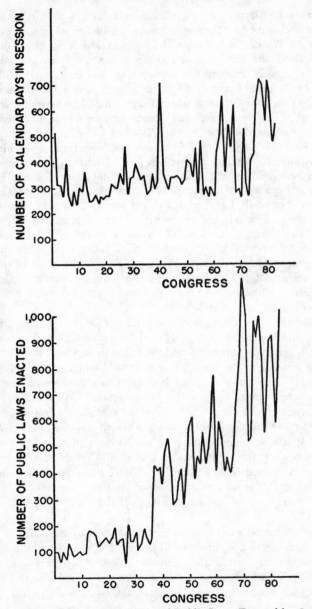

Fig. 9. Calendar Days in Session and Public Laws Enacted by Congress, 1st through 84th Congresses

dance and eat caviar in Washington."[32] Senator Warren Magnuson of Washington returned home a few years ago to campaign for re-election to find the state saturated with campaign leaflets which began: "Once upon a time there was a Senator who loved the purr of a Cadillac, the genial clink of ice cubes late at night, the company of lovely ladies . . . ."[33]

WORK LOAD

"I had expected deliberation," one newly elected senator explains. "Instead, I have found haste and even a certain amount of frenzy."[34] His colleagues agree that theirs is an impossible job. Most work at it about twelve hours a day, some as long as sixteen or eighteen hours, day in and day out.

The volume of legislation which comes before the Senate is almost beyond belief and grows steadily (Figure 9). Until recent years, the Congress convened on March 4 and adjourned within four months, usually by the Fourth of July. Today, the Congress convenes during the first week in January and seldom goes home until August. Yet the longer sessions have not cleared up the legislative calendars; only a constantly increasing pace has made it possible for the House and Senate to dispose of the mounting tide of legislative proposals—this despite the fact that the legislative problems of today are incomparably more complex than those of twenty years ago.

Yet legislating is only a small part of most senators' work; getting and staying elected is considerably more than a full-time job as well. The present-day long sessions of Congress make it difficult, if not impossible, for most senators to restrict their campaigning and fence-mending to the months when the Senate is adjourned. Most members of the Senate make regular trips to their home states for brief, hectic rounds of personal appearances and speechmaking during the session. While in Washington, a sizeable share of their time is devoted to such activities as answering mail (and running the errands and doing the favors which so many of the letters request), writing news letters and preparing press releases, taping radio and filming TV shows for home consumption. Some constituents do not write, they come ("The poor

32. *Current Biography* (New York: H. W. Wilson, 1943), p. 50.

33. *New York Times,* October 19, 1956. An assistant to a Midwestern conservative tells a story about the time his boss had his picture taken at a wedding reception holding a glass of champagne. "The next day he called me in and asked if I could get hold of the picture and have it destroyed. 'If it had been a plain old glass of bourbon,' he explained, 'they wouldn't care in [home state]. But champagne . . . !'"

34. R. L. Neuberger, "Mistakes of a Freshman Senator," *American Magazine,* CVXI (June, 1956), p. 100.

bastards from nearby get them by the hundreds," as one Western senator put it); and at least the more important ones must be greeted,
listened to, and shown around the city and the Capitol. Then, too,
there are the endless dinners, cocktail parties, banquets, and receptions
which many senators feel "you can't stay away from . . . if you want
to know what's going on beyond the end of your nose."[35] The senators' social obligations sometimes get out of hand. Senator Green,
Rhode Island's spry nonagenarian and inveterate party-goer, was once
spied by a colleague consulting a little black book while at a party.
"Senator Green," his colleague asked, "are you looking in your book
to find out where you go next?" "No," he replied, "I am trying to
find out where I am now."[36]

Finally, at the end of the session, more and more senators (perhaps
half of them in an off-election year) take off for extended travel abroad.
Some of these "junkets" may be little more than expense-account vacations—the number of statesmen who have found it necessary to inspect
American facilities in Paris and Rome is amazing—but most of them
have a serious purpose and an extensive and exhausting itinerary.

"But it's not the hard work or the long hours that wear you down,"
one senator explained, "it's the *uncertainty*. You never know when
there will be a crisis, a roll call, when the session will run into the
evening, or if there will be a Friday or Saturday session. You don't
even know when Congress will adjourn. . . ."

No senator has a really fixed schedule of work. As representatives
they are expected to respond to the often unpredictable wants of their
constituents, and, as members of a group of one hundred equals, anyone of whom can shatter the plans of the other ninety-nine, they find
that "You just can't make plans. . . ." Regardless of the reasons, the
senators have largely lost control over their own time.[37]

Look, for example, at how Senator Richard Neuberger describes a
more or less typical day during the 1956 Congressional session.

6:45-7:45 A.M. Rise, read *Congressional Record* of the previous day which
was left on doorstep during night, also two daily newspapers.
7:45-8:30 A.M. Take orange juice with my wife, drive to Capitol building.
8:30-9:30 A.M. Have breakfast with leader of Railroad Brotherhoods from

35. An anonymous senator quoted in C. Phillips, "The High Cost of Our Low-Paid
Congress," *The New York Times Magazine*, February 24, 1952, p. 41.

36. This story was told by Senator Gore, *Congressional Record* (Daily Edition),
June 10, 1956, p. 9409.

37. The importance of this in the analysis of congressional behavior is effectively
stressed by L. Dexter, "Congressmen and the People They Listen To" (unpublished MS,
1955).

Oregon and his wife; take them onto Senate floor and show them my desk—which is permitted only when the Senate is not in session.

9:30-10:00 A.M. Confer with administrative assistant and other members of my staff about day's agenda, important letters and telegrams.

10:00-12:00 A.M. Attend Senate Public Works Committee hearings on government water-power policies.

Noon. Go to floor for opening of the day's Senate business, make two-minute speech urging adherence to Supreme Court ruling in school-segregation cases.

12:30-1:30 P.M. Relieve Senator George, president pro-tem in chair, and preside over Senate.

1:30-2:15 P.M. Have as guests in Senate Restaurant college coed from Oregon who is studying drama in New York City and her girl friend, a delegate to Young Republican meeting. (Because I was late for lunch, as usual, my wife was present to get our guests started.)

2:15-3:15 P.M. Attend Senate session and participate in debate on amendments to farm bill. Called off floor four times for interviews with delegations from "home" and once to be questioned by Associated Press reporter about campaign spending bills.

3:15-4:30 P.M. Preside again over Senate, relieving Democratic Senator Bible of Nevada in chair.

4:30-5:30 P.M. Dictate to secretary in alcove just off Marble Reading Room, answering personally more than forty letters and telegrams.

5:30-6:30 P.M. Return to office to sign mail and be briefed by staff about information and messages brought by steady stream of callers during day.

6:30-6:45 P.M. Phone government officials at their homes about matters of vital importance to my state.

6:45-7:30 P.M. Return to Senate floor to make insertions in *Record* of several editorials from Oregon papers, prior to close of day's debate.

8:00-10:00 P.M. Dinner at downtown Washington hotel with Oregon's Chancellor of Higher Education, in city for conferences with Veterans Administration on GI training.

10:00-12:00 P.M. Return home with brief case full of documents, work in study for two full hours on draft of major Senate speech urging reduction in Social Security age for women.

12:00-1:00 A.M. Go to bed, discuss with wife events of day . . . the telephone can ring at any moment [during the night], and often does. I have been awakened by a constituent who wanted me to facilitate his bidding on a Defense Department contract, by an Oregon GI who ran afoul of MP's in Louisiana for alleged drunken driving, and by a female voter 3,000 miles away who wondered if my wife . . . would be good enough to compute her income tax. . . ."[38]

38. Neuberger, "Mistakes of a Freshman Senator," *Am. Mag.*, p. 104.

While, no doubt, this was a fairly ordinary day for Senator Neuberger, other senators were equally busy doing quite different things. The nature of the senators' work varies considerably, partly because of their different conceptions of the role and partly as a result of such other factors as the size of their states, the security of their seats, their positions in the chamber's hierarchy, and the level of their political ambitions. The senators from the most populous states, for example, face the greatest burden of correspondence and constituent errand running. Those from nearby states have the largest number of visiting "customers" with whom to contend. The members of the Senate with insecure seats, as well as almost all the others during the last two years of their terms, tend to invest a larger share of their time and energy in fence-mending, public relations, and publicity-seeking. The senior senators from one-party states, who have a relatively light mail load and need not worry too much about re-election, monopolize most of the important and time-consuming committee chairmanships. The large handful of serious presidential hopefuls follow an exhausting routine of speech-making, travel, and politicking throughout the country. Thus the sort of work the senators do varies, but almost all the senators work long and hard at some aspects of their many-faceted job.

Most of them feel that the job is slipping out of control. "I just don't have time to study bills as I should, and as the people back home *think* I'm doing," one of them complained. "I'm just dealing off the top of the deck all the time."

THE SENATOR'S OFFICE

Some of the fastest-growing "bureaucracies" in Washington are to be found in the Senate Office Building. Within the memory of Senate old-timers, a typical senator's office staff consisted of an executive secretary and a typist or two. The average postwar senator, with his vastly increased work load, has a staff of a dozen or so people squeezed into his three- or four-room office suite.[39]

39. Senate offices are assigned on the basis of seniority. During the postwar decade, all new senators save those from the very largest states—New York, California, Illinois, Pennsylvania, Texas, and Ohio—were assigned three connecting rooms. The big-state senators received a fourth room, often in the basement of the building, regardless of seniority. The choice four-room offices—convenient to the Capitol subway, roomier, lighter, and overlooking the Mall—were generally monopolized by senior senators.

The opening of the New Senate Office Building in 1959 has eased the office-space problem, at least temporarily. All office suites are now five rooms, and additional non-attached space may be granted to members from larger states or with high seniority. Many senators' offices are still overcrowded—especially, of course, the offices of those from the larger states—and there is already talk of the need for a "new" New Senate Office Building.

On the surface, these miniature bureaucracies appear to be much the same. One walks in the door and there is a receptionist, eager to have you sign the guest book, to give you a gallery visitor's card and a tourist's map of Washington, to talk about "home." In the same narrow room, decorated with pictures of the state's industries and tourist attractions, are three or four other girls (at least in the Helen E. Hokinson sense) typing and answering the constantly ringing telephone. Next door in another room or two there are more typists, the senator's administrative assistant, a legislative assistant or two, and perhaps an executive secretary. Beyond this, a tranquil oasis amid the noise and clutter of the "outer" and "working" rooms, is the senator's private office. Here one finds a large, well-worn desk, several Victorian couches and leather chairs, often a huge wall map of the world, autographed pictures of politicians, framed citations and awards, and more pictures of scenic attractions.

But the similarity between the senators' offices ends right there— with the titles of his assistants, with the worn parlor-car furniture, and the pictures on the wall. Save for the limitation of his allowance for clerical help and a statutory limitation on the maximum salaries he may pay, the senators are entirely free to hire and fire, pay and organize their personal staff as they see fit. As a consequence, no two offices are quite the same. Staff members with identical titles may have very different responsibilities. While most of them are lawyers and former newspapermen, the top staff men vary considerably in their backgrounds, political experience, and qualifications. Some senators hire only home-state people; others pick up their staffs in Washington without regard to their origins or residences. Indeed, the way a senator staffs and organizes his office is a kind of political Rorschach test which, when studied with some care, tells a great deal about him as a man, what his problems and preoccupations are, and how he defines his role.

It is possible to distinguish between two types of Senate offices, the bureaucratic and the individualistic. While very few offices are pure examples of either, most offices can be easily classified as tending toward one or the other. In the bureaucratic offices, the senator has delegated considerable nonroutine responsibilities to his staff, established a fairly clearcut division of labor and chain of command. The administrative assistant is really a "senator, junior grade,"[40] and under his direction other members of the staff specialize in such things as legislative research and speechwriting, answering the mail, press rela-

40. P. Wyden, "Ghosts on Capitol Hill," *Newsweek,* January 28, 1957, p. 33.

tions, or patronage matters. At the opposite end of the spectrum are the individualistic offices, "vest pocket" operations in which the senator has delegated only routine tasks and in which the staff has little influence and less authority. In these offices, a division of labor is relatively amorphous—"everyone does a little bit of everything in this office"—and the administrative assistant's job is reduced to that of a "paper shuffler."

In both types of offices, the staff serves at the pleasure of the senator and there is a fairly rapid turnover. "We sometimes wonder," one legislative assistant said, "what we are doing here. The job leads nowhere. We all view our jobs as temporary interruptions in some other career." The small proportion of Congressional staff members who join the Hill's voluntary retirement system seem to bear him out.

The staff's lack of job security is probably necessary and proper. Their work is both sensitive and confidential and "above all [a good staff member] must be loyal. Hell, this is politics. If he is not 100 per cent loyal, he's no good no matter how able he may be. Indeed without loyalty an administrative assistant with brains is more dangerous than one without them. . . ." At the same time, the staff member's total dependence upon the senator may make him so subservient as to greatly diminish his usefulness. "There is one thing I believe everyone who works on the Hill has to some degree and that is a sensitivity to the political cues and moods of their bosses . . . ," one career woman working for a Southern Democrat explained. "They like to pigeon-hole you and are very good at it. If you end up in the wrong pigeon hole you do not last very long. Of course, after you have worked for a senator for a while, you begin to see things his way."

A new member of a Midwestern Republican's staff put the same thought a little differently. "Part of my job is to know what the boss thinks. I suppose that I am somewhat more liberal than he is. Sometimes I overcompensate. . . . I really don't know if I approve of what I am doing. . . . I just haven't time to think about it."

A Border state senator's public relations man was even more outspoken: "They are like a hundred princes," he said. "I'll tell you one thing, their staffs are all terrified of them. You just don't say no to senators as you might to other people. I did once—and got the real treatment. Now I've learned more subtle ways to imply it. They are surrounded by 'yes men' who jump whenever, and in whichever direction, the senator wants."[41]

41. One executive secretary once complimented his boss by saying, "This guy is

The hectic schedules, long hours, and unpredictability of the senator's work vastly complicate and confuse the staff's job. When their
boss jumps from one crisis to another, so must they, and their pattern
of work soon contains as little discipline and regularity as his. Even
the senator's own staff members find it "a real battle to see him," and
when they do it is likely to be for so short a period, and in competition
with so many other demands on his time, that the staff's value is
greatly diminished. Then, too, the typical senator is insensitive to the
problems and needs of his staff. "On the hustings, they are all good
Joes," one staff member remarked ruefully, "but when they are here
a good many of them try to play God." When a senator gets an urge
to impersonate the Deity, there is no more convenient audience than
his own staff. "I suppose," one rather unreflective staff member reflected one day, "there is some tendency for them to take their frustrations out on us. On the floor, he is dealing with peers and he can't
boss them around. No matter how mad he gets he's got to call them
'honorable' and 'distinguished.' He may be simultaneously embroiled
in a primary fight and this, too, creates tension, yet he can't tell his
constituents to go to hell. But he can give his staff a very hard time
indeed. . . ."

The senators' personal office staffs are important; on routine matters
they *are* the senators. But their importance in the policy-making
process varies considerably, according to the type of office. In the
relatively bureaucratic offices, the senator's staff serves as a major
channel of communication between the senator and his colleagues,
constituents, lobbyists, journalists, and bureaucrats. The role of the
senator's staff in these relationships will be presented in more detail
later, but it needs to be said now that in these offices a senator sees
and personally answers only a tiny fraction of his mail. His staff
prepares analyses of pending bills and ghost-writes most of his speeches
and newsletters, press releases, and statements. If the senator's staff
has real influence and inside knowledge, journalists and lobbyists often
prefer to deal with them rather than with their busier employers.
Much of the communication between senators and the executive departments takes place on the staff level. As many visiting constituents
as possible are channeled to a member of the senator's staff who tries,
as one of them said, "to leave them smiling." In the process of selecting
the "important" things out of this vast stream of communications,
the staff has considerable influence on the senator and his decisions.

different, you can argue with him. Why, just yesterday I disagreed with him and I
almost won."

In the less bureaucratic offices, however, the staff is less significant. The senator reads and answers far more of his own mail; he does most of his own research and speech writing. Since his staff is not so influential, those who seek information or a decision go to the senator rather than to his staff. In these offices, the staff may not even try to conserve their boss's time by screening persons wishing personal interviews. "In our office," one member of a highly individualistic staff put it, "if anyone wants to see the senator and he isn't talking to someone else, we send them right in. We figure the sooner the senator sees them the sooner he can get back to work. We don't make appointments or anything. Why in some offices they have an *appointment book!* [said in a horrified tone] . . . We've had some constituents tell us that it is easier to see ———— than it is their county sheriff, and that's the way we want to keep it."

Basically, two major factors seem to determine the type of office a senator has. First there is his work load. The more work to be done and the larger the senator's staff, the more likely it is to at least approximate the bureaucratic model. This means, of course, that the senators from the larger states are more likely to have bureaucratic offices than those from small ones. They have a far heavier burden of mail and cases, and senators from them receive slightly larger allowances for clerical assistance. The extra amount they receive is not, however, proportional to the size of their states—a senator from New York, with almost one hundred times the population of Nevada, receives only about half again as large an allotment—so it is necessary for the large-state senators to get more work out of every member of the staff. The more highly developed division of labor and hierarchy of a bureaucratic office is a means to that end.

A senator's work load is not an automatic reflection of the size of the state he represents. A senator from a very insecure seat tends to work harder at getting publicity than one whose seat is relatively safe. So, too, does a senator running for the presidency, and this places greater burdens on both him and his staff. A senator who defines his role as being a national leader rather than a state representative is in the same boat. There is a decided tendency for these various factors to converge on many of the same senators—the big-state senators tend to come from two-party states, to suffer as a consequence from extreme political insecurity, to be nationally oriented, and to be potential, or actual, presidential candidates.

A second factor which shapes a senator's use of his staff is his own previous experience. Senators who have had long political careers in local politics, in state legislatures, or in the House of Representatives generally have rather individualistic offices. Men with such careers have become accustomed to all the "snafus" of local and political voluntary organizations.[42]   Usually, they have developed great faith in the personal touch—they have found the many hours "wasted" in shaking hands and idle conversation to have high political pay-offs— and try to maintain their old ways of acting, even in a drastically altered situation. Nor have men with this kind of political background ever before had to depend upon a staff. Moreover, most of these men are lawyers, and lawyers do most of their work themselves.[43] "Lawyers, by definition, are lousy administrators," one staff member declared, and the Senate provides a good deal of support to his claim. The situation is somewhat different for the former business executives, mayors, cabinet officers, and state governors in the Senate. They have used a staff before and, as a consequence, are more willing to delegate responsibilities and to organize their offices along more bureaucratic lines.

THE SENATORS' PAY

During most of the postwar decade, United States senators were paid $15,000 a year. In addition they received a travel allowance of twenty cents per mile for one round trip each session between Washington and their homes, an annual $800 stationery allowance (the unexpended portions of which could be withdrawn in cash), and allowances for such necessities as clerical help and telephone and telegraph expenses (unexpended portions of which reverted to the Treasury).

To the average man in the street this remuneration seems adequate. Most United States senators, however, found that it rarely covered their expenses.[44]

In an earlier era, when Congress met for only a few months of each year, senators and representatives came to Washington without their families and lived in hotel rooms and rooming houses. Today, when they spend almost all year at their jobs, only those who live within week-end commuting distance of the capital can continue this transient existence. The others move their families to Washington and rent or buy an additional residence there. At the same time, they can ill afford to sell the old homestead, for to do so is to run the risk of being

42. Dexter, "Congressmen and the People They Listen To," Chap. III, pp. 35-36.

43. Cf. F. M. Marx, "Congressional Investigations: Significance for the Administrative Process," *University of Chicago Law Review*, XVIII (1951), 505, n. 7.

44. Phillips, "High Cost of Our Low-Paid Congress," *NYT Mag.*, pp. 1 ff.

labeled a "hotel-room senator," a charge most members prefer not to face.[45]   Of course, the place at home can be rented, but the uncertain length of Congressional sessions makes this difficult.   Besides, the senator's wife and children often prefer to escape the Washington heat by going home at the conclusion of the school year—to await his arrival later in the summer.   If the session is a long one, the senator returns home just as his wife and children leave for the September reopening of school in Washington.   For this reason, most senators maintain two residences, a costly consequence of their jobs.

The senator's "social" expenses are very high as well.   Most senators like to go to parties and, as we have already observed, find it politically useful to do so; "and if you go to them, you must give one occasionally."[46]   Important constituents must be entertained at dinner and less important visitors at lunch at the Capitol dining room; the senators habitually pick up the check.   Witness, for example, the following exchange which took place during a hearing concerned with the heavy burden of senatorial expenses:

SENATOR MORSE.   You take . . . the question of entertaining.   It is to be expected, and I think it ought to be done, but you cannot get the average citizen to realize what that adds up to in a year.
SENATOR DOUGLAS.   May I invite the witnesses to lunch with us today?[47]

In the course of a year, similar invitations may cost the average senator about $1,500.[48]

The senators' political expenses are likely to be heavy, too.   Most candidates for the Senate become one of their own largest campaign contributors, especially, of course, if they are relatively well-to-do Patricians or Amateurs.   The senators' political expenses do not end on election day, however, they go on "month after month, as inexorably as taxes."   They are expected to contribute substantially to local and national campaigns and to show up regularly at $100-a-plate party dinners.   "They must keep up their memberships in the Elks, Masons, Rotary and make free speeches at their conventions and clambakes.   They must subscribe to the building fund for that new church, lodge hall or orphanage; buy tickets to the civic rallies and school plays;

45. "The Hotel Room Senator," *Democratic Digest*, IV (August 1956), 95.
46. Anonymous senator quoted in Phillips, "High Cost of Our Low-Paid Congress," *NYT Mag.*, p. 41.
47. Subcommittee to Study Senate Concurrent Resolution 21 of the Senate Committee on Labor and Public Welfare, 82nd Congress, 1st Session, *Hearings*, p. 450.
48. Phillips, "High Cost of Our Low-Paid Congress," *NYT Mag.*, p. 41.

contribute prizes for the charity bazaars and bingo tournaments; buy space in countless programs and fraternal papers."[49]

Finally, the senators' travel expenses are heavy. Those from nearby may go home every week end; all save those solidly entrenched in their seats or from the Far West make a trip home once every month or six weeks, each trip costing several hundred dollars. Small wonder, then, that in 1952 a *New York Times* survey found that the average senator or congressman's expenses exceeded his salary by over $3,000 a year.[50]

Where, then, did the money come from? A good many of the postwar senators were wealthy enough to make up their personal deficits from income on investments, but to the others, the only solution to their financial dilemma was some form of part-time money-making activity. Many of the lawyers kept a finger in their old law practices, and some of the businessmen managed to play active roles in their old concerns. Others made sizeable amounts from writings and lecture tours. "I have to scrounge the countryside like the Russian Army, making speeches and lectures along the way," one of these explained.[51] A sizeable number of senators—no less than twenty-eight in 1950[52]—put members of their immediate families on their office payrolls. A few, including Richard M. Nixon, accepted outright subsidies from well-heeled political supporters.

Most of these practices consume a considerable amount of time and, as we have already seen, time is already in critically short supply in the Senate. All of these practices raise serious ethical problems as well. A senator's name on the office door and letterhead of a law firm can have an amazing effect on the firm's practice. Some of these new-found clients are out to buy influence, and others, perhaps, are merely impressed by the firm's prestige. But in either event, is it right for a senator, through his firm, to be retained by a corporation vitally interested in his decisions as a senator? The part-time businessmen in the Senate are hardly in a better ethical situation. Even the Senate's week-end writers and lecturers—certainly harmless pursuits in normal circumstances—occasionally are presented with a very large fee for a very small lecture or article. Few members of the Senate care to defend nepotism or the acceptance of subsidies on any grounds other than financial necessity.

49. *Ibid.*
50. *Ibid.*, p. 42.
51. Anonymous senator quoted in *ibid.*, p. 1.
52. *Washington Post*, April 13, 1950. Seventeen senators had relatives on the payroll in 1959, *New York Times*, December 1, 1959.

Yet, even as the postwar inflation made their financial situation more and more uncomfortable, the members of both the Senate and House were reluctant to act. Their last efforts to raise their own salaries had been mocked into oblivion by the slogan "Bundles for Congressmen," and the most vocal advocates of higher Congressional pay had suffered heavily at the polls. Finally, an elaborately staged procedure was devised to make a pay raise as politically palatable as possible. First, the question of Congressional pay was linked with that of federal judges. Then a distinguished group of private citizens appointed by the president, vice-president, and speaker of the House was given the task of studying the matter. To no one's surprise, the Commission on Judicial and Congressional Salaries found that Congressional salaries had not been adjusted to keep pace with the growing responsibilities of the offices, that the discrepancy between Congressional salaries and the earnings of men of comparable ability in private industry was too great, that salary adjustments for congressmen lagged far behind those made for other officials of the federal government, that the over-all level of compensation of congressmen was "grossly inadequate" and "tended to confine those positions to persons of independent wealth or outside earnings," and that the net cost to the government of making a Congressional and judicial pay raise would be small. They recommended that the salaries of representatives and senators be raised to $27,500.[53] After an embarrassed debate, the Congress settled for a 50 per cent raise, and in 1955 voted themselves a salary of $22,500.

This new level of payment has made it possible, today, for a frugal senator at least to break even. While many senators continue supplementing their incomes through part-time business or professional activity, some of the financial pressure is off.

The way of life of a United States senator is an extraordinary one. Its rewards—power, prestige and sometimes fame, an extraordinary opportunity to render public service—are both obvious and substantial. Yet the price of power is high. Few Americans could live with the job's tensions, moral dilemmas, intrigue, and insecurity. Its effect on the individual's personality is, when judged by the dominant values of American society, unfortunate. An almost superhuman energy and

53. *Report of the Commission on Judicial and Congressional Salaries* (H. Doc. 300), 83rd Congress, 2nd Session (Washington: Government Printing Office, 1954).

vitality is needed to cope with the job's work load. Certainly, few could be attracted to the job by the pay.

Typically, the senators' own reactions to the job are ambivalent. As one of them said, "I don't know why anyone would want this job— *Don't quote me on that, I'm running for re-election!*"

CHAPTER V

The Folkways of the Senate

THE SENATE of the United States, just as any other group of human beings, has its unwritten rules of the game, its norms of conduct, its approved manner of behavior. Some things are just not done; others are met with widespread approval. "There is great pressure for conformity in the Senate," one of its influential members said. "It's just like living in a small town."

What are the standards to which the senators are expected to conform? What, specifically, do these unwritten rules of behavior say? Why do they exist? In what ways do they influence the senators? How, concretely, are they enforced? What kinds of senators obey the folkways? Which ones do not, and why?

These are difficult questions for an outsider to analyze. Only those who have served in the Senate, and perhaps not even all of them, are likely to grasp its folkways in all their complexity.[1] Yet, if we are to understand why senators behave as they do, we must try to understand them.

APPRENTICESHIP

The first rule of Senate behavior, and the one most widely recognized off the Hill, is that new members are expected to serve a proper apprenticeship.

1. Significantly, the only major work on the Senate which gives much attention to these questions is W. S. White, *Citadel: The Story of the United States Senate* (New York: Harper and Brothers, 1956). At the time he wrote this book, Mr. White was chief Congressional correspondent for the *New York Times* and very much an "insider." White's book both gains and suffers from the intimate position from which he viewed the Senate. On this point see Chapter IX.

The freshman senator's subordinate status is impressed upon him in many ways. He receives the committee assignments the other senators do not want. The same is true of his office suite and his seat in the chamber. In committee rooms he is assigned to the end of the table. He is expected to do more than his share of the thankless and boring tasks of the Senate, such as presiding over the floor debate or serving on his party's Calendar Committee. According to the folkways of the Senate, the freshman is expected to accept such treatment as a matter of course.

Moreover, the new senator is expected to keep his mouth shut, not to take the lead in floor fights, to listen and to learn. "Like children," one freshman said, "we should be seen and not heard." Just how long this often painful silence must be maintained is not clear, but it is certainly wiser for a freshman to postpone his maiden efforts on the floor too long than to appear overly aggressive. Perhaps, ideally, he should wait until pushed reluctantly to the fore. "I attended the floor debates and voted for a year without giving a single speech" a senior senator said with pride. "Finally, one day, a matter came up with which I had had considerable experience in the House. My part in it had gotten some publicity. ———— leaned over to me and said, '————, are you going to speak on this?' I said, 'No.' 'You know a great deal about this,' he replied. 'I think you should speak.' I answered that I had not prepared a speech and that I would rather not speak on the bill. 'Look,' he said, 'I am going to get up on the floor and ask you a question about this bill. Then you will *have* to speak!' And that's how I made my first speech in the Senate."

Freshmen are also expected to show respect for their elders ("You may think you are smarter than the older fellows, but after a time you find that this is not true") and to seek their advice (" 'Keep on asking for advice, boy,' the committee chairman told me. 'That's the way to get ahead around here' "). They are encouraged to concentrate on developing an acquaintanceship in the Senate. ("Young senators should make a point of getting to know the other senators. This isn't very hard: there are only ninety-nine of them. And if the other senators know and like you, it increases your effectiveness.")

The freshman who does not accept his lot as a temporary but very real second-class senator is met with thinly veiled hostility. For instance, one old-timer tells this story: "When I came to the Senate, I sat next to Senator Borah. A few months later, he had a birthday. A number of the older men got up and made brief, laudatory speeches about it. Borah was pleased. Then a freshman senator—one who had only been in the chamber three or four months—got to his feet and started on a similar eulogy. He was an excellent speaker. But between each of his laudatory references to Borah, Borah loudly whispered, 'That son-of-a-bitch, that son-of-a-bitch.' He didn't dislike the speaker, personally. He just didn't feel that he should speak so soon."

Even so, the veterans in the Senate remark, rather wistfully, that the practice of serving an apprenticeship is on the way out, and, to some extent, they are undoubtedly correct. The practice seems to have begun well before the popular election of senators and the exigencies of the popularly elected official have placed it under considerable strain. As one very senior senator, whose service extends back almost to the days before popular election, ruefully explained: "A new senator today represents millions of people. He feels that he has to *do* something to make a record from the start."

This judgment is also colored by the tendency in any group for the old-timers to feel that the younger generation is going to hell in a handbasket. To the present-day freshmen in the Senate, the period of apprenticeship is very real and very confining. As one of them put it, "It reminds me a little of Hell Week in college." Indeed, the nostalgic talk of the older senators regarding the unhappy lot of the freshman in the good old days is one way the senior senators keep the younger men in their place. One freshman Democrat, for example, after completing a floor speech found himself sitting next to Senator George, then the dean of the Senate. Thinking that he should make polite conversation, the freshman asked the Georgia patriarch what major changes had taken place in the Senate during his long service. Senator George replied, "Freshmen didn't use to talk so much."

LEGISLATIVE WORK

"There are two kinds of Congressmen—show horses and work horses. If you want to get your name in the papers, be a show horse. If you want to gain the respect of your colleagues, keep quiet and be a work horse."[2] Senator Carl Hayden of Arizona remembers being told this when he first came to the Congress many years ago. It is still true.

The great bulk of the Senate's work is highly detailed, dull, and politically unrewarding. According to the folkways of the Senate, it is to those tasks that a senator *ought* to devote a major share of his time, energy, and thought. Those who follow this rule are the senators most respected by their colleagues. Those who do not carry their share of the legislative burden or who appear to subordinate this responsibility to a quest for publicity and personal advancement are held in disdain.

This results, at first, in a puzzling disparity between the prestige of senators inside and outside the Senate. Some of the men most highly respected by their colleagues are quite unknown except on the Hill and in their own states; others whose names are household words are thought to be second-raters and slackers.[3] The words used to describe those senators who seem to slight their legislative duties are harsh—"grandstanders," "demagogues," "headline hunters," "publicity seekers," "messiahs." They are said to do nothing but "play to the galleries," to suffer from "laziness" and "verbal diarrhea," and not to be "team players." It is even occasionally hinted that they are mentally or emotionally deranged.

But this does not mean that all publicity is undesirable. It takes publicity to get, and stay, elected. This publicity, as long as it does not interfere with the performance of legislative duties, is considered necessary and desirable. Nor is there any objection to publicity calculated to further the cause of a program or policy or to publicity which flows from a senator's position or performance. But the Senate folkways do prescribe that a senator give first priority to being a legislator. Everything else, including his understandable desire for personal and political publicity, must be secondary to this aspect of his job.

SPECIALIZATION

According to the folkways of the Senate, a senator should not try to know something about every bill that comes before the chamber nor try to be active on a wide variety of measures. Rather, he ought to specialize, to focus his energy and attention on the relatively few matters that come before his committees or that directly and immediately affect his state. "When you come to the Senate," one administrative assistant said, "you have to decide which street corner you are going to fight on."

In part, at least, senators ought to specialize because they must: "Thousands of bills come before the Senate each Congress. If some senator knows the fine details of more than half a dozen of them, I've never heard of him." Even when a senator restricts his attention

3. Cf. Harry S. Truman's comments. "I learned [upon entering the Senate] . . . that the estimates of the various members which I formed in advance were not always accurate. I soon found that, among my ninety-five colleagues the real business of the Senate was carried on by unassuming and conscientious men, not by those who managed to get the most publicity." *New York Times*, October 3, 1955.

to his committee work, the job is more than one man can do. "I belong to twelve or thirteen committees and subcommittees," a leading senator says. "It's physically impossible to give them all the attention I should. So I have picked out two or three subcommittees in which I am especially interested and have concentrated on them. I believe that this is the usual practice around here."

The relatively few senators who have refused to specialize agree. One of these, a relatively young man of awesome energy, says, "I'll be perfectly frank with you. Being active on as wide a range of issues as I have been is a man-killing job. In a few years I suspect that I will be active on many fewer issues. I came down here a young man and I'm gradually petering out." The limit of human endurance is not, however, the only reason for a senator to specialize. By restricting his attention to matters concerning his committee work and his home state, the senator is concentrating on the two things he should know best. Only through specialization can he know more about a subject than his colleagues and thus make a positive contribution to the operation of the chamber.

Moreover, speaking too much tends to decrease a senator's legislative impact. "Look at ———," one of them said. "He came in here with his mouth open and he hasn't closed it yet. After a while, people stop listening." Furthermore, a senator who is too active outside his specialty may destroy his influence within his area of special competence. "When ———, one of my best friends in the Senate, came here he was known as an expert on ———, and they used to listen to him as such. But then he began talking on many other issues as well. As a result, he lost some of his effectiveness on ——— matters as well as on the other issues to which he addressed himself."

Almost all the senators are agreed that: "The really effective senators are those who speak only on the subjects they have been dealing with at close quarters, not those who are on their feet on almost every subject all the time."[4] Why this pressure for specialization? Why does this folkway exist? There would seem to be a number of reasons.

The formal rules of the Senate provide for what amounts to unlimited debate. Even with the folkways limiting the activity of freshmen, discouraging "playing to the galleries," and encouraging specialization, the Senate moves with glacial speed. If many more senators took full advantage of their opportunities for debate and discussion, the tempo of action would be further slowed. The specialization

4. *Providence* (R.I.) *Evening Journal,* February 8, 1956.

folkway helps make it possible for the Senate to devote less time to talking and more to action.

Moreover, modern legislation is complex and technical, and it comes before the Senate in a crushing quantity. The committee system and specialization—in a word, a division of labor within the chamber—increase skill and decrease the average senator's work load to something approaching manageable proportions. When a senator refuses to "go along" with specialization, he not only challenges the existing power structure but also decreases the expert attention which legislative measures receive.

COURTESY

The Senate of the United States exists to solve problems, to grapple with conflicts. Sooner or later, the hot, emotion-laden issues of our time come before it. Senators as a group are ambitious and egocentric men, chosen through an electoral battle in which a talent for invective, righteous indignation, "mud-slinging," and "engaging in personalities" are often assets. Under these circumstances, one might reasonably expect a great deal of manifest conflict and competition in the Senate. Such conflict does exist, but its sharp edges are blunted by the felt need—expressed in the Senate folkways—for courtesy.

A cardinal rule of Senate behavior is that political disagreements should not influence personal feelings. This is not an easy task; for, as one senator said, "It's hard not to call a man a liar when you know that he is one."

Fortunately, a number of the chamber's formal rules and conventions make it possible for him to approximate this ideal—at least so far as overt behavior is concerned. The selection of committee members and chairmen on the basis of their seniority neatly by-passes a potential cause of grave dissention in the Senate. The rules prohibit the questioning of a colleague's motives or the criticism of another state. All remarks made on the floor are, technically, addressed to the presiding officer, and this formality serves as a psychological barrier between antagonists. Senators are expected to address each other not by name but by title—Earle C. Clements does not disagree with Irving M. Ives, but rather the Senior Senator from Kentucky disagrees with the Senior Senator from New York.

Sometimes the senators' efforts to achieve verbal impersonality become ludicrous in their stilted formality. For example:

MR. JOHNSON of Texas. The Senator from Texas does not have any objection, and the Senator from Texas wishes the Senator from California to know that the Senator from Texas knew the Senator from California did not criticise him. . . .[5]

Few opportunities to praise publicly a colleague are missed in the Senate. Senators habitually refer to each other as "The distinguished Senator from ———" or "The able Senator from ———." Birthdays, anniversaries, re-election or retirement from the Senate, and the approach of adjournment are seized as opportunities for the swapping of praise. Sometimes, on these occasions, the sentiment is as thick as Senate bean soup. For example, the following recently took place on the Senate floor and was duly printed in the *Record:*

MR. JOHNSON of Texas. Mr. President, if the Senate will indulge me, I should like the attention of members of both sides of the aisle for a bipartisan announcement of considerable importance. It involves the minority leader, the distinguished Senator from California (MR. KNOWLAND).

For many years, I have been closely associated with the Senator from California. Like every member of this chamber—on either side of the aisle—I have found him to be able, patriotic, courteous, and thoughtful.

But I wonder how many of my colleagues know that he is also a five-time winner in the contest for the proudest granddaddy in the Senate?

His fifth victory was chalked up last Monday when Harold Jewett II discovered America. Anybody who has found buttons lying on the floor in front of the minority leader's desk in the past few days can know now that they popped right off BILL KNOWLAND's shirt.[6]

This kind of behavior—avoiding personal attacks on colleagues, striving for impersonality by divorcing the self from the office, "buttering-up" the opposition by extending unsolicited compliments—is thought by the senators to pay off in legislative results.[7] Personal attacks, unnecessary unpleasantness, and pursuing a line of thought or action that might embarrass a colleague needlessly are all thought to be self-defeating—"After all, your enemies on one issue may be your friends on the next." Similar considerations also suggest the undesirability of excessive partisanship. "I want to be able to pick up votes from the other side of the aisle," one Republican said. "I hope that a majority of the Republicans will vote for anything I sponsor. But always some of them are going to have special problems that impel

5. *Congressional Record* (Daily Edition), April 24, 1956, p. 6148.
6. *Congressional Record* (Daily Edition), June 13, 1956, pp. 9147-48.
7. For example, witness the following exchange from the *Congressional Record* (Daily Edition), June 11, 1956, p. 8990.
MR. HILL. Mr. President, although I greatly love the Senator from Illinois and although he has been very generous toward me in his remarks on the bill, —
MR. DOUGLAS. I had hoped I would soften up the Senator from Alabama. (Laughter).

them to vote against the party." They also suggest, despite partisan differences, that one senator should hesitate to campaign against another. "The fellows who go around the country demagoguing and calling their fellow senators names are likely to be ineffective senators. It's just human nature that the other senators will not cooperate with them unless they have to."

In private, senators are frequently cynical regarding this courtesy. They say that "it doesn't mean a thing," that it is "every man for himself in the Senate," that some of their colleagues "no more should be senators than I should be Pope," that it is "just custom." Senator Barkley's advice to the freshman senator—if you think a colleague stupid, refer to him as "the able, learned and distinguished senator," but if you *know* he is stupid, refer to him as "the *very* able, learned and distinguished senator"—is often quoted.[8] Despite its blatant hypocrisy, the practice persists, and after serving in the Senate for a period of years most senators grow to appreciate it. "You discover that political self-preservation dictates at least a semblance of friendship. And then before you know it, you really *are* friends. It is rather like the friendships that might develop within a band of outlaws. You all hang together or you will hang separately."

Courtesy, far from being a meaningless custom as some senators seem to think it is, permits competitors to cooperate. The chaos which ensues when this folkway is ignored testifies to its vital function.

RECIPROCITY

Every senator, at one time or another, is in a position to help out a colleague. The folkways of the Senate hold that a senator should provide this assistance and that he be repaid in kind. The most important aspect of this pattern of reciprocity is, no doubt, the trading of votes. Occasionally this is done quite openly in the course of public debate. The following exchange, for example, took place during the 1956 debate on acreage allotments for burley tobacco:

MR. LANGER [North Dakota]. We don't raise any tobacco in North Dakota, but we are interested in the tobacco situation in Kentucky, and I hope the Senator will support us in securing assistance for the wheat growers in our State.

MR. CLEMENTS [Kentucky]. I think the Senator will find that my support will be 100 per cent.

MR. BARKLEY [Kentucky]. Mr. President, will my colleague from Kentucky yield?

8. Alben W. Barkley, *That Reminds Me* (Garden City: Doubleday and Co., 1954), p. 255.

MR. CLEMENTS. I yield.

MR. BARKLEY. The colloquy just had confirms and justifies the Woodrow Wilsonian doctrine of open covenants openly arrived at. (Laughter).[9]

Usually, however, this kind of bargain is either made by implication or in private. Senator Douglas of Illinois, who tried unsuccessfully to combat this system, has analyzed the way in which a public works appropriation bill is passed.

... This bill is built up out of a whole system of mutual accommodations in which the favors are widely distributed, with the implicit promise that no one will kick over the applecart; that if Senators do not object to the bill as a whole, they will "get theirs." It is a process, if I may use an inelegant expression, of mutual backscratching and mutual logrolling.

Any member who tries to buck the system is only confronted with an impossible amount of work in trying to ascertain the relative merits of a given project; and any member who does ascertain them, and who feels convinced that he is correct, is unable to get an individual project turned down because the senators from the State in which the project is located, and thus is benefiting, naturally will oppose any objection to the project; and the other members of the Senate will feel that they must support the Senators in question, because if they do not do so, similar appropriations for their own States at some time likely will be called into question.[10]

Of course, *all* bills are not passed as the result of such implicit or explicit "deals."

On the other hand, this kind of bargaining (or "logrolling" or "backscratching" or "trading off," phrases whose invidious connotations indicate the public's attitude toward these practices) is not confined just to the trading of votes. Indeed, it is not an exaggeration to say that reciprocity is a way of life in the Senate. "My boss," one highly experienced administrative assistant says, "will—if it doesn't mean anything to him—do a favor for any other Senator. It doesn't matter *who* he is. It's not a matter of friendship, it's just a matter of I won't be an S.O.B. if you won't be one."

It is this implicit bargaining that explains much of the behavior of senators. Each of them has vast power under the chamber's rules. A single senator, for example, can slow the Senate almost to a halt by systematically objecting to all unanimous consent requests. A few, by exercising their right to filibuster, can block the passage of all bills. Or a single senator could sneak almost any piece of legislation through the chamber by acting when floor attendance is sparse and by taking

9. *Congressional Record* (Daily Edition), February 16, 1956, pp. 2300-2301.
10. *Ibid.*, June 13, 1956, p. 9153.

advantage of the looseness of the chamber rules. While these and other similar powers always exist as a potential threat, the amazing thing is that they are rarely utilized. The spirit of reciprocity results in much, if not most, of the senators' actual power not being exercised. If a senator *does* push his formal powers to the limit, he has broken the implicit bargain and can expect, not cooperation from his colleagues, but only retaliation in kind. "A man in the Senate," one senator says, "has just as much power as he has the sense to use. For this very reason he has to be careful to use it properly or else he will incur the wrath of his colleagues."

To play this game properly and effectively requires tolerance and an understanding of the often unique problems and divergent views of the other senators. "No man," one highly placed staff assistant says, "can really be successful in the Senate until he has adopted a *national* point of view. Learning what the other senators' problems are and working within this framework to pass legislation gives him this outlook. If he assumes that everyone thinks and feels the same way he and his constituents do, he will be an ineffective legislator." It demands, too, an ability to calculate how much "credit" a senator builds up with a colleague by doing him a favor or "going along." If a senator expects too little in return, he has sold himself and his constituents short. If he expects too much, he will soon find that to ask the impossible is fruitless and that "there are some things a senator just can't do in return for help from you." Finally, this mode of procedure requires that a senator live up to his end of the bargain, no matter how implicit the bargain may have been. "You don't *have* to make these commitments," one senator said, "and if you keep your mouth shut you are often better off, but if you *do* make them, you had better live up to them."

These are subtle skills. Some men do not have them in sufficient quantity to be successful at this sort of bargaining. A few take the view that these practices are immoral and refuse, with some display of righteous indignation, to play the game that way. But these men are the exceptions, the nonconformists to the Senate folkways.

INSTITUTIONAL PATRIOTISM

Most institutions demand an emotional investment from their members. The Senate of the United States is no exception. Senators are expected to believe that they belong to the greatest legislative and deliberative body in the world. They are expected to be a bit suspicious of the President and the bureaucrats and just a little disdainful of the House. They are expected to revere the Senate's personnel, organization, and folkways and to champion them to the outside world.

Most of them do. "The most remarkable group that I have ever met anywhere," "the most able and intelligent body of men that it [has] been my fortune to meet," "the best men in political life today"; thus do senators typically describe their colleagues.[11] The Senate as an institution is usually described in similar superlatives.[12]

A senator whose emotional commitment to Senate ways appears to be less than total is suspect. One who brings the Senate as an institution or senators as a class into public disrepute invites his own destruction as an effective legislator. One who seems to be using the Senate for the purposes of self-advertisement and advancement obviously does not belong. Senators are, as a group, fiercely protective of, and highly patriotic in regard to, the Senate.

This, after all, is not a great deal different from the school spirit of P.S. 34, or the morale of a military outfit, or the "fight" of a football team. But, as we shall see, its political consequences are substantial, for some senators are in a better position than others to develop this emotional attachment.

INFLUENCES ON CONFORMITY

We have seen that normative rules of conduct—called here folkways—exist in the Senate. Moreover, we have seen that they perform important functions.[13] They provide motivation for the performance of legislative duties that, perhaps, would not otherwise be performed. They discourage long-windedness in a chamber of one hundred highly verbal men who are dependent upon publicity and unrestrained by any formal limitations on debate. They encourage the development of expertism and division of labor and discourage those who would challenge it. They soften the inevitable personal conflict of a legisla-

11. William Benton, "For Distinguished Service in Congress," *The New York Times Magazine,* July 24, 1955, p. 38; Ralph E. Flanders, "What Ails the Senate?" *The New York Times Magazine,* May 9, 1954, p. 13.

12. This "institutional patriotism" extends down to the staff level. "I'm an apologist for the Senate and senators," one staff member said in the course of an interview. "When I came here I thought just like the normal liberal that the Senate was bumbling and incompetent, that senators were strictly from Kokomo and that if you wanted something done, you had to go to the Executive Branch. Well, all that is a lot of stuff. It's just not true."

13. That is, the folkways contribute to the survival of the system without change. For a brilliant analysis of the promise and pitfalls of functional analysis see R. K. Merton, *Social Theory and Social Structure* (Glencoe, Illinois: The Free Press, 1949), Ch. 1.

tive body so that adversaries and competitors can meet (at the very least) in an atmosphere of antagonistic cooperation or (at best) in an atmosphere of friendship and mutual respect. They encourage senators to become "compromisers" and "bargainers" and to use their substantial powers with caution and restraint. Without these folkways the Senate could hardly operate in anything like its present form.

Yet the folkways are not universally accepted or adhered to; indeed, there is some covert hostility toward them in certain circles. If most senators do observe them, why not all?

Previous Training and Experience

Senators often express pride in the fact that their chamber is "democratic." "No matter," one senior senator says, "what you were before—a rich man or a poor man, a man with a good reputation or an unknown—you've got to prove yourself in the Senate. It's what you do when you arrive and not what you've done before that determines the amount of respect you get from your colleagues." Or as another has expressed it, everyone "must begin at the foot of the class and spell up."[14] This point of view overlooks the fact that it is a great deal harder for some men than others to start at the foot of the class.

A former governor who becomes a senator is often accustomed to a higher salary, more power and perquisites, a grander office, a larger staff, and more publicity than the freshman senator enjoys. He is likely to find the pace of legislative life slow and to be frustrated by the necessity of cooperating with ninety-nine equals. To move from the governorship of one of the larger states to the role of apprentice senator is, in the short run, a demotion. The result for the one-time governors is a frequent feeling of disillusionment, depression, and discouragement. "I moved from one world to another," a former governor now in the Senate says. "Back home everything revolved, or seemed to revolve, around the Governor. I had a part in practically everything that happened. There was administration. There was policy making. But down here there was just a seat at the end of the table."[15] At the same time, the other senators complain that the former governors "are the hardest group to handle; they come down here expecting to be big shots" and that they often are unwilling to realize that "they are just one of the boys." Some governors, they feel,

14. Tom Connally [as told to Alfred Steinberg], *My Name is Tom Connally* (New York: Thomas Y. Crowell Co., 1954), p. 88.
15. *Providence Evening Journal*, February 8, 1956.

never make the adjustment; a larger number make it slowly and painfully.[16]

It is possible to subject this hypothesis to a rough empirical test. Crude indices of conformity can be obtained by counting the number of speeches senators make and by determining the extent to which the bills they introduce are on similar or disparate subjects.[17]

These measures of the former governors' floor activity and legislative specialization were calculated and are compared to those of men elected from other offices in Tables 33 and 34.

In giving floor speeches during the Eighty-third and Eighty-fourth Congresses, the former governors were more vocal than the former congressmen, state legislators, judges, and men with no officeholding experience. The former local government officials and federal executives, on the other hand, gave even more floor speeches than the onetime governors. In legislative specialization, only the former judges appear to have had a narrower range of legislative interests than the governors. Indeed, of the other senators, only the former congressmen and state legislators came even close to matching them in this respect. If our indices of conformity are of any value, the

16. The same situation seems to occur when a man enters the Senate after long and distinguished service in the House of Representatives. Witness this passage from F. Crissey, *Theodore E. Burton: American Statesman* (New York: World, 1956), pp. 235-36:

"Possibly no man had entered the United States Senate with a feeling of more profound satisfaction and assurance than had Theodore E. Burton. His every personal characteristic marked him as predestined for this high place. 'A born Senator' was a phrase repeatedly on the lips of his friends.

"Yet few Senators have found their service in the 'American House of Lords' more disappointing than Burton did. He met with a disillusionment which irritated and often wounded him. He had become accustomed to being treated with almost unprecedented deference in the House. The entire membership often arose to its feet when he was about to deliver an address and he was listened to with rare attentiveness. Any bill which he opposed was in doubt until the vote was taken.

"He was, in fact, a House institution. . . .

"Accustomed, for years, to this position of power, he was unable, on entering the Senate, to realize that his reputation would not secure for him a consideration not enjoyed by most of the newer members.

"He knew, theoretically, that the seniority rule was applied in the Senate as in no other legislative body; but failed to realize that it was inexorable and undiscriminating; that his many years of service at the other end of the long Capitol corridor could not soften its application. . . . Suddenly, on his promotion to the Senate, he was 'put in his place.' "

It is a rare occurrence indeed when a leader of the House of Representatives runs for the Senate—most of the former congressmen in the Senate served in the lower house for only a few terms. Thus this particular problem of adjustment does not occur with the great regularity that the problem of the former governors does.

17. These indices are described in detail in Appendix D.

Table 33
LAST PUBLIC OFFICE AND FREQUENCY OF FLOOR SPEAKING
(83rd and 84th Congresses)

Last Public Office	Frequency of Floor Speaking			
	High	Medium	Low	
Governor	10%	35%	55%	100% (20)
U.S. Representative	0%	52%	48%	100% (23)
State Legislator	0%	33%	67%	100% (6)
State Executive	17%	17%	67%	100% (6)
Local Official	50%	50%	0%	100% (6)
Judge	0%	60%	40%	100% (5)
Federal Executive	33%	22%	45%	100% (9)
None	0%	50%	50%	100% (4)

NOTE: The two floor leaders, Johnson (Dem., Tex.) and Knowland (Rep., Cal.) have been omitted from this and all subsequent tables on frequency of floor speaking. A high level of floor activity is an inevitable consequence of their positions and is not considered a breach of the folkways.

governors as a whole seem to "go along" with the Senate folkways fairly well.

But it is the governors from the larger states, coming to the Senate with national reputations, who seem to find their initial experiences in the chamber especially trying. Moreover, their record for conformity to the folkways is bad. While they do tend to specialize quite

Table 34
LAST PUBLIC OFFICE AND INDEX OF SPECIALIZATION
(83rd and 84th Congresses)

Last Public Office	Index of Specialization			
	High	Medium	Low	
Governor	35%	15%	50%	100% (20)
U.S. Representative	8%	46%	46%	100% (24)
State Legislator	28%	43%	28%	100% (7)
State Executive	0%	33%	67%	100% (6)
Local Executive	0%	50%	50%	100% (6)
Judge	40%	40%	20%	100% (5)
Federal Executive	0%	44%	56%	100% (9)
None	0%	25%	75%	100% (4)

Table 35

FREQUENCY OF FLOOR SPEAKING OF BIG-STATE SENATORS,
BY LAST PUBLIC OFFICE

(83rd and 84th Congresses)

	Frequency of Floor Speaking		
Last Public Office	*High + Medium*	*Low*	
Governor	50%	50%	100% (6)
U.S. Representative	20%	80%	100% (6)
All Other	38%	62%	100% (8)

NOTE: "Big state" is defined as one with more than 4,000,000 population in 1950. See note to Table 33.

highly, they are extremely active on the floor, even when compared to other senators from similar states (Table 35).

There is another peculiar feature of the former governors in the Senate: those with low seniority conform to the folkways more closely than those with high seniority. In Table 36, we can see that the higher the seniority of the former governors, the more active they were in floor debate, while just the opposite is true among the former representatives. Both the former governors and former representatives are more specialized as seniority increases, yet the former congressmen with high seniority specialize considerably more than the high seniority governors. While the numbers involved are too small to warrant generalization, the same pattern is suggested for the former local officials and federal executives: those with high seniority conform less than the junior men. The onetime judges and state legislators, on the other hand, seem to follow the pattern of congressmen: the senior men conform more than the youngsters.

Among the present crop of senators at any rate, prolonged exposure to the folkways seems to have resulted in a high degree of conformity among the former congressmen, state legislators, and judges but *not* among former governors, federal executives, and local government officials.[18]

The Amateur Politicians, distinguished business and professional men who entered politics relatively late in life and became senators with little political experience, face many of the same problems that the former governors do, compounded by their relative ignorance of

18. This conclusion must be treated with more than the usual scholarly caution. Only a longitudinal study or one using far more elaborate cross tabulation than is possible here can adequately isolate the effects of seniority on conformity to the folkways.

Table 36

LAST PUBLIC OFFICE, FREQUENCY OF FLOOR SPEAKING, AND INDEX OF
SPECIALIZATION, BY SENIORITY LEVEL

(84th Congress)

Last Public Office	Seniority	Percentage Low, Floor Speaking	Percentage High, Index of Specialization	
Governor	High	78%	45%	(9)
	Medium	88%	25%	(8)
	Low	100%	20%	(5)
U.S. Representative	High	100%	67%	(6)
	Medium	88%	22%	(9)
	Low	94%	0%	(17)
State Legislator	High	66%	100%	(3)
	Medium	50%	0%	(2)
	Low	50%	0%	(2)
State Executive	High	100%	0%	(1)
	Medium	50%	0%	(2)
	Low	100%	0%	(4)
Local Official	High	0%	0%	(1)
	Medium	0%	0%	(2)
	Low	25%	0%	(4)
Judge	High	100%	50%	(2)
	Medium	0%	33%	(3)
	Low	100%	0%	(1)
Federal Executive	High	25%	0%	(4)
	Medium	0%	0%	(2)
	Low	100%	33%	(3)
None	High	0%	0%	(1)
	Medium	0%	0%	(1)
	Low	100%	0%	(2)

political ways. One must learn to be a senator and the Amateurs have a great deal to learn. As can be seen in Table 37, they are more likely to ignore the folkways regarding floor activity and legislative specialization than are the Professionals. Moreover, the Amateurs usually must learn how to be legislators in less time than those who follow other career lines to the Senate; they are the oldest group of freshmen. A relatively young man can afford to be patient, to devote two or four or six years to learning the ropes and climbing the seniority ladder. A sixty year old man, with sufficient vigor to win election to the Senate and a distinguished career behind him, is not so likely to take the long view. At any rate, a larger proportion of the men elected to the Senate

Table 37
PERCENTAGE OF PRE-SENATE ADULT LIFE IN PUBLIC OFFICE, FREQUENCY OF
FLOOR SPEAKING, AND INDEX OF SPECIALIZATION
(83rd and 84th Congresses)

Percentage of Pre-Senate Adult years in Public Office	Frequency of Floor Speaking			
	High	Medium	Low	
Under 40%	21%	37%	42%	100% (36)
40%-60%	0%	48%	52%	100% (21)
60% plus	5%	35%	60%	100% (20)

	Index of Specialization			
	High	Medium	Low	
Under 40%	10%	31%	59%	100% (39)
40%-60%	10%	43%	48%	100% (21)
60% plus	33%	38%	29%	100% (21)

NOTE: See note to Table 33.

relatively late in life tend to "talk too much" than is the case with the others (Table 38).

We find a curious situation in the Senate. The greater a man's pre-Senate accomplishments (either in or out of politics) and the greater his age at election, the less likely he is to conform. For these reasons, a sort of reverse snobbism is quite widespread in the Senate. As one old-timer said, "We are skeptical of men who come to the

Table 38
AGE AT FIRST ELECTION/APPOINTMENT TO THE SENATE
AND FREQUENCY OF FLOOR SPEAKING
(83rd and 84th Congresses)

Age at First Election/ Appointment	Frequency of Floor Speaking			
	High	Medium	Low	
30-39	8%	54%	38%	100% (13)
40-49	4%	46%	50%	100% (28)
50-59	17%	33%	50%	100% (30)
60 plus	25%	25%	50%	100% (8)

NOTE: See Note to Table 33.

Senate with big reputations." From the standpoint of protecting the Senate folkways, this skepticism is justified.

Political Ambitions

Higher political ambitions—and for senators this means a desire to become either president or vice-president—can also lead to nonconformity.

First of all, strong and exalted ambitions are likely to lead to restiveness during the period of apprenticeship. A national following is seldom acquired by "being seen and not heard" or through faithful service on the District of Columbia Committee. In order to overcome this initial handicap, the highly ambitious freshman may resort to extreme and unsettling tactics, as, for example, Senator Kefauver is thought by his colleagues to have done in his crime investigation and Senator McCarthy certainly did in his "crusade" against communism. His legislative duties are likely to be neglected in the ceaseless quest for publicity and personal advancement. His ears are likely to be "attuned to noises outside the workaday drone of the Senate chamber."[19] Since the senator with higher ambitions is almost invariably shooting for the presidency, he is likely to be attuned to the voices of somewhat different groups than are most senators. Close presidential elections are won and lost in the doubtful states containing large metropolitan populations. Popularity in these areas is generally a prerequisite for nomination and election to the presidency. Yet these very groups are the ones underrepresented in the Senate, the ones most often at odds with its present power structure. To the extent that ambitious senators anticipate the wants of possible future constituents, they find themselves challenging the Senate *status quo*.

In Table 39 we see that of the most obvious presidential aspirants during the Eighty-third and Eighty-fourth Congresses, all save Symington, gave more floor speeches than the average senator and pursued a wider range of legislative interests.

It should be immediately admitted, however, that Table 39's list of presidential aspirants is based entirely upon reports in the public press, even though latent presidential ambitions no doubt smolder in the breasts of senators not included. Moreover, the list includes both floor leaders, and the folkways regarding floor speaking and specialization are necessarily and greatly relaxed for the incumbents of these specialized positions. Finally, an occasional senator is able to be both a

19. Douglass Cater, "Estes Kefauver, Most Willing of the Most Willing," *The Reporter*, November 3, 1955, p. 16.

Table 39

FREQUENCY OF FLOOR SPEAKING AND INDEX OF SPECIALIZATION OF
ACTIVE PRESIDENTIAL ASPIRANTS
(83rd and 84th Congresses)

Active Presidential Aspirants	Number of Speeches	Index of Specialization
Humphrey (Dem., Minn.)	1528	.32
Johnson (Dem., Tex.)	1203	.41
Kefauver (Dem., Tenn.)	446	.49
Kennedy (Dem., Mass.)	359	.47
Knowland (Rep., Calif.)	1317	.37
Symington (Dem., Mo.)	248	.43
Median for all senators	272	.52

serious presidental candidate and a highly regarded and effective senator; Senators Taft, Johnson, and Knowland are the most conspicuous examples within recent years. Yet Taft was never nominated, at least in part because he was a "Senate man." Knowland obviously found the conflict between the expectations of his Senate colleagues and his presidential ambitions difficult to bear. Senator Johnson's presidential chances are low for somewhat the same reason that Taft's were. As a general rule, it seems that a man who entirely adheres to the Senate folkways has little chance of ever becoming President of the United States.

Constituency Problems

A third factor which encourages nonconformity to Senate folkways is a competitive two-party, or a large and complex, constituency.

The political insecurity of a senator from this kind of state is likely to result in a shortened time perspective, an eagerness to build a record quickly, an impatience with the slowness of the seniority system. The approved attitude for the new senator was voiced by a freshman: "I want to be a *Senator*. I want to gain the respect of my colleagues so that I can represent my state better. I want to establish a reputation as a hard-working committee member who does his homework, who has integrity and good judgment rather than to get my name in the paper every morning. This is taking the long view. It takes time to establish this kind of a reputation in the Senate. It's rather like starting a law practice in a new and small town, as I did in ———, ———. You can't rush it." A senator whose seat is in grave danger is much more likely to try to "rush it" than one who can count on re-election unless he makes a major blunder.

Table 40 seems to support this line of reasoning. The senators from two-party states are a little more likely to be frequent floor speakers than those from modified one-party constituencies. Both are considerably more vocal than those from pure one-party states. The picture is a little different so far as legislative specialization is concerned. One-party state senators seem to be the most specialized; those from modified one-party states, least specialized; while the senators from two-party areas fall between.

Table 40

TYPE OF PARTY SYSTEM IN HOME STATE, FREQUENCY OF FLOOR SPEAKING, AND INDEX OF SPECIALIZATION

(83rd and 84th Congresses)

Type of Party System	Frequency of Floor Speaking			
	High	Medium	Low	
Two-Party	16%	35%	49%	100% (43)
Modified One-Party	11%	39%	50%	100% (18)
One-Party	0%	50%	50%	100% (18)
	Index of Specialization			
	High	Medium	Low	
Two-Party	16%	41%	43%	100% (44)
Modified One-Party	6%	33%	61%	100% (18)
One-Party	26%	26%	47%	100% (19)

NOTE: See note to Table 33.

The size and complexity of a senator's state also influences the likelihood of his conforming to Senate norms. A senator from a large state has a far greater burden of "case work" to process and errands to run, mail to answer, and speeches to give back home than the man from a small state; and he has to do this without a proportionately larger staff. He is just not likely to have as much time for legislating as a senator from Nevada, Wyoming, or Delaware. The large states also tend to be the politically complex states, shot through with sectional, religious, economic, and ethnic conflicts. As a result, a senator from one of these states is subject to greater cross pressures than is a man representing a homogeneous state with only one or two real issues, as, for example, has been the case for the Southern states. He is also expected by his constituents to be active on more issues than the man from the smaller and simpler states, and so he will be tempted to challenge the specialization folkway. Generally he is forced to grapple with these problems without the benefit of substantial seniority, which men from closely contested, large, and complex states seldom achieve.

Table 41 appears to reinforce this speculation; the larger in size and the more urban a senator's state, the more likely he is to be hyperactive on the Senate floor. Table 42 presents the relationships between the same two variables and legislative specialization. Urban state senators definitely specialize less than ones from rural states. The size of a senator's state, however, does not seem to have any effect on the range of his legislative interests.

Table 41
SIZE AND COMPLEXITY OF HOME STATE AND FREQUENCY OF FLOOR SPEAKING
(83rd and 84th Congresses)

	Frequency of Floor Speaking			
	High	Medium	Low	
Percentage Urban, State Population (1950)				
80% plus	38%	12%	50%	100% (8)
60%-79%	13%	33%	54%	100% (24)
40%-59%	6%	48%	46%	100% (33)
Under 40%	7%	43%	50%	100% (14)
Size of State Population (1950)				
4,000,000 plus	40%	13%	47%	100% (15)
2,000,000-4,000,000	6%	54%	40%	100% (35)
Less than 2,000,000	10%	35%	55%	100% (31)

NOTE: See note to Table 33.

Political Ideology

Senators are, of necessity, tolerant of differences of opinion. A senator's political views make less difference to his acceptance or nonacceptance by his colleagues than is generally realized. Yet a senator's stance on political issues *does* make it easier (or harder) for him to conform to the folkways and thus, indirectly, influences his prestige and effectiveness in the chamber.

Table 42

SIZE AND COMPLEXITY OF HOME STATE AND INDEX OF SPECIALIZATION
(83rd and 84th Congresses)

	Index of Specialization				
	High	*Medium*	*Low*		
Percentage Urban, State Population (1950)					
80% plus	11%	33%	55%	100%	(9)
60%–79%	8%	32%	60%	100%	(25)
40%–59%	15%	42%	42%	100%	(33)
Under 40%	36%	29%	36%	100%	(14)
Size of State Population (1950)					
4,000,000 plus	13%	33%	53%	100%	(15)
2,000,000–4,000,000	17%	40%	43%	100%	(35)
Less than 2,000,000	16%	32%	52%	100%	(31)

The folkways of the Senate, as we have already seen, buttress the *status quo* in the chamber, and the distribution of power within the chamber results in moderate to conservative policies. The liberals are more likely to challenge Senate norms than the conservatives. "A reformer's life is perhaps not easy anywhere," one close observer of the Senate has remarked. "In the Senate it can be both bitter and fruitless. . . ."[20]

A man elected to the Senate as a "liberal" or "progressive" or "reformer" is under considerable pressure to produce legislative results in a hurry. The people who voted for him are not likely to be happy with small favors—dams built, rivers dredged, roads financed—but want major national legislative policy changed. Yet as a freshman or a junior senator, and many never become anything else, the liberal is in no position to do this alone. If he gives in to the pressure for conformity coming from the folkways, he must postpone the achievement of his liberal objectives. If he presses for these objectives regardless of his junior position, he will become tabbed as a nonconformist, lose popularity with his colleagues and, in most cases, his legislative effectiveness as well.

The conservative does not face this problem. He has committed himself to fewer changes in basic policies; he finds the strategic positions in the Senate occupied by like-minded senators regardless of

20. William S. White, "Realistic Reformer from Tennessee," *The New York Times Magazine*, March 4, 1956, p. 32. On the same point, cf. Jerry Voorhis, *Confessions of a Congressman* (Garden City: Doubleday and Company, 1947), especially at p. 62.

which party organized them. He is able to identify more strongly with the folkways of the chamber and side more easily with Congress in its running feud with a generally more liberal president. Nor is he, as is the liberal, so dependent on the support of broad, often unorganized groups which can be reached only through the mass media. At any rate, the liberals seem to talk considerably more and to specialize somewhat less than do senators of different political persuasion (Table 43).[21] Conservatives can afford to be quiet and patient. Reformers, by definition, find it difficult to be either.

Table 43
POLITICAL IDEOLOGY, FREQUENCY OF FLOOR SPEAKING, AND
INDEX OF SPECIALIZATION

Political Ideology	Frequency of Floor Speaking			
	High	Medium	Low	
Liberal	12%	23%	65%	100% (34)
Moderate	0%	0%	100%	100% (19)
Conservative	0%	8%	92%	100% (37)
	Index of Specialization			
	High	Medium	Low	
Liberal	20%	31%	49%	100% (35)
Moderate	21%	37%	42%	100% (19)
Conservative	24%	42%	34%	100% (38)

NOTE: See note to Table 33 and Appendix D.

CONFORMITY AND "EFFECTIVENESS"

All this would be very "interesting" but not particularly important to serious students of politics if the Senate folkways did not influence the distribution of power within the chamber.

The senators believe, either rightly or wrongly, that without the respect and confidence of their colleagues they can have little influence in the Senate. "You can't be effective," they said over and over again, "unless you are respected—on both sides of the aisle." The safest way to obtain this respect is to conform to the folkways, to become a "real Senate man." Those who do not run a serious risk. "In the Senate, if you don't conform, you don't get many favors for your state. You are never told that, but you soon learn."

21. For a detailed discussion of the construction of the Index of Conservatism-Liberalism see Appendix D.

In order to test this hypothesis, a crude index of "Legislative Effectiveness" was constructed for the Eighty-third and Eighty-fourth Congresses by calculating the proportion of all public bills and resolutions introduced by each senator that were passed by the Senate.[22] While such an index does not pretend to measure the over-all power or influence of a senator, it does seem to reflect his efficiency as a legislator, narrowly defined. To the extent that the concept as used on Capitol Hill has any distinct meaning, "effectiveness" seems to mean the ability to get one's bills passed.

The "effectiveness" of the conforming and nonconforming senators is presented in Table 44. The less a senator talks on the Senate floor, and the narrower a senator's area of legislative interest and activity, the greater is his "effectiveness." Conformity to the Senate folkways does, therefore, seem to "pay off" in concrete legislative results.[23]

Table 44
FLOOR SPEAKING, INDEX OF SPECIALIZATION, AND LEGISLATIVE EFFECTIVENESS
(83rd and 84th Congresses)

Level of Floor Speaking	Index of Legislative Effectiveness			
	High	Medium	Low	
High	0%	33%	67%	100% (9)
Medium	3%	68%	29%	100% (31)
Low	15%	59%	26%	100% (39)
Index of Specialization				
High	23%	69%	8%	100% (13)
Medium	10%	62%	28%	100% (29)
Low	8%	51%	41%	100% (39)

NOTE: See note to Table 33.

22. See Appendix D for a description and discussion of the Index of Legislative Effectiveness.

23. It should be pointed out, as one friendly critic remarked after reading a draft of this analysis, that it is possible that "concentration and silence may be a product of legislative effectiveness, rather than the other way around." Statistical analysis is unable to tell us which came first. However, our Capitol Hill informants *overwhelmingly* argued that conformity leads to effectiveness and not the other way around. Until such time as a more refined analysis is possible, this seems to be the best evidence we have upon which to determine which is cause and which is effect.

See Appendix E, Table 7, for evidence that the types of senators which tend not to conform to the folkways also tend to be relatively "ineffective" senators.

There are unwritten rules of behavior, which we have called folk-ways, in the Senate. These rules are normative, that is, they define how a senator ought to behave. Nonconformity is met with moral condemnation, while senators who conform to the folkways are re-warded with high esteem by their colleagues. Partly because of this fact, they tend to be the most influential and effective members of the Senate.

These folkways, we have suggested, are highly functional to the Senate social system since they provide motivation for the performance of vital duties and essential modes of behavior which, otherwise, would go unrewarded. They discourage frequent and lengthy speech-making in a chamber without any other effective limitation on debate, en-courage the development of expertness and a division of labor in a group of overworked laymen facing unbelievably complex problems, soften the inevitable personal conflicts of a problem-solving body, and encourage bargaining and the cautious use of awesome formal powers. Without these folkways, the Senate could hardly operate with its present organization and rules.

Nonetheless, the folkways are no more perfectly obeyed than the nation's traffic laws. Men who come to the Senate relatively late in life, toward the close of a distinguished career either in or out of politics, have a more difficult time fitting in than the others. So do those elected to the Senate with little prior political experience. The senators who aspire to the presidency find it hard to reconcile the expectations of their Senate colleagues with their desire to build a national following. Finally, all senators belong to, or identify with, many other groups beside the Senate, and the expectations and de-mands of these groups sometimes conflict with the folkways. This seems to happen most often with the liberals from large, urban two-party states. When confronted with such a conflict situation, a senator must choose between conforming to the folkways, and thus appearing to "sell out," or gaining popularity back home at the expense of good-will, esteem, and effectiveness in the Senate, a course which diminishes his long-run ability to achieve what his followers demand. For this reason, conflicts between the demands of constituents and legislative peers are by no means automatically resolved in favor of constituents.

It would be a mistake to assume that the folkways of the Senate are unchangeable. Their origins are obscure, but sparse evidence scat-tered throughout senatorial memoirs suggests that they have changed very little since the nineteenth century.[24] Certainly the chamber's small membership and gradual turnover is conducive to the transmission of such rules virtually unchanged from one generation to the next. Yet the trend in American politics seems to be toward more competitive two-party politics; a greater political role for the mass media of communications and those skilled in their political use; larger, more urban constituencies. All these are factors which presently encourage departure from the norms of Senate behavior. In all likelihood, therefore, nonconformity to the folkways will increase in the future if the folkways remain as they are today. Moreover, the major forces which presently push senators toward nonconformity tend to converge upon a relatively small group of senators. Certainly, this is a more unstable situation than the random distribution of such influences—and, hence, of nonconforming behavior—among the entire membership of the Senate.

24. "Should the new legislator wish to be heard, the way to command the attention of the House," George Washington wrote to his favorite nephew, Bushrod, upon Bushrod's election to the Virginia House of Delegates in 1787, "is to speak seldom, but to important subjects, except such as relate to your constituents and, in the former case, make yourself perfectly master of the subject. Never exceed a decent warmth, and submit your sentiments with diffidence. A dictatorial style, though it may carry conviction, is always accompanied with disgust." J. A. Carroll and M. W. Ashworth [continuing D. S. Freeman's biography], *George Washington* (New York: C. Scribner's Sons, 1957), VII, 591. At least some of the folkways are very old and not restricted to the Senate of the United States!

CHAPTER VI

Party Leadership

"IT'S ORGANIZED just like a string of sausages," one lady lobbyist has said of the United States Senate. "Its lack of a chain of command was quite a shock to an ex-bureaucrat like me." A Capitol Hill journalist, whose acquaintance with the Senate has been both long and intimate, argues quite the opposite. "The Senate," he says, "is essentially an hierarchical institution." Both observers are partly right.

Formally all senators are equal in their rights. Each has one vote. The rules of the chamber give each member highly individualized power. "Senators are like a hundred barons. They do not owe each other a damned thing. Except insofar as they find it expedient to work together, they are completely independent of one another." No one, save their constituents—and they only after a considerable time lag—can order them to do anything. These features of the Senate cause both observers and participants to stress its "individualism," its lack of hierarchy, its tendency to do business on the basis of bargaining by equals.

At the same time, the Senate of the United States is a group which, just as any other, operates in accordance with a complex of norms shaping the behavior of its members; in the last chapter we saw how these norms affect the distribution of prestige and power within the chamber. Moreover, the Senate has been assigned a task which can be performed only cooperatively; this necessitates internal organization, division of labor, leadership. In this and the following chapter we shall examine how this fact affects the Senate's structure of power.

According to popular mythology, the Democratic and Republican parties formulate "principles" and select candidates who "stand" on them at election time. Then "the people" choose the party which most nearly represents their opinions at the polls. The victorious party, backed by a popular "mandate," enacts the program into legislation. If the majority party fails to live up to its commitments or if the people, on second thought, do not care for its policies they may be defeated at the next election.[1]

The realities of American party politics are different. The parties are loose coalitions of state and local organizations with divergent policy aims, leadership groups, and electoral followings. Senators who belong to the same national party are elected at different times, by different electorates, on different platforms. Both Senate parties contain "liberals" and "conservatives," "radicals" and "reactionaries," no matter how these much abused terms are defined. Nevertheless, the ideological center of gravity of the two parties *is* different; the Democrats' is toward the "Left," and the Republicans' is toward the "Right" of the abbreviated American political spectrum. This is clearly—if crudely—demonstrated in Figure 10, which shows the ideological make-up of the two parties during the postwar Congresses.

There is not much that the national leadership of the parties can do about this situation. With rare exceptions the senators are not beholden to the party leaders; they had little to do with the senators' nomination or election. The tradition of localism and popular reverence for legislative "independence" largely frustrate any efforts by the president, national chairman, or Senate leaders of a party to "purge" unfaithful members.[2] As a result, the political parties in the Senate are,

1. The notion that American party politics *ought* to be conducted in this fashion is not restricted to the politically uninitiated. For scholarly critiques of American party politics based, either implicitly or explicitly, on such a model see E. E. Schattschneider, *Party Government* (New York: Rinehart, 1942), and Committee on Political Parties, American Political Science Association, *Toward a More Responsible Two-party System*, Supplement to the *American Political Science Review*, XLIV (September, 1950). For an important statement of a contrary view see E. P. Herring, *The Politics of Democracy* (New York: Rinehart, 1940).

2. "When a seat is held by the opposition, the national party leadership may help recruit and support the nomination of a strong candidate to challenge the incumbent," V. O. Key writes in *Politics, Parties and Pressure Groups* (4th ed.; New York, Thomas Y. Crowell Company, 1958), at p. 481. "Yet when a sitting senator seeks renomination, the prevailing etiquette demands non-intervention by the national leadership" (p. 484). The most famous effort by a recent president to purge irregular senators was Franklin Roosevelt's ill-fated attempts in 1938. For an analysis of the role of national party leadership in making Senate nominations, see *ibid.*, Ch. 16.

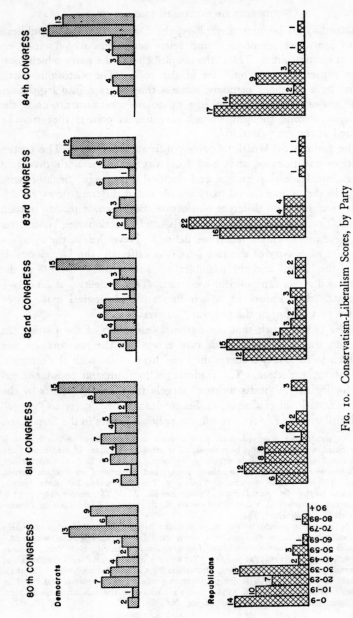

Fig. 10. Conservatism-Liberalism Scores, by Party

when compared with the parties in most parliamentary democracies and a number of American states, rather disunited organizations.[3]

Look, for example, at Figure 11. The percentage of the time Democratic and Republican senators voted with a majority of their party on roll call votes, in which a majority of one party voted against a majority of the other, is presented in this figure for each Congress during the postwar decade.[4] On the whole, the figures show that the "average" senator voted with his party about 75 or 80 per cent of the time on party-line roll calls. But notice also the wide range of party-unity scores to be found within both political parties. While the bulk of the senators seem to have been fairly regular party supporters, a few voted with the opposition more often than with their own party.

On the other hand, most senators do identify strongly with their party. They do want to be "good" Democrats or Republicans even though their definition of this state of grace does not always coincide with those of their colleagues. "None of us," one senator remarked, "likes to see the party split, openly and repeatedly." Another, whose voting record hardly indicates an addiction to party regularity, confessed with real emotion that "it's not pleasant to vote against a majority of your party." The Senate is organized in a way which reinforces and intensifies these feelings. After being in the Senate only briefly, one senator has written he saw "how party spirit develops. The Republicans and Democrats sit on the floor of the Senate in separate groups, the Republicans on the right, the Democrats on the left. Most members eat their lunch in a small dining room 'For Senators Only,' and there the Republicans and Democrats eat separately. Republicans and Democrats even have separate lounges so that the contacts a freshman senator makes are largely with members of his own party. He loafs, he even takes a nap in this lounge, but it is a Republican—or Democratic—nap."[5] Moreover, the party leaders have a dominant influence—"control" would be too strong a word—over the legislative schedule and the utilization of the chamber's time. In a body faced with a permanent overload of work, this is especially significant. The

3. See J. Turner, *Party and Constituency: Pressures on Congress* (Baltimore: The Johns Hopkins Press, 1951), Ch. 2, and M. E. Jewell, "Party Voting in American State Legislatures," *The American Political Science Review*, XLIX (September, 1955), 773-91.

4. These party-unity scores were obtained from the *Congressional Quarterly Almanac*. Unfortunately for our purposes, the *CQ* changed its definition of a party-unity vote during the 84th Congress making comparison between this Congress and the earlier ones impossible. Comparisons between the Republicans and Democrats during the 84th Congress can, of course, still be made. See Appendix D.

5. D. P. Griswold, "A Freshman Senator Makes a Report," *New York Times Magazine,* March 8, 1953, p. 53.

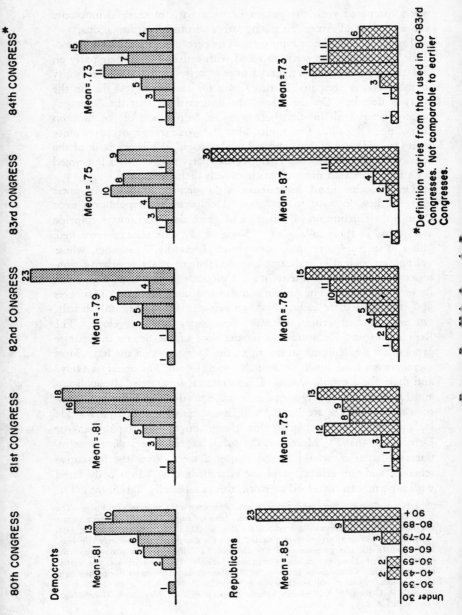

*Definition varies from that used in 80-83rd Congresses. Not comparable to earlier Congresses.

importance of a senator's committee assignments to him and his political future can hardly be overestimated. This, too, is a party matter.

The division of the senators into two political parties is, therefore, a very significant feature of the chamber. Party "discipline" may be weak, but party "identification" is strong. Party affiliation, as we shall see in this and subsequent chapters, is a major influence on the senators' voting behavior. The parties provide the chamber with its members, have considerable influence on its procedure, and allocate members to fill its different positions. In the process, the parties help determine the distribution of power within the Senate.

PARTY ORGANIZATION: DEMOCRATIC AND REPUBLICAN CONTRASTS

Both parties in the Senate are elaborately organized. The formal machinery, however, rarely operates in the manner one thinks, and the similar formal organizations of the Democrats and Republicans obscure the fact that the leadership of the two parties is quite different.[6]

Democratic party leadership is highly personalized, informal, centralized in the hands of the floor leader. He may not be the most powerful Democrat in the chamber—indeed only Lyndon Johnson has come close to being so during the postwar era—but he, his staff, and his assistant (the whip) provide the party with whatever general and central leadership originates in the Senate itself. The Conference, a meeting of all Democratic senators, which officially serves as the supreme governing body of the party in the Senate, almost never meets. When a vacancy occurs in the leadership, it convenes to elect a successor who thenceforth directs the day-to-day tactics of the party as floor leader, appoints members to the important party committees and presides over the party as Conference chairman, directs the formulation of party strategy and the scheduling of bills for floor debate as chairman of the Policy Committee, and directs the appointment of Democrats to Senate committees as chairman of the Steering Committee.

The Conference (often, unofficially referred to by its earlier title of caucus) rarely meets again during the session. Moreover, policy is

6. The following analysis draws upon two first-rate recent analyses of party operation in the Senate: H. B. Westerfield, *Foreign Policy and Party Politics* (New Haven: Yale University Press, 1955), Ch. 6; and H. A. Bone, "An Introduction to Senate Policy Committees," *The American Political Science Review*, L (June, 1956), 339-59, both published after the author's interviews on this subject were completed. The similarity between my conclusions and those of Westerfield and Bone are therefore especially reassuring. D. B. Truman, *The Congressional Party: A Case Study* (New York: John Wiley and Sons, 1959), the most intensive and systematic study of the Congressional parties made to date, was published after this chapter was written. For the most part, the analysis which it contains is compatible with the findings presented here. Those places at which the two analyses diverge are pointed out in the footnotes to follow.

almost never discussed when it does meet, largely for fear of advertising the party's sharp internal divisions. "We hold few caucuses and they are almost always unsatisfactory," one senator explained. "While they are supposedly secret, an account of what happens always appears in Drew Pearson's column the next day." Debates on policy, furthermore, merely exacerbate personal relations and solidify the conflicting policy stances of different members of the party. Any effort to obtain a binding commitment from members is bound to fail ("Can't you see us trying to bind Eastland to the Democratic FEPC plank? *That* would be a fine day in Hell!") except where it is not needed anyway. To take an official party stand on this kind of issue would, in all likelihood, merely alienate like-minded Republicans. "Personally," one Democrat said, "I can't see any purpose in a caucus. You can't bind anyone. All you can do is talk. The same speakers would say the same things on the floor a little later on." Of course, the inactivity of the Conference serves to enhance the influence of the leader for "it's awfully hard to fight the party leadership when there are no caucuses." Since the leader appoints the members (and the staffs) of the Policy and Steering Committees and serves as their chairman, his wishes carry great weight in these agencies of party leadership as well.

The extent of the leader's influence varies, of course, from one leader to the next. Senator Barkley, who was Democratic leader during the Eightieth Congress before becoming vice-president, and Senator Johnson of Texas, widely recognized as the most technically proficient floor leader the Senate has seen in this generation, operated with very little guidance from the Policy Committee, the Conference, or any other formal organs of party governance. For all practical purposes, they were the Democratic party organization in the Senate. Senators Scott Lucas and Ernest McFarland, who served during the Eighty-first and Eighty-second Congresses, were both able enough leaders but neither possessed the prestige of a Barkley nor the manipulative skill of a Johnson. Both depended a great deal more on formal party agencies for advice, guidance, and the generation of support.

Even when compared with the Democratic party under a relatively weak leader, the Republican leadership is more formalized, institutionalized, and decentralized. In the first place, the elective jobs of floor leader, chairman of the Conference, chairman of the Policy Committee, and chairman of the Committee on Committees are held by different men. Even when separated, these positions bestow considerable influence: that of the floor leader flowing from his tactical control over procedure; and that of the chairman of the Conference from his ability to nominate members for party offices who are generally ratified by the Conference without controversy. The Republican Policy Committee, very large and characterized by a rapid turnover in personnel, is dominated by its chairman. He is, therefore, of considerable importance in determining party strategy and the legislative schedule. Only the Republican chairman of the Committee on Committees gains little influence from his party post because of the party's strict adherence to the seniority rule.[7]

In the second place, the Republican Conference, while it suffers from many of the same debilities as that of the Democrats, is considerably more active and significant. During much of the Eisenhower administration, for example, weekly Conference luncheons were held at which the party leaders reported on their legislative discussions with the president. While no binding votes were attempted—indeed, veteran Republicans can never remember such a vote—some efforts were made, from time to time, to arrive at consensus.

Just as within the Democratic party, the actual pattern of Republican leadership depends in large measure upon the personalities, prestige, and skills of the men who hold the positions of leadership. There was, for example, a period during the postwar years when Senator Taft, first as chairman of the Policy Committee and later as floor leader, lead his party as single-handedly as any Democratic leader. But most of the time, the leadership of the GOP is more nearly corporate than individual.[8]

7. Truman, *Congressional Party*, pp. 99 ff., includes the Chairmen of the Senate Campaign Committees and Patronage Committees, as well as the President *Pro Tempore* among the "elective" party leaders in the Senate. Neither Professor Truman's data nor my own interviews suggest that the incumbents of these offices play a significant role in Senate party leadership.

8. The language is suggested by Westerfield, *Foreign Policy and Party Politics*, p. 84. This conclusion differs, at least in emphasis, from that contained in Truman, *Congressional Party*, Ch. 4. Truman argues, and the supporting evidence his elaborate cluster-bloc method of analysis supplies is impressive, that the pivotal leadership position in *both* parties is that of floor leader. My own interviews and observation suggest that the Republican floor leaders' power is not as great as that of the Democrats and that Republican leadership in the Senate is usually supplied by a small group, rather than by the floor leader alone. Truman also found (*ibid.*, p. 122) that the "elective" leaders of the Republican party were less cohesive as a group than the Democratic "elective" leaders. This finding may reflect the extremely broad definition of "elective" leader which Truman adopted (see above, note 7) and the fact that in the 81st Congress—the single Congress he studied—the Republicans were more disunited than in any other postwar Congress (see Figure 11). But even if these possibilities are ignored, his finding does not necessarily contradict the notion that Republican leadership tends to be "corporate." The Republican leaders may or may not agree with one another; the point is that they are a group—of which the floor leader is generally the most important—while in the Democratic party the leader is an individual.

PARTY LEADERS IN ACTION

Senate party leaders generally conceive of their jobs not as creating an over-all party program of legislative action (this is generally supplied by the president) but as achieving as much party unity as possible on discreet pieces of legislation. Under modern conditions, the more ambitious role is no doubt beyond their power. Even the limited goals they set for themselves are very difficult to achieve. They have no control over the raw material they are expected to unify; new party members appear on the Hill and old members are defeated quite independently of the leaders' actions or desires. They have no major sanctions to employ against party dissidents. "I didn't," one former leader remarked, "have anything to threaten them with, and it wouldn't have worked even if I had tried . . . sure as hell, someone would have gotten up on the floor and accused me of trying to become a dictator." Moreover, as another senator said, "When the party division in the Senate is close (and the need for party discipline therefore greatest) the party leaders want every Democrat or every Republican they can get—no matter how irregular his voting record." Often, the leader has little control over the content of the measures on which he seeks party agreement. To do so, he must exert influence at the committee stage of the legislative process, and "committee chairmen are independent cusses, highly jealous of their prerogatives." Some leaders do not even try to exert influence until after the committee has made its report. "I always believed," the same former leader said, "that it wasn't the leader's job to try to influence committee decisions. The leader's job is to take bills which have already been reported out of committee and placed on the Calendar and try to obtain as much party backing for them as he can."[9]

The party leader's principal weapon is his own persuasiveness. A major share of his time is devoted to lobbying—flattering, cajoling, appealing to the senators' sense of party loyalty, arguing the merits of legislative measures. The more effective leaders are, in fact, "conducting a continuous caucus on the floor, in the corridors and cloakrooms, over the telephone." If all efforts at persuading a straying party

9. Despite these protestations, most senators feel that the floor leaders do, at times, have influence on committee chairmen. Truman, *Congressional Party*, pp. 136 ff. finds that committee chairmen and floor leaders vote together more often on measures reported from the chairman's committee than they do on other legislation. Of course, one cannot be certain from this whether the chairman "went along" with the floor leader or vice versa. Indirect indications of the relative strength of the two parties (*ibid.*, pp. 139 ff.) suggest that the floor leader is more likely to be dominant, and the principal votes upon which the majority leader and committee chairmen are likely to show agreement are on administration supported measures (*ibid.*, pp. 286-87).

member fail, and they do with some senators on almost every vote in which the leadership takes an interest, the leaders seek to persuade the maverick to absent himself from the chamber during the vote, or to pair,[10] or, at least, not to dramatize the party split by playing an active role in floor debate.

Much of this lobbying is done through emissaries. "The leader often sends a friend of mine around to see if he can change my mind. He drops in—not saying that the leader sent him, of course—and talks to me about the bill. But if I say that I have definitely made up my mind one way or the other, that's all there is to it." Some senators who are close both to the leader and to a group with which the leader has limited influence can develop a position of substantial power by playing the role well.

"Most of the time," one senator explained, "the leader is cast in the role of someone trying to help you with your problems." Does a senator want an office overlooking the Mall? Is he looking for an administrative assistant? Does he need to be out of town when an important roll call vote is likely to be taken? Does he desire a seat on the Foreign Relations Committee? Wish to make a four-hour speech next Thursday? Is he looking for a pair on the agriculture bill? Does he need to get his pet bill passed in order to stand a chance for re-election? Or does he want to know what S. 123 would *really* do to his constituents? The leader can be of at least some help, and often of very great assistance, in grappling with questions of this sort. As a result, the leader is in an excellent position to know every member's problems, ambitions, and idiosyncracies. If the leader makes a firm commitment to be of aid, a senator can count on his battling to keep his word—and reminding the senator of the favor if it should ever be necessary to do so!

Undoubtedly the biggest favor a party leader can do for a senator is to get him a desirable committee assignment. On initial assignments, the party leaders sometimes have a little maneuverability. Beyond this point, however, the leader's discretion is bound by the seniority rule; that is, once a senator is appointed to a committee he may serve on it as long as he desires and committee vacancies are given to the

10. A "pair" is a means by which a senator can register his opinion on a particular vote, even though he is absent. In order to pair, a senator needs only to enter into a private agreement with another senator that he will not vote if the other is absent. These pairs are announced at the conclusion of the roll call and printed in the *Record*, showing one for and another against the issue. Pairs are not counted, however, in determining how many senators voted for, and how many against, a measure.

senator requesting them who has served longest in the chamber.[11] The principal advantage of this system, of course, is that it almost automatically allocates the limited supply of desirable committees in an entirely "objective" way, thus minimizing intra-Senate conflict and logrolling. But it also largely eliminates a potential lever for the leaders to use against party irregulars.

The seniority system is not entirely automatic, since two or more party members with identical seniority may apply for the same vacancy. This dilemma is often solved by relatively weak leaders by ranking these men according to their previous political experience (former governors first, former representatives second, and so on), by resorting to the alphabet, or even by flipping a coin. Yet given the seniority system, a party leader can sometimes, within severely restricted limits, use his influence over committee assignments to punish friends and reward enemies. He can, for example, use his knowledge of the wants of his party's members to block the "promotion" of an uncooperative senator simply by persuading a man with greater seniority to apply for the committee assignment the recalcitrant senator desires. One rather independent Democrat applied three times for a seat on a major committee for which his seniority seemed more than sufficient. Each time he was beaten out by a surprise applicant with greater seniority. "I feel," the senator ruefully remarked, "that they are scouting around for men senior to me to put on that committee." Too much stress should not be placed on this point. If a committee assignment is really desirable a senior man will snap it up without any urging, but the party leaders can sometimes facilitate this process to serve their own ends.

Senator Johnson, as Democratic leader, has gone considerably further than this. By persuading many of the senior senators to give up one of their two desirable committees, he has been able to assure every senator, regardless of seniority, that he will quickly receive one important committee assignment. Here is no mean incentive to party regularity, although one which can be used only with relatively junior senators who have not yet achieved the committee assignments they prefer. It cannot affect the men who are already entrenched in good committee posts, and these tend to be the most powerful members in the Senate.

In addition to persuasion and the granting and withholding of favors, the party leaders have other methods of maximizing party

11. Occasionally, the party ratios on committees will change so drastically from one Congress to the next that one or more members must be "bumped" off a committee. This is done in the inverse order of seniority.

unity. Their control over the parliamentary situation can be used for this purpose. "No Southern Senator—except perhaps the two from Alabama—", explained one member of a Democratic leader's staff, "can afford to vote for a public housing bill. The Northern Democrats can't afford to vote against one. You can't ask a senator to slit his own throat. So you bring up the bill in such a way that the Southerners can vote for it because it provides less housing than the alternative (or because it does not contain an FEPC provision) and the Northerners vote for it because it is better than nothing." Sometimes, the most petty floor maneuvers can make the difference between passage or defeat of a party measure. In a recent Congress, for example, Senator Johnson was positive that an important bill would pass if a certain Southern senator would vote for it, but according to a careful canvass of the situation the senator was still undecided. Abruptly, in the middle of floor debate, Johnson approached the wavering senator, announced that he had to leave the chamber for an hour or so and casually asked the potential dissenter to take over as floor manager of the bill. The senator hesitated and then agreed as Johnson left the floor. The undecided senator voted for the bill.

The party leaders can refuse to bring a bill to the floor if they are not satisfied that it will pass in a form acceptable to the party. Occasionally, they can even afford to ignore the bills of uncooperative members. "They don't dare do this often or they will have a revolt on their hands," but the threat of studied inaction can be potent even if rarely carried out.

Above all, the party leader must seek to anticipate intraparty controversy and "find a basis upon which the party can agree. This requires that he understand the problems of every member of his party and try to find a way of reconciling them." A good leader must be able to find "the bargaining point," the "common denominator of party accord."[12]

THE RECRUITMENT OF PARTY LEADERS

The leader's job requires vast energy, tolerance, patience, a willingness to pay infinite attention to details, manipulative ability, a sense of "news," and a talent for creative compromise, but the exact mixture of these skills needed for effective leadership varies from one situation to another.

12. The language is from F. M. Riddick, *United States Congress: Organization and Procedure* (Manassas, Va.: National Capitol Publishers, Inc., 1949), p. 93; and D. Cater, "The Trouble in Lyndon Johnson's Backyard," *The Reporter*, December 1, 1955, p. 32 Chapter Five of Riddick's volume contains a realistic description of the floor leaders and whips in action.

On the whole, the Republican leaders, at the head of a more unified party with a less experienced and politically skilled membership, need less manipulative ability and skill at compromise than the Democratic leaders. As a general rule, the Republican leader is not as smooth a legislative "operator" as the Democrat. Senator Taft, for example, had no patience for trivia, nor an ingratiating personality, nor a liking for petty politicking, yet he was, in his own abrasive way, a brilliant leader for the GOP.[13] Senator Knowland, rock-like in his patience and personal integrity, did not engage in the cloakroom politicking so essential to the effective operation of most Democratic leaders. Yet it was generally agreed by Republicans (Taft and Eisenhower wings) that he was the best man in the party for the job. Of the recent Republican floor leaders perhaps only Styles Bridges possessed the manipulative style of the postwar Democratic leaders.[14]

The division of seats between the two parties also affects the kinds of men likely to emerge as leaders in both parties. Back in the 1930's, when the Democrats controlled all but a relative handful of the Senate seats and the New Deal was at the crest of its popularity, the majority leader's most important function was that of dramatizing administration measures. The minority leader, leading a small and homogeneous band of senators from irreconcilably Republican states, hardly needed vast manipulative abilities either. This was a time for what one present day leader has called the "rock 'em, sock 'em, damn the opposition"[15] kind of leader in both parties.

The period following World War II, on the other hand, was one of paper-thin majorities ("We don't *really* have a majority," one Democrat said during the Eighty-fourth Congress, "but they haven't found out yet"), few rousing issues, and slack presidential leadership. The situation placed a heavy premium on parliamentary and manipulative skills, a talent for compromise and raiding the other side of the aisle. "Mechanics!" one Democrat admiringly exclaimed, while contemplating his party's postwar leaders. "They are fascinated by the process

13. On Taft as a party leader see W. S. White, *The Taft Story* (New York: Harper, 1954), Chs. 16-21.

14. Kenneth Wherry, more of a back-room operator than either Taft or Knowland, suffered as a floor leader from his position near the extreme right wing of the Republican party. It is difficult, if not impossible, to play the role of honest broker from an extremist ideological position. See Truman's comments, *Congressional Party*, pp. 104-17.

15. Senator Lyndon Johnson, in a memorandum published in Arthur Krock's *New York Times* column for July 13, 1956. This entire memorandum, or at least that part of it published by Krock, provides considerable insight into Johnson's definition of the legislative party leader's role.

of politics. It's their whole life—occupation, hobby, family, everything. Yet they aren't particularly interested in or knowledgeable about issues. They just like to tinker with the legislative machinery and see it go."

Fourteen men held important positions of party leadership during the 1947-57 decade.[16] When their backgrounds and careers are compared to those of all senators serving during the same period, these generalizations gain considerable support.

In the first place, the recruitment of party leaders favored "moderates" in both parties. In Table 45, the differences in political ideology and party-line voting of Democratic and Republican leaders and rank and file are presented, using the now familiar index of overrepresentation. The extreme ends of the ideological spectrum were underrepresented among the leaders of both parties; moderate Democrats and Republicans were favored as leaders. While middle-of-the-roaders, the leaders tended to be quite partisan before election to the party office. In both parties, senators with low party-unity scores were not elected to party leadership positions at all. On the other hand, the most highly partisan Democrats and Republicans (while slightly overrepresented in their respective party's leadership groups) were not chosen in as disproportionately large numbers as men with high but not the highest records in party-line voting. Paradoxically, election to positions of party leadership encouraged, under postwar conditions, a less partisan stance: the leaders' party unity scores noticeably declined after their election to party office—this despite the fact that the party leaders' ideological positions tended, after their election, to shift slightly away

16. These positions and their incumbents during each Congress were:

	80th Cong.	81st Cong.	82nd Cong.	83rd Cong.	84th Cong.
Democrats					
Leader	Barkley	Lucas	McFarland	Johnson	Johnson
Whip	Lucas	Myers	Johnson	Clements	Clements
Republicans					
Leader	White	Wherry	Bridges	Taft, Knowland	Knowland
Whip	Wherry	Saltonstall	Saltonstall	Saltonstall	Saltonstall
Chairman, Policy Committee	Taft	Taft	Taft	Knowland, Ferguson	Bridges
Chairman, Conference	Millikin	Millikin	Millikin	Millikin	Millikin

Table 45

RECRUITMENT OF SENATE PARTY LEADERS: PARTISANSHIP AND IDEOLOGY

(index of overrepresentation of leaders compared with all
senators, 1947-57)

Mean Conservatism-Liberalism Scores Before Election	Democratic Leaders (n-6)	Republican Leaders (n-8)	All Leaders (n-14)
0-19	0	0.4	0.4
20-39	0	2.8	1.7
40-59	3.2	0	2.3
60-79	1.4	0	1.2
80 plus	0.5	0	0.5
Mean Party-Unity Scores Before Election			
0-69	0	0	0
70-79	0	1.6	0.8
80-89	2.7	1.1	2.2
90 plus	1.4	1.3	1.1

from the political center toward the centers of gravity of their respective parties.[17]

In the second place, the party leaders were far more often experienced politicians, born and bred to the craft, than were the ordinary senators. There were three times the number of Patricians, and 1.3 the number of Professionals in positions of party leadership as one would expect on the basis of chance (Table 46). Moreover, the party leaders were very apt to have had legislative experience before their election to the Senate: the group of party leaders contained 1.5 the number of former congressmen and 1.1 times the number of former state legislators as were to be found in the Senate as a whole.[18] There

17. The mean party-unity and conservatism-liberalism scores of the party leaders before and after their election to positions of party leadership are as follows:

	Before Becoming Party Leader	After Becoming Party Leader
Party-Unity Scores	86	80
Conservatism-Liberalism Scores		
Democrats	63	79
Republicans	26	13

18. Underscoring the preference for men with prior legislative experience is the fact that three of the eight members of the Senate who had once been Congressional staff members were party leaders. The index of overrepresentation of former Congressional staff members among the party leaders is 5.4.

are interesting differences between the parties, too. Leadership selection within the GOP favored "old family" Patricians, while *all* the Democratic party leaders were Professional Politicians. The Democrats favored former congressmen as leaders; the Republicans, former state legislators.

Table 46

RECRUITMENT OF SENATE PARTY LEADERS: CAREER TYPES

(index of overrepresentation of leader compared with all senators, 1947-57)

Career Type	Democratic Leaders (n-6)	Republican Leaders (n-8)	All Leaders (n-14)
Professionals	1.6	1.1	1.3
Patricians	0	5.4	3.0
Amateurs	0	0.3	0.2
Agitators	0	0	0

THE EFFECTS OF PARTY LEADERSHIP

Sometimes the leaders begin to wonder if they really have any effect on the unity of their party in the Senate. For one thing, when the leadership of one party decides to make a bill a "party issue,"— which occurs on only a small minority of all bills and resolutions that come to the floor—this often stimulates the opposition party to do the same thing; the harder one set of leaders works to unify their party and to split the opposition, the harder the opposition tries to counteract their efforts. Moreover, it is difficult to separate the "natural" unity, which a party would have because of the coincidence of views of its members even if the party leaders did nothing, from the fruits of the leaders' efforts.

It seems quite clear that the unity which the parties display in the Senate is far more a result of the similarity of their members' attitudes than of either "pressure" or persuasion from party leaders. There is an impressively strong tendency for liberal Democrats to have relatively high party-unity scores and for conservative Democrats to stray from the fold. Quite the opposite is the case for the Republicans: the conservative Republicans tend to be party "regulars" while the liberal members of the GOP do not vote with their party nearly so often (Figure 12). A senator's over-all ideological stance is usually set by the time he becomes a senator and is largely beyond the powers of the leaders significantly to change it.

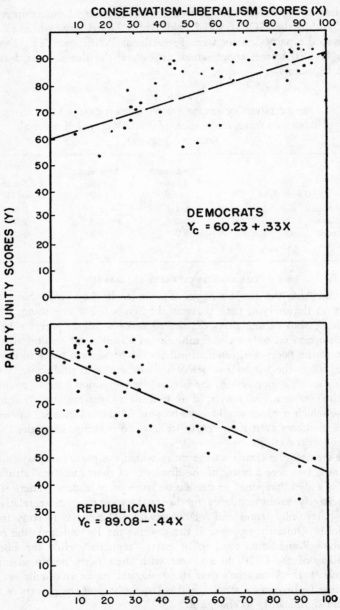

FIG. 12. Ideology and Party Voting, by Party, 81st Congress

However, the unity within each party in the Senate cannot be explained entirely on this basis. While a senator's party regularity is largely a function of his ideological position, it is not entirely determined by this factor. Another look at Figure 12 shows this clearly. Some senators have higher party unity scores, given their ideological position, than others. In the figure this is symbolized by the scattering of dots (each representing a senator) above and below the broken line (called a line of regression) which represents the usual relationship between a senator's liberalism-conservatism score and the extent of his party voting. The difference between how often a senator actually votes with his party and how often he would be expected to on the basis of his over-all ideological stance, we shall call party effort. Some senators display high party effort, some about the average amount, while still others seem to put forth relatively little.[19] Why?

Indebtedness to the party leader is one possible reason, and Senator Johnson's recent departures from the strict seniority rule in making Democratic committee assignments gives us an excellent opportunity to see if this is true.

In Table 47 the names of all Democratic senators who received "premature" committee assignments (i.e., their seniority was less than that normally required for the appointment) under Johnson's leadership are presented along with their party-effort scores before and after receiving the committee plum. In every case save two—and one of these was Senator Clements, the Democratic whip, a position which we have already seen tends to result in a drop-off in party-line voting—the recipient senators increased their party effort *after* receiving the assignment. As a group, their party effort scores increased from +0.5 to +5.5.[20]

If, as this evidence seems to indicate, a senator's party effort depends, at least to some degree, on his relations with the party leader, we should expect it to vary considerably with seniority; swapping of favors is likely to be more effective in dealing with junior men than with the entrenched and powerful. Table 48 shows that freshmen senators start out with relatively high party-effort scores and become even a little more faithful to the party during the middle years of service. Their party effort, however, falls off very sharply as they achieve high seniority. Moreover, this is especially the case among the Democrats, a fact which jibes with what we know of the leader-

19. For a more technical discussion of the Index of Party Effort see Appendix D.
20. All other Democratic senators who received high prestige committee assignments during the 83rd and 84th Congresses (but who had sufficient seniority to "earn" the appointments) increased in their mean party effort scores from +0.2 to +3.6.

Table 47

DEMOCRATS RECEIVING "PREMATURE" ASSIGNMENTS TO
IMPORTANT COMMITTEES
(83rd and 84th Congresses)

Name of Senator	Committee Assignment	Mean Seniority of All Senators at Appointment to Committee (in years)	Senator's Seniority at Appointment (in years)	Mean Party Effort Scores	
				Before Appointment	After Appointment
Mansfield	Foreign Relations	8.1	0	—	+10.0
Morse	Foreign Relations	8.1	0*	—	+ 3.0
Humphrey	Foreign Relations	8.1	4	−1.3	+ 6.0
Scott	Agriculture	2.8	0	—	+ 7.0
Symington	Armed Services	2.1	0	—	+ 7.5
O'Mahoney	Judiciary	2.0	0	−1.7**	+ 9.0
Ervin	Armed Services	2.1	1	+7.0	+ 5.0
Clements	Appropriations	5.8	5	+2.5	− 6.0
Jackson	Armed Services	2.1	2	−2.0	+12.0
Long	Foreign Relations	8.1	8	−4.0	+ 2.0
	Mean Party Effort Score			+0.5	+ 5.5

* Senator Morse, while previously a senator, became a Democrat at the beginning of the Eighty-fourth Congress. His Democratic seniority was, therefore, nil.

** Senator O'Mahoney was defeated at the end of the Eighty-second Congress and returned to the Senate in the Eighty-fourth. His "before appointment" party effort scores were figured for the Eightieth to the Eighty-second Congresses. Senator Barkley, technically a "freshman" upon his return to the Senate in the Eighty-fourth Congress although a former vice-president and Senate Democratic leader received choice assignments to Foreign Relations and Finance. Insufficient data makes the figuring of his party-effort scores impossible and he has been omitted.

ship styles in the two parties. The Republican leaders are less prone to favor-swapping, hence the party effort of the rank and file among the Republicans varies less with seniority than is the case in the Democratic party.

Another factor which affects the party effort of senators is the electoral cycle (Figure 13). Six years is a long time, especially in the perspective of elective politicians, but as the time for re-election closes in, a senator—especially a relatively junior one—tends to become panicky. The party leaders can often help a senator running for re-election look good back home, and a senator's sense of partisanship is likely to be enhanced by the impending electoral struggle. Thus, the senator's party effort tends to rise sharply during his term, hitting its

Table 48
PARTY EFFORT AND SENIORITY
(percentage "high" of all party-effort scores)

	Term of Service				
	1st	*2nd*	*3rd*	*4th*	*5th*
All Senators	42%	45%	37%	28%	10%
Democrats	44%	49%	34%	27%	18%
Republicans	39%	41%	46%	33%	0%

NOTE: "High" party effort is defined as a score of +4.0 and above.

peak the last two years before re-election, drops off sharply during the first Congress of his second term, and then begins rising again. The rise and fall of the senator's party effort parallel to the cycle of elections tend to level out if he serves long enough, but then those senators who serve through more than two complete cycles tend to come from states in which re-election is relatively certain and the hot winds of party conflict blow feebly if at all.

Indebtedness to party leaders, seniority, and the imminence of a re-election bid all affect a senator's party effort, but, during the postwar decade at least, this was more the case within the Democratic party than the Republican. Does this mean that Democratic leaders had a greater impact on their colleagues than the Republican leaders? Our data makes it possible for us to hazard a very tentative answer to this question.

First of all, examine Figure 14 which presents several hypothetical lines of regression, figured for the party unity and conservatism-liberalism scores of legislators. In the first hypothetical situation, the line of regression is horizontal: members of party "A" tend to have high party-unity scores regardless of their over-all stance on issues. In the second situation, the line of regression is vertical: the members of party "B" have similar political ideologies but varying degrees of attachment to their party. The third situation is more complex: there are two parties, both with members ranging from highly liberal to highly conservative. Party "A," however, tends to be a liberal party and its liberal members vote with their party more often than the conservatives. In party "B," which tends toward conservatism, the reverse is true; the conservative members of party "B" are more devoted to party regularity than are the liberal members. A close examination of this figure also shows that party "A," given the ideo-

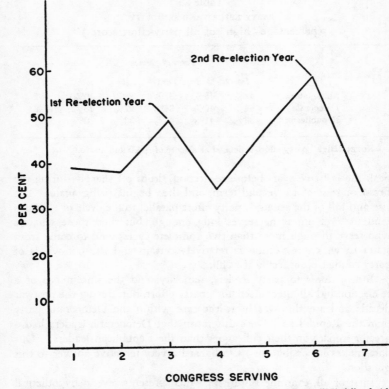

FIG. 13. Electoral Cycle and Party Effort, in Per Cent "High" of All Party Effort Scores

logical heterogeneity of its members, has achieved greater party unity than party "B." The conservatives in party "A" vote with the party almost as often as do the liberals—the fact that party "A's" line of regression is almost flat shows that ideology has relatively little effect on party voting. In party "B," however, there is a vast difference in the party regularity of conservatives and liberals; witness the fact that its line of regression is almost vertical.

Let us now look at the actual situation in the Senate. In Figure 15, the lines of regression between the party-unity and conservatism-liberalism scores of Democrats and Republicans have been plotted for the Eightieth through the Eighty-fourth Congresses. While, of neces-

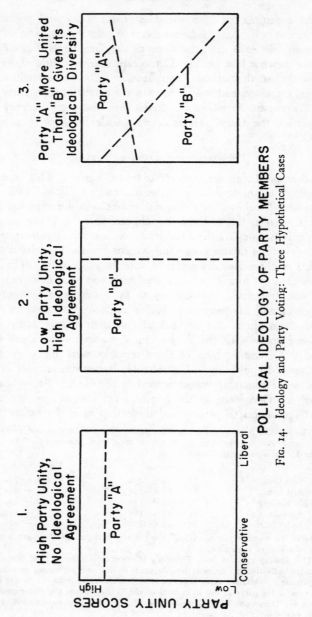

POLITICAL IDEOLOGY OF PARTY MEMBERS

Fig. 14. Ideology and Party Voting: Three Hypothetical Cases

sity, the measures for both variables—party unity and political ideology—are very inexact, the figure seems to point firmly to an important conclusion. In each case, the slope of the Democrats' line of regression is somewhat less, i.e., the Democratic line is a little closer to the horizontal than that of the Republicans.[21] The Democratic senators' ideology, therefore, had less to do with the extent of their party voting than was true for Republicans. Given the ideological diversity within both parties, the Democrats achieved a little more party unity than the GOP.[22]

PRESIDENT AND PARTY LEADERSHIP

Modern presidents are expected to lead Congress. This expectation, with all of its ambiguities, is as widespread on Capitol Hill as anywhere else. "I believe," one senior Republican said during the Eighty-fourth Congress, "that if the Republican party is going to stay in power it must support the President. As a result, I sometimes 'hold my nose'—as the saying goes—and go along with the Administration, though I might personally prefer to vote the other way." The administrative assistant to a Republican freshman was even more outspoken: "The most important 'pressure' on us in this office is Dwight David Eisenhower and his program. We've a file of his messages and we refer to them often. It's not a matter of their calling us up or anything—we know what the White House wants and we don't have to be told." Of course, both of these remarks were made by devoted "Eisenhower Republicans." Considerably less enthusiasm for President Eisenhower's leadership was expressed by the old-line Republicans and most of the Democrats in the Senate. Yet few, if any, senators expressed opposition to presidential leadership as such; rather, if they

21. The statistically equipped reader can, perhaps more accurately and easily, see this from the equations for the lines of regression than from Figure 15. The regression equations for each party and Congress are:

	Democrats	Republicans
80th Cong.	$Yc = 55 + .43x$	$Yc = 102 - .64x$
81st Cong.	$Yc = 60 + .33x$	$Yc = 89 - .44x$
82nd Cong.	$Yc = 56 + .37x$	$Yc = 89 - .47x$
83rd Cong.	$Yc = 43 + .46x$	$Yc = 95 - .54x$
84th Cong.	$Yc = 37 + .42x$	$Yc = 92 - .90x$

The smaller the number preceding "x," the less is the slope and the more nearly horizontal is the line of regression.

22. This finding conflicts with Truman's (*Congressional Party*) basic thesis that the party leaders' effectiveness depends heavily upon having the presidency controlled by a fellow partisan. While we agree that the party leaders' position in the Senate is greatly strengthened if his party is also in control of the White House, the above analysis suggests that the Democratic leaders were more effective than the Republicans even when they did not enjoy that advantage.

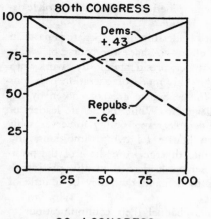

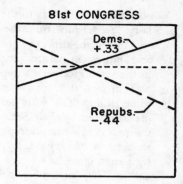

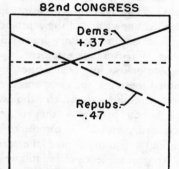

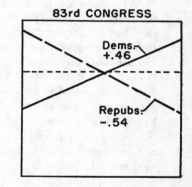

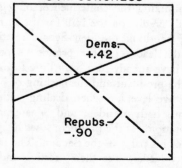

PARTY UNITY SCORES

CONSERVATISM–LIBERALISM SCORES

FIG. 15. Ideology and Party Voting

objected at all, it was to the direction, ineffectiveness, or lack of legis-lative "leadership" from the White House.

Most of the time, the president's leadership of the Senate is partisan and indirect in nature. In their efforts to shape the course of events in the often recalcitrant upper chamber, presidents mostly "work with and through their party leaders." This mode of operation occasions some strain. The party leaders in the Senate are not chosen by the president but by their Senate colleagues. While the Senate leaders of the president's party accept considerable responsibility to serve as his spokesmen, they have their own Senate following, ambitions, and legislative interests which sometimes diverge from those of the presi-dent. They are more nearly Senate leaders than the president's leaders, although the role seems to demand that they be a little of both.[23]

Why, then, do most presidents channel their communications to the Senate through the party leaders? The reasons are clear. No president has the time, energy, or detailed knowledge of the constantly shifting legislative terrain requisite for direct and personal leadership. He has too many other things to do. Moreover, the president is in-terested in a legislative package of more or less interrelated measures publicly supported in his budget, annual messages, speeches, and press conferences. The committee and sub-committee chairmen who will handle these proposals are legion. Almost invariably, they possess limited spans of attention and specialized perspectives, competencies, and influence. In order to get a general program adopted, the presi-dent needs to deal with generalists. As a consequence of the folkways, few if any influential generalists exist in the Senate aside from the party leaders. Moreover, to deal with the Senate indirectly has the advantage of minimizing the consequences of legislative defeat and saving his personal "credit" on the Hill for use in major crises.

This mode of handling president-Senate relationships is equally advantageous to the leaders of the president's party in the Senate. They have, as we have already seen, very little formal authority. Their regular access to the president and the backing of his prestige provides them with impressive leverage when dealing with their followers in the Senate.[24] Thus both president and Senate party leaders benefit from close collaboration. If the president loses his power and prestige, so do the leaders of his party in the Senate. The opposite is also true: if the Senate party leaders lose their prestige and effectiveness—and

23. Cf. *ibid.*, pp. 298-99.
24. *Ibid.*, Ch. 8.

this they will certainly do if they are perceived merely as presidential messenger boys—the president and his program are in serious trouble.

The importance of presidential backing to the Senate party leaders can be demonstrated in several different ways. In the first place, the party effort of the senators from the president's party is closely related to their willingness to support the president's legislative program (Table 49). Some of the time, then, loyalty to the president and his administration leads a senator to vote with his party more regularly than his ideological position necessitates or than he would if his party did not control the executive branch.

Table 49

SUPPORT FOR EISENHOWER ADMINISTRATION MEASURES AND PARTY EFFORT OF REPUBLICANS

(83rd Congress)

Administration Support	Index of Party Effort			
	High	Medium	Low	
High	63%	26%	11%	100% (19)
Medium	38%	44%	19%	100% (16)
Low	22%	11%	66%	100% (19)

NOTE: Figures on the senators' support of Eisenhower administration measures are from the *Congressional Quarterly Almanac*. See Appendix D.

In the second place, both parties achieve their highest degree of party unity when the White House is controlled by a member of their own party. If the reader will turn back to Figure 11 on page 122, he will see that the Democratic senators were most united in their voting during the Eightieth, Eighty-first, and Eighty-second Congresses while Harry Truman was president. The Republicans, on the other hand, achieved their greatest party unity in the Eighty-third Congress, the Eisenhower honeymoon. (The figures for the Eighty-fourth Congress are not comparable to those for other years.) The same figure suggests that majority status in the Senate encourages party unity, even if the presidency is controlled by the opposition party. The Republicans were a majority during the Eightieth Congress, and the Democrats, a majority during the Eighty-fourth, while the White House was controlled by the opposition. In both instances, their unity was unusually high for the nonpresidential party.[25]

25. This again diverges from Truman's conclusions, *ibid.*, p. 312. This and other

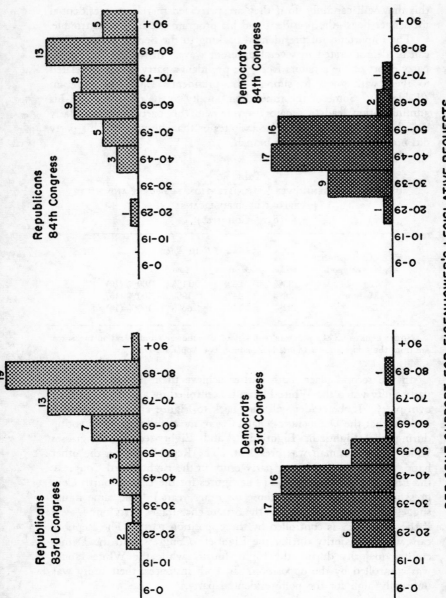

PER CENT SUPPORT FOR EISENHOWER'S LEGISLATIVE REQUESTS

Finally, the president's most consistent supporters in the Senate are almost invariably drawn from the members of his own party. The frequency with which members vote for the president's proposals varies a good deal within each party, of course, yet the central tendency is clear (Figure 16). The hard core of a president's support in the Senate comes from his own party. Indeed, the *average* member of the president's party usually votes for his proposals more often than the most "Republican minded" Democrat or most "Democratically minded" Republican.

On Capitol Hill everyone is a partisan. Yet the Democratic and Republican parties are quite different in the Senate. The Democrats incline toward a highly personalized rule by the floor leader; the Republicans, toward leadership by a handful of party officials. In neither party do the leaders conceive of their jobs as regularly requiring the development of an over-all legislative program or regular intervention into committee proceedings. Rather, their principal efforts are directed toward maximizing party unity during the floor consideration and voting on bills.

The party leader's principal weapon is his own intra-Senate standing and personal persuasiveness. The leader of the president's party, however, possesses a major additional source of influence—the president's prestige.

The political style and skills of the party leaders vary according to the party and the situation. During the postwar years, however, party leaders tended to be quite manipulative (especially the Democrats), moderate in their policy stances (in both parties), and highly experienced legislative politicians before their election to the Senate. Leadership selection within the GOP favored Patricians, within the Democratic party, Professionals.

Party unity in the Senate is more the result of the correspondence of views of the senator and the actions of his party than the result of "pressure" from the leadership. However, the party leaders do have an effect on their parties' unity. Generally speaking, the more indebted a senator is to the party leaders, the less seniority he has, the closer his next re-election bid, the more sensitive he is to the party

differences between the conclusions reached here and by Professor Truman may be the result of the different time periods studied and the different statistical techniques used in the two studies. Additional testing and refinement of the statistical measures used in this chapter and replication of Truman's admirable study in other Congresses are both in order.

leader's cues. Given both parties' ideological diversity, the Democrats achieve more unity in the Senate than the Republicans do.

Finally, presidential leadership of the Senate is partisan leadership most of the time: each president habitually works through the leaders of his party in the Senate; the president's party is usually more nearly united than the opposition; and the hard core of presidential supporters is made up of members of the president's own party.

Clearly, then, parties have a considerable impact on the distribution of power in the Senate and on the behavior of senators, but parties are not the only significant sub-groups in the Senate. The Senate's system of standing committees provides another, often competing, structure of power. It is to the Senate committees that we must now turn our attention.

CHAPTER VII

The Committees

"THE COMMITTEES are where the *real* work of the Senate is done," so goes a familiar Capitol Hill refrain. Its constant repetition seems justifiable. Virtually all legislative measures are referred to one of the Senate's fifteen subject-matter committees before being taken up by the chamber as a whole.[1] The consideration of matters not previously studied by a committee ("writing legislation on the floor") is frowned upon. Only a small fraction of the bills and resolutions referred to committees ever emerge from the committee room (Woodrow Wilson once called them "dim dungeons of silence"),[2] and those that do usually bear indelible marks of committee struggle. In the subsequent floor debate, voting, and reconciliation of differences between the Senate and the House, the recommendations of committee members carry great weight. Moreover, the committees are highly autonomous organizations; the spirit of reciprocity suggests that it is best to allow other committees to go their own way if one's own committees are to enjoy a similar freedom.

Thus a senator's committee work is of paramount importance to him. It is here that he makes his reputation with his colleagues and leaves his mark on legislation.

1. These committees are: Agriculture and Forestry, Appropriations, Armed Services, Banking and Currency, District of Columbia, Finance, Foreign Relations, Government Operations, Interior and Insular Affairs, Interstate and Foreign Commerce, Judiciary, Labor and Public Welfare, Post Office and Civil Service, Public Works, Rules and Administration. A sixteenth standing committee on Aeronautical and Space Sciences was created during the 85th Congress.

2. Woodrow Wilson, *Congressional Government* (Boston: Houghton Mifflin Company, 1925), p. 69.

Each senator normally serves on two standing committees; a few receive a third seat on a minor committee as well.[3] These assignments, as we have already seen, are made by the party Committee on Committees, and the senior senator who requests a vacant seat almost always gets it.   There may not, however, be two senators from the same party and state on the same committee.[4]

Given the strategic role of committees in the legislative process, it is not surprising that the senators are eager to receive good committee assignments.   Moreover, there is substantial consensus as to which committees are the desirable ones.   The resultant ranking of committee desirability and prestige—one informant referred to it as the "committee caste system"—is one of the Senate's most important structural features.

The "Committee Caste System"

One indication of the differences in committee prestige is the continual movement of senators from one committee to another during the course of their careers; it is a rare senator, indeed, who is content to sit on a committee to which he was initially assigned during the entire length of his service.   In order to obtain a new committee assignment, a senator must normally resign from one of the two committees on which he already serves.   Since any change in committee assignment involves a loss of committee seniority, thereby diminishing the senator's chance of becoming a committee chairman, a change usually indicates that a senator prefers the new committee considerably more than the old.   Now, if there were no consensus on the desirability of committees, we would expect all of the changes in committee assignments over a period of years to cancel out.   For every senator who preferred the Armed Services Committee over Banking and Currency, there would be another who saw things in just the opposite way.

This is very far from the case.   Figure 17 shows the net effects of all changes in Senate committee assignments during the entire 1947-57

3. The minor committees, as stipulated in Rule XXV, are the committees on the District of Columbia, Government Operations, and Post Office and Civil Service.   The new Aeronautical and Space Sciences Committee is also a minor committee.

4. As a matter of fact, two senators from the same state and different parties seldom serve on the same committee.   As G. Goodwin, "The Seniority System in Congress," *American Political Science Review*, LIII (June, 1959), 415, points out, this practice not only assures some geographical distribution of committee seats but also "eliminates what otherwise might be a source of intrastate jurisdictional disputes between the two senators."

period. Looking first at the extreme right-hand column, we can see that eight committees—Foreign Relations, Appropriations, Finance, Armed Services, Agriculture, Judiciary, Commerce, and Banking and Currency—recorded net gains in the decade-long game of "musical chairs," while the remaining seven committees—Interior, Public Works, Labor and Public Welfare, Government Operations, Rules and Administration, Post Office and Civil Service, and District of Columbia—suffered a net loss of membership. The differences in committee attractiveness, at least insofar as they are reflected in these figures, seem to be substantial. The Foreign Relations Committee gained sixteen members and Appropriations, fifteen, while the Post Office and Civil Service and the District of Columbia committees suffered net losses of nineteen and seventeen members, respectively.

COMMITTEE	For. Relations	Appropriations	Finance	Armed Ser.	Agri. & For.	Judiciary	Int. & For. Comm.	Banking & Curr.	Interior	Public Works	Labor & Pub. Wel.	Govt. Operations	Rules & Admin.	P.O. & Civ. Ser.	Dist. of Col.	NET TOTALS
1. Foreign Relations		+2	+2	+1	+2	+1	+1	+1	+1	+1	+1	+2		+1	+1	+16
2. Appropriations	-2		+1	+2		+1	+1		+3	+1	+3	+1	+3	+1		+15
3. Finance	-2	-1		+1	+1		0	+2	+2	+1	+1	+2	+1	+2		+10
4. Armed Services	-1	-2	-1		+1		+2		+1			+3		+1		+4
5. Agriculture & Forestry	-2		-1	-1		+1	+1		+1			+3	+1	+1	+3	+7
6. Judiciary	-1	-1					+1		+2	+2	+2	+1	+1	+1		+8
7. Interstate & Foreign Comm.	-1	-1	0		-1	-1		0	+2	+1	0	+2	+2	+4	+1	+8
8. Banking & Currency	-1			-2			0		0	+1		+2	+3	0	-1	+1
9. Interior	-1		-2				-2	0		+1		+1		+1		-2
10. Public Works	-1	-3	-2	-1	-1	-2	-1	-1	-1		+1		+1	+4	+2	-5
11. Labor & Public Welfare	-2	-1	-1		-2		0			-1		+2			-1	-6
12. Government Operations		-3	-1		-3	-2	-2	-2	-1		-2		+1	+1	+3	-11
13. Rules & Administration	-1		-1	-2	-3	-1	-1	-2	-3		-1	-1		+3	+4	-9
14. Post Office & Civil Service	-1	-3	-1		-1	-1	-4	0	-1	-4		-1	-3		+1	-19
15. District of Columbia		-1	-2	-1	-3	-1	-1	-1	+1		-2	+1	-3	-4		-17

FIG. 17. Net Gain or Loss of Committee Membership through Change of Assignment, 80th through 84th Congresses

Considerably more important and revealing, however, are each committee's net gains from, and losses to, every other committee. There are, after all, many ways in which a committee could build up a sizeable net gain (or loss) of members. Committee "A," for example, might have been chosen by so many members of Committee "B" that its net gain was the highest of all committees, even though it had no drawing power from Committees "C," "D," and "E." Nor do over-all net gain and loss figures demonstrate agreement among senators as to desirability of committees or any clear-cut hierarchy of prestige. Committee "A" may be preferred to Committee "B," which drew members from Committee "C," which in turn gained members at the expense of Committee "A"!

When one looks at the remainder of the figure, which presents the net gains and losses of each committee vis-à-vis all of the others, it is quickly evident that the senators displayed both consistency and agreement in their choice of committee posts. Note that Foreign Relations, to begin at the top, gained members from every other committee in the Senate save two—the Government Operations and the District of Columbia committees—and there were no changes in either direction between these two committees and Foreign Relations. The second-ranking committee, Appropriations, lost members to Foreign Relations and gained from every other committee with which it exchanged members, and so on down the committee pecking-order, each committee tending to lose members to those ranked above it while tending to gain members from those ranking below. The pattern is by no means perfect,[5] but there is sufficient agreement in committee preferences to say that the committees are clearly stratified.

The consequences of this fact are considerable. In the first place, it means that apprentice senators are heavily concentrated in a rela-

5. A good many of the possible changes in committee seats did not occur. When the difference in prestige of the two committees—as judged by their standings relative to the other committees—seems large, it is probably safe to assume that if the opportunity arose, members of the low-prestige committee (i.e., District of Columbia) would gladly resign for a seat on the desirable committee (i.e., Foreign Relations). But where the difference in relative ranking of the two committees seems small (as between Interior and Labor, for example), the lack of movement in either direction may well indicate differing opinions among senators concerning their relative desirability or indicate that the payoff obtained by a change is so small that it was not worth the sacrifice in committee seniority required to make the move. In the second place, there are two cases in which committee-membership flows contrary to the ranking: Banking and Currency (ranked eighth) and Labor (ranked eleventh) each lost one member to District of Columbia (ranked fifteenth). Moreover, since the rankings suggested here are based on *net* movements, there was some changing of committee assignments contrary to the general pattern that is not revealed in the figure. Finally, in five cases the flow of members from committee "A" to committee "B" was exactly equalled by the flow from "B" to "A," thereby revealing no agreed-upon preference. On the other hand, the practice that two senators from the same state and party may not serve on the same committee bars many senators from the more attractive seats. If this custom did not exist, the pattern of preferences presented in Figure 17 would probably be much more striking.

G. Goodwin, "Seniority System in Congress," *APSR*, p. 433, contains a slightly different ranking of committee desirability. The inconsistencies between Goodwin's analysis and the present one seem to be the result of the different time-spans covered and Goodwin's reliance upon total net shifts of membership "corrected" for the size of the committee as his index of committee desirability.

tively few committees. The committees on the District of Columbia, Post Office and Civil Service, Government Operations, Public Works, Interior, and Labor tend to be staffed almost entirely by Senate newcomers.[6] Turnover is high, skill is lacking, and morale among those members covetously eyeing other committee posts is frequently low. True, some senators choose to serve on low-prestige committees well beyond the time their seniority requires. In some cases, this is because the low-prestige assignment is a good one for them, even if not for most other senators. Others may decide to shoot for a quick chairmanship in a relatively unimportant committee rather than to go to the bottom of the long and slow seniority ladder of an important committee.[7]

Even so, when compared with the high ranking committees, those which are less desirable are often woefully weak in parliamentary skill, prestige, and experience. Moreover, their members rarely hold other positions of power in the Senate. The Foreign Relations and Appropriations committees, for example, are made up largely of chairmen of other committees.[8] The party leaders are also concentrated in the elite committees. Thus the caste system tends to feed on and perpetuate itself; the most influential committees tend to be composed of the most esteemed senators, which lends the committee even more prestige.

In the second place, the consensus on committee desirability reinforces the seniority system by making it more "functional" than it otherwise would be. As long as the senators tend to agree on the relative desirability of committee seats, there will be a permanent shortage of good assignments. Allocating these scarce seats on some

6. Ninety-one per cent of all assignments to the Labor Committee were *initial* assignments. The corresponding figure for the other committees were: District of Columbia, 90%; Post Office and Civil Service, 85%; Interior and Insular Affairs, 81%; Government Operations, 79%; Public Works, 72%; Banking and Currency, 64%; Rules and Administration, 56%; Interstate and Foreign Commerce, 44%; Armed Services, 39%; Judiciary, 36%; Agriculture and Forestry, 29%; Finance, 20%; Foreign Relations, 14%; Appropriations, 4%.

7. This seems especially to be the case if the senator is already a member of one important and influential committee. In making his committee choices, a senator's first committee choice is very likely to affect his second. It has not been possible to take this factor into account in the following analysis.

8. The Appropriations Committee, during the 2nd Session of the 84th Congress, contained nine chairmen or ranking minority members of other committees, the Democratic floor leader and whip, the Republican floor leader, whip, and Policy Committee chairman. Foreign Relations included seven committee chairmen plus the Republican floor leader. Finance contained four committee chairmen and the chairman of the Republican Conference. Armed Services included two committee chairmen, the Democratic floor leader, and the Republican floor leader and whip.

nonautomatic basis would have the result of greatly increasing intra-Senate tensions and centralizing power into the hands of the person or group who makes the assignment. Even the rather limited departures from the seniority system made by Senator Johnson in recent years have had both consequences. As long as the present level of agreement on committee desirability persists, it seems unlikely that the seniority pattern will be basically or permanently altered.

This, of course, means that senators from competitive two-party states are seldom able to achieve chairmanships or senior positions on important committees. On the average, during the postwar years, a senator had to be well into his second term before he could reasonably expect an appointment to the Foreign Relations Committee (Table 50). An appointment to the Appropriations Committee, on the average, needed about six years of seniority; Finance and Agriculture, three, and so on down the line. Once such an assignment is attained, and especially in the high-prestige committees, many more years are required before a senator's committee seniority is great enough for him to become an important member, to say nothing of chairman. The advantages which thereby accrue to the nation's one-party states are obvious.

The structure of committee prestige also affects, and in turn is affected by, the distribution of power outside the Senate in other ways. Note, for example, the Senate's ranking of the "interest" committees: Agriculture is first; Judiciary, second; Commerce, third; Banking and Currency, fourth; Labor, a very poor last. This ranking of committee desirability is undoubtedly influenced by the relative political power of these groups in the senators' constituencies, but the senators' ranking of these committees tends to reinforce the relative power of these groups outside the Senate: if the Labor Committee had more prestige, it could attract and hold a larger number of the chamber's powerful members, labor interests outside the Senate would benefit, labor would become politically more powerful, the Labor Committee would be more attractive to senators, and so on and on. The Senate's "Committee Caste System" is worth a good hard look. It can tell a great deal about the distribution of power both in and out of the Senate chamber.

Influences on Committee Preferences

To say that the standing committees of the Senate are ranked in terms of their relative desirability and prestige does not mean that all senators agree on their committee preferences. The situation is anala-

Table 50

SENIORITY AT TIME OF APPOINTMENT TO STANDING COMMITTEES
(80th through 84th Congresses)

Committee	Mean Seniority at Appointment in Years	Median Seniority at Appointment in Years
Foreign Relations	8.1	8.5
Appropriations	5.8	5.0
Finance	3.0	2.0
Agriculture and Forestry	2.8	3.0
Armed Services	2.1	1.0
Judiciary	2.0*	2.0
Interstate and Foreign Commerce	1.4	1.0
Banking and Currency	1.1	0
Rules and Administration	1.1	0
Interior and Insular	1.1	0
Post Office and Civil Service	0.6	0
Public Works	0.5	0
Government Operations	0.5**	0
District of Columbia	0.5	0
Labor and Public Welfare	0.2	0

* Excluding Senator Wagner of New York. At the close of his service, Senator Wagner was too ill to attend either committee or floor sessions. In order to make a place for another on Foreign Relations, Wagner was reassigned to a vacancy on Judiciary.

** Excluding Senator Vandenberg of Michigan. While chairman of the Foreign Relations Committee, Vandenberg—reportedly at his own request—was relieved of all other duties on major committees and assigned to a Republican vacancy on Government Operations. His seniority was so great at the time that, as in the case of Wagner above, its inclusion would greatly alter the mean.

gous to that in American society as a whole. Few thoughtful Americans would deny that a class system exists in their country, yet there is considerable disagreement on its exact configurations. While Americans, on the average, may agree that Supreme Court justices and medical doctors have the most desirable of all occupations,[9] fortunately not all of us think so.

The standard, Capitol Hill explanation of the senators' committee preferences is "political advantage." The tendency for senators to be attracted by committees of especial importance to their constituents is well known. The postwar Committee on Interior and Insular Affairs, for example, was overwhelmingly made up of senators from the public

9. "Jobs and Occupations: A Popular Evaluation," *Opinion News*, IX (September 1, 1947), 3-13.

land states: there were about three times more members from the Rocky Mountain and Pacific states than one would expect on the basis of chance. Or take the Senate Agriculture Committee: there were almost three times the proportion of senators from the Great Plains, and one-half again as many Southern senators on the Agriculture Committee as there were in the Senate as a whole. The committees on Labor, Commerce, Finance, and Banking had a special appeal to senators from the highly industrialized Northeastern and Great Lakes states. The committee with the greatest contingent of senators from rural states was Agriculture, and the committee with the greatest urban representation was Labor and Public Welfare.

To say that "political advantage" greatly influences a senator's preference in committee assignments is not to say very much. Senators from virtually identical states can have quite different electoral followings and thus define "political advantage" quite differently. Moreover, senators differ in their political aspirations. Service on Foreign Relations, for example, does not help many senators back home in their states—indeed, in most cases, it is a distinct liability—but it provides the best committee position from which to build a national reputation and launch an assault on the presidency. Then, too, some committee assignments confer considerable influence in the Senate. While this can sometimes be converted into constituency appeal or a national reputation, the major immediate and visible payoff is peer group respect and deference. Senators differ in their political styles. Playing an important and well-publicized role in the making of national policy is one way in which a politician can attempt to build and hold an electoral following; the "top" committees—Foreign Relations, Appropriations, Finance, and Armed Services—provide the best positions from which to do this. Or a close and sympathetic cooperation with one or more organized interests can also be advantageous; to those who choose this method, the "interest" committees are especially attractive. Finally, a liberal, but still judicious, distribution of federal loaves and fishes is another way in which to get ahead in politics: Appropriations, Interior, Public Works, and Post Office and Civil Service are the most strategic positions for those interested in "pork" and patronage.[10] In order to discover the influences of the senators' committee preferences, we must go considerably beyond the crude notion of political advantage.

10. The typology of Congressional committees used here was originated by Dwaine Marvick, "A Quantitative Technique for Analyzing Congressional Alignments," (Ph.D. dissertation, Columbia University, 1950). The "top" committees are Foreign Relations, Appropriations, Armed Services, and Finance. The "interest" committees are Agri-

There are, for example, differences in the committee preference hierarchies of Democrats and Republicans (Table 51). Both rank the four committees concerned with broad national and international policy—Foreign Relations, Appropriations, Finance, and Armed Services—very high on their lists, but the Democrats seemingly value a seat on Appropriations or Finance more highly than the Republicans do. On the other hand, the Agriculture Committee is considered highly desirable by more Republicans than Democrats. This is not because of a larger share of Republicans than Democrats coming from rural states; when the proportion of Republicans and Democrats serving on the Agriculture Committee is figured for states of different degrees of ruralism, we find that the Republicans from the most rural states serve on Agriculture twice as often as do the Democrats. The proportion of Republicans serving on Agriculture, on the other hand, declines sharply as their constituencies become more urban until, in the relatively urban states, the committee has more appeal for Democrats than for Republicans (Figure 18).

Of the other interest committees, the Republicans rate the Judiciary Committee second; Banking and Currency, third; Commerce, fourth; and Labor, fifth in desirability. The Democrats see things quite differently; Agriculture and Labor are tied for first place, Judiciary next, followed by Banking and Currency and, at the bottom of the heap, the Commerce Committee. Even with these differences in party ranking, the Republicans prefer all of the interest committees except Labor more than the Democrats do.

A senator's previous experience, skills, and interests also affect his committee preferences. There are sizeable differences in the committee preferences of senators with different occupational backgrounds. Among the top four committees, all requiring substantial seniority as a precondition of membership, the lawyers favor Foreign Relations most and Finance least. The opposite is the case for the businessmen; they prefer Finance, Armed Services coming next, then Appropriations, and finally Foreign Relations. Farmers rank the two fiscal committees over the foreign-military-policy committees. Among the college professors, Foreign Relations is by far the most desirable of the top committees, and there were over three times the proportion of them on Foreign Relations as in the Senate as a whole. Shifting our attention to the interest committees, we find the same kind of

culture, Banking and Currency, Interstate and Foreign Commerce, Judiciary, and Labor. The "pork" committees are Interior, Post Office and Civil Service, and Public Works. The "duty" committees are Rules and Administration, Government Operations, and District of Columbia.

Table 51

MEAN CONTINUOUS SERVICE OF COMMITTEE MEMBERS: JANUARY 3, 1955

	Democrats			Republicans	
Rank	Committee	Mean Service in Years	Rank	Committee	Mean Service in Years
1.	Appropriations	13.9	1.	Foreign Relations	11.8
2.	Foreign Relations	10.7	2.	Agriculture	8.9
3.	Rules and Administration	10.5	3.	Judiciary	8.3
4.	Finance	10.3	4.	Appropriations	7.8
5.	Armed Services	8.5	5.	Armed Services	7.7
6.-7.	Agriculture	8.0	6.	Finance	7.6
6.-7.	Labor	8.0	7.	Interior	5.7
8.	Judiciary	7.5	8.	Banking and Currency	5.1
9.	Banking and Currency	7.1	9.	Rules & Administration	4.5
10.	Public Works	4.3	10.	Post Office & Civil Service	4.3
11.	Interior	4.2	11.	Commerce	4.0
12.	Post Office & Civil Service	4.0	12.	Labor & Public Welfare	3.7
13.	District of Columbia	3.7	13.	Government Operations	3.3
14.	Government Operations	3.6	14.	Public Works	2.7
15.	Interstate & Foreign Commerce	3.1	15.	District of Columbia	0.5

thing: farmers are heavily overrepresented on the Agriculture Committee; lawyers, on Judiciary; businessmen, on Banking and Currency and Finance; and college professors (a notoriously pro-underdog group) are overrepresented on Labor. The occupational distributions of the members of the lower-prestige committees, where committee service is less a matter of choice than lack of seniority, follows that of the Senate as a whole fairly closely.[11]

These occupational differences between the Senate committees hold up even when the effect of the senators' constituencies are held constant. In Figure 19, for example, the proportion of farmers and sons of farmers serving on the Agriculture Committee is presented for

11. One cannot, of course, merely compare the characteristics of all the members of a committee with the characteristics of all senators and conclude from that alone that the characteristics statistically overrepresented among committee members predisposed them to seek out membership on that committee. For committee assignments are made on the basis of seniority as well as personal choice. Thus, if we find a larger proportion of lawyers in a committee than in the Senate as a whole, this may not be a reflection of the preferences of lawyers but the result of the fact that lawyers tend to have relatively high seniority. If we are to determine influences on committee preferences, comparisons can be made only between committees which require approximately the same seniority as a requisite for membership. The tables upon which much of the discussion in this section is based may be found in Appendix E.

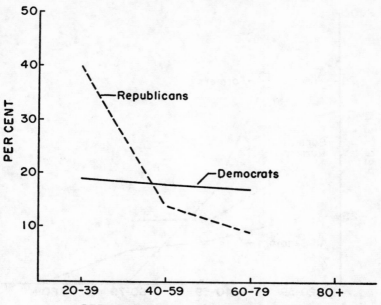

FIG. 18. Party and Service on Agriculture Committee, in Per Cent Serving on Committee, 80th through 84th Congresses

states of different degrees of ruralism. Note that less than 25 per cent of all senators from the most rural states served on Agriculture, but 100 per cent of the senator-farmers from these states did so. Over 40 per cent of the sons of farmers from these states belonged to the committee. In all but the most urban states, the farmers and sons of farmers choose Agriculture in larger numbers than do the other senators.[12]

The senator's career type is also related to his preference in committee (Figure 20). The Professional Politicians, for example, tend to seek assignments to Finance and Appropriations rather than Foreign Relations and Armed Services. Certainly the two fiscal committees have more political "mileage" in them—conceived in the traditional sense of positions from which one can do economic favors for one's friends—than the committees concerned with foreign and military policy. Among the interest committees, the Professionals prefer Agri-

---

12. Evidently urban state senators with rural backgrounds prefer to play this fact down.

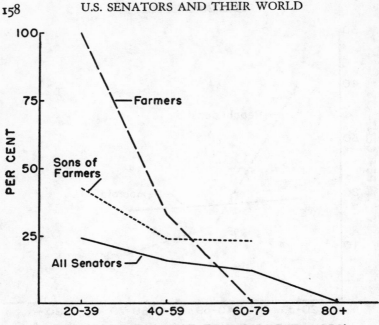

Fig. 19. Farm Background and Service on Agriculture Committee, in Per Cent Serving on Committee, 80th through 84th Congresses

culture and Commerce to Labor and Judiciary. Of the lesser committees, they tend toward Rules and Government Operations, committees which are concerned with the subject they know best, the internal functioning of the government. The Amateurs, most of whom have spent the lion's share of their adult life in business or law, are especially attracted to Finance, Judiciary, Banking and Currency. They are noticeably underrepresented on Appropriations, Armed Services, Agriculture, Government Operations, and Rules. The "old family" concern with the military is reflected in the Patricians' clear preference for the Armed Services Committee over all others; there were almost four times as many of them on this committee as in the Senate as a whole. Appropriations and Foreign Relations fall next in popularity among Patricians while the traditional old family disdain for "trade" may be reflected in the small number of them who served on Finance. The Patricians are conspicuously underrepresented on all the other committees in the Senate save Labor, on which a small group of Patrician reformers served during the postwar years.

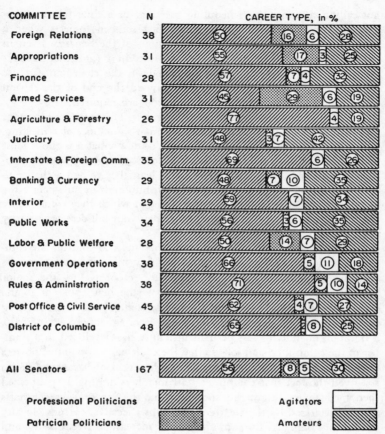

Fig. 20. Career Type and Committee Assignments, 80th through 84th Congresses

THE COMMITTEE CHAIRMAN

At first glance, the committee chairman's formal powers are not particularly impressive. Yet the chairman, with rare exceptions usually caused by gross senility or incompetence, is the most influential member of a Senate committee.

Sources of the Chairman's Power

The rules of some committees provide that the committee meet at the call of the chair. This permits the chairman to kill bills simply by not calling meetings, by scheduling meetings at a time when a quorum cannot be obtained, or by seeing that someone objects when a meeting will require the unanimous consent of the Senate. Even in the committees with regularly scheduled meetings (and this includes virtually all of the Senate committees today), the chairman can use these stalling tactics quite successfully toward the end of the session when time is short and additional meetings are required.

He also controls the committee's agenda. This, too, is important for, as one senator says, "They [the chairmen] announce at a meeting, 'We shall now take up S. 1111.' You don't know what it is about most of the time. By bringing it up without forewarning, their recommendation is likely to have great weight. At least they've had a chance to read it in advance." Since there are often hundreds of bills before the committee, the chairman chooses the order in which they come before the committee, "It's hard to *prove* to him that your bill deserves priority over all the others."

Within certain limits, the chairman appoints and controls the committee staff. Committee staffs contain a few minority staff members who are appointed by, and are especially responsive to, the senior committee member of the minority party (the heir apparent to the chairmanship, should control of the Senate change) called the ranking minority member. Since the Legislative Reorganization Act of 1946, a tradition of more or less permanent tenure has developed in a number of the committee staff jobs so that the chairman's appointive powers may be exercised only intermittently in the event of vacancies. Even so, given the fact that committee staff members are highly politicized men and women, thoroughly socialized into the Senate ways, the staffs are characterized by their extreme, perhaps excessive, personal loyalty to the chairman. As the committee staffs increase in size, quality, and importance, the chairman's power to appoint, organize, and direct the staff becomes increasingly significant.[13]

Most committees are further divided into standing subcommittees. The competition for these subcommittee posts is sometimes as intense as for committee seats. The chairman of the committee appoints the chairmen of these subcommittees and, in consultation with the ranking minority member, the other members as well. While seniority has some effect on subcommittee assignments, the chairman has wide discretion in making these appointments. At any time he can shuffle subcommittee personnel at will.

13. While there is noticeable variation from one committee to the next, the caliber of the professional committee staff members is already high.

Some committees operate largely through *ad hoc* subcommittees, a procedure which enhances the chairman's influence. In others, some measures do not fall within the jurisdiction of any of the standing subcommittees and are referred to *ad hoc* groups appointed by the chairman. "Usually," according to the chief clerk of one committee which uses *ad hoc* subcommittees a great deal, "the chairman, in appointing subcommittees, will either take the chairmanship himself or appoint the member of his party who is most interested in the matter—often the sponsor of the original legislation. Then—if it is to be a three-man subcommittee—he canvasses the others to get the second majority member. The *way* he does this is important. If he wants a senator to get the seat, he says that ———— has expressed an interest in the assignment and he's sure that you don't care if he takes it. . . ."

The relationships between subcommittees and committees vary a great deal. In a committee faced by a huge work load—the best example is Appropriations—the subcommittees are relatively independent of the full committee. Also, subcommittees are most influential on highly technical pieces of legislation and nonpartisan matters. Within these limits, the subcommittee's autonomy "depends entirely upon the committee chairman." In the last analysis, he controls the subcommittee's membership and the referral of bills to it; "he can follow either a hands-off policy or keep close control."[14]

Finally, the committee chairman either manages, or names the floor manager for, all bills reported to the floor from the committee. He is invariably appointed to conference committees and, if strict seniority is not followed in the appointment of the other conferees, his recommendations are considered authoritative.

By using these rather limited procedural powers and perquisites to the hilt, a chairman can—"if he wants to be a bastard," as one chairman said—turn the committee into a tight little oligarchy in which the other members, especially those of junior status, feel "like first graders at a seventh grade party."[15] But, as one senator said, "Most committee chairmen don't use their formal powers a great deal," because they do not have to. They generally get their way without using these powers.

The committee chairman is always the most experienced majority

14. The growth in numbers of standing subcommittees since the Legislative Reorganization Act is generally viewed with alarm. What is usually overlooked in all this is that they have "usually been an outgrowth of the internal friction and resentment generated by one-man rule" by the committee chairman. S. L. Udall, "A Defense of the Seniority System," *New York Times Magazine,* January 13, 1957, p. 64.

15. *Ibid.,* p. 17.

party committee member if not always the most expert. Committees consider bills, not policy in the round, and this places a premium on detailed and highly technical knowledge of earlier statutes, the legislative history of similar bills, relevant administrative rulings and court decisions, and the like. Congress rarely considers an entirely new issue. Years of service on the same committee is a liberal education in the politics of a particular field. Most committee chairmen know more about the work of the committee than junior members.

Secondly, the chairman as a necessary consequence of his position is more active and involved in the work of the committee than are the others. Most senators, as we have already seen, tend to narrow their focus of attention to a very few policy areas and to the work of only some of the committees and subcommittees to which they belong. The chairmanship forces the chairman to concentrate the bulk of his time and attention on the committee's business. Few other members of the committee—particularly if it is one of the less desirable committees—may be similarly interested and active. In some committees, absenteeism and apathy are rife.[16]

Finally, while the chairman's decisions, rulings, and appointments always could be overruled by the committee membership (many times, it would take merely the switch of a single majority member's vote, for committee votes on organizational and procedural matters are often, as on the floor of the Senate itself, strictly partisan), it is "just not done." Why? "Mainly," one shrewd committee staff director said, "it's just tradition. But like most traditions in the Senate there is a reason behind it. Challenging the power of the chairman is not done because it doesn't pay off. There's no percentage in it. He could make a committee member's life miserable and futile for a long, long time." Such considerations, rather than the vigorous use of his procedural powers, usually account for the chairman's power in the Senate. The chairman's formal powers remain latent; their excessive use is more often a sign of weakness than of strength.

Seniority and the Recruitment of Chairmen

The senior (in committee service) member of the majority party is chairman of the committee. Outside the Senate this practice has

16. This is another reason for the luxuriant subcommittee growth in recent years. "In our committee," a staff director said, "subcommittees are a good way of keeping up interest and attendance of the members and for getting the thankless jobs done. By appointing one man chairman and giving him responsibility, you can be sure that the job will be done. In return, the subcommittee chairman gets his name in the paper. If we didn't have subcommittees, I suspect that the chairman would be the only man at our meetings."

few defenders, but among senators, it is almost universally approved. According to them, the most likely alternative to the seniority system, the election of the chairman by the committee, would lead to excessive logrolling and petty politicking. "The seniority system sometimes results in strange chairmen but not half so strange as we would get without it. Why, the backscratching—you know, you help me become chairman this year and I'll help you next—would be unbelievable." The election of committee chairmen also would result in "grave dissension . . . we must, in order to get things done reasonably well, have a minimum of personal animosities and emotion. This is not always easy to achieve under present conditions. If you tried to elect chairmen from among a group of men so sensitive to any public sign of approval or disapproval, the end result would be disastrous." Of course, the junior men grumble, but then, as some senior senators are fond of saying with a laugh, "the longer I serve in the Senate, the more I think of the seniority rule."

The seniority system of selecting committee chairmen places a premium on being elected to the Senate early in life, thus an early political start and a rapid ascent to the Senate are distinct advantages.[17] An important consequence of this is a class bias in the recruitment of committee chairmen. Patrician Politicians, members of wealthy political families, start a political career with substantial advantages, are elected to the Senate relatively early in life, and thus are heavily overrepresented among the chairmen (Table 52).

The seniority system also places a premium upon regular re-election to the Senate once a seat is won. This means, of course, that senators

Table 52

CAREER TYPES OF COMMITTEE CHAIRMEN AND ALL SENATORS
(80th through 84th Congresses)

	Chairmen	All	*Index of Overrepresentation*
Professional	42%	55%	0.8
Patrician	17%	7%	2.4
Amateurs	37%	34%	1.1
Agitators	4%	4%	1.0

17. The index of overrepresentation of chairmen holding their first public offices in their twenties is 1.2; in their thirties is 0.9; and in their forties is 1.1. No committee chairman held his first public office at age fifty or above. The index of overrepresentation of chairmen elected to the Senate in their thirties is 1.5; in their forties, 1.2; fifties, 0.8; and sixties, 0.6.

from small, rural one-party states are substantially overrepresented among the chairmen.[18] Senators from closely divided urban states containing the nation's large metropolitan areas—so important in presidential politics—are at a substantial disadvantage in the Senate. As a result, the senators most out of step with their respective parties tend to be favored somewhat in the recruitment of chairmen (Table 53).

Table 53

MEAN PARTY-UNITY SCORES OF COMMITTEE CHAIRMEN
AND ALL SENATORS
(80th through 84th Congresses)

Party-Unity Scores	Chairmen	All	Index of Overrepresentation
90+	10%	18%	0.6
80-89	40%	45%	0.9
70-79	17%	16%	1.1
60-69	12%	10%	1.2
50-59	4%	4%	1.0
Under 50	4%	2%	2.0

Moreover, once a senator becomes a committee chairman and obtains all the power which goes along with it, he usually becomes an even less "regular" party member than before. Of the twenty-seven senators for whom it was possible to obtain party-unity voting scores both before and after they became committee chairmen, twenty-one showed less frequent voting with their party after becoming a chairman, two showed no change, and only four increased in their party voting. All four of these senators who voted with their party more often as chairmen than before were "modern" Republicans who became committee chairmen as Eisenhower entered the White House.[19]

18. The index of overrepresentation of large-state senators among the chairmen is 0.6; for medium-sized states, 1.0; and for small states, 1.3. The same index, according to the percentage urban of the senators' states' population is as follows: 80-100% urban, 0.8%; 60-79% urban, 0.8; 40-59% urban, 1.1; 20-39% urban, 1.2. The index of overrepresentation of two-party state senators among the chairmen is 1.0; modified one-party states, 0.8; one-party states, 1.5.

19. The index of party effort, which provides a relative picture of the senator's party loyalty given his ideological position, may actually be a better measure. Of the twenty-seven cases, fifteen of the chairmen declined in their party effort after becoming a chairman, one made no change, and eight improved. Five of these were Eisenhower Republicans who became chairmen during the 83rd Congress. This finding appears to conflict with D. B. Truman, *The Congressional Party: A Case Study* (New York: John Wiley and Sons, 1959), 136 ff. But cf. Goodwin "Seniority System in Congress," *APSR*, pp. 427-29.

The seniority system results in the underrepresentation of liberals among the chairmen of both parties (Table 54). Moderates are over-represented in both parties, and conservatives overrepresented among the Democratic chairmen.

Table 54

COMPARISON OF THE MEAN CONSERVATISM-LIBERALISM SCORES OF COMMITTEE
CHAIRMEN AND ALL SENATORS
(80th through 84th Congresses)

| | Index of Overrepresentation | |
	Democrats	Republicans
Liberals	0.5	0.98
Moderates	1.4	1.3
Conservatives	1.1	0.97

The seniority system's bias against urban liberals of both parties tends to be self-perpetuating. As one Northern Democrat explained, "The Southerners become committee chairmen because enough Northern Democrats in close states manage to win. But these Northern Democrats whose victories gave them their power are not, originally, in positions of enough seniority to obtain the legislation needed to keep on winning in the North. Therefore, they often lose and cannot earn enough seniority to wrest control of Congress from them. The same thing happens in the Republican party." On the other hand, it seems reasonable to suppose that the committee chairmen are entirely aware of this fact and hence, if for no other reason than to hold on to their chairmanships, might be more sensitive to the political problems of the urban liberals than our informant suggests. At any rate, this is apparently the case where the problem is most serious—in the Democratic party. The moderate to conservative Democrats who became committee chairmen during 1947-57, with but one exception, were more liberal after becoming chairmen than they were before. This is not the case with the Republican conservatives, however; all but one of them became more conservative upon achieving a committee chairmanship.[20]

20. "Before" and "after" conservatism-liberalism scores were available for eight moderate to conservative Democratic chairmen; seven of them became more liberal upon assuming the chairmanship. The same scores were available for eight moderate to conservative Republican chairmen; seven of them were more conservative after becoming committee chairman.

COMMITTEE ACTION AND FLOOR VOTES

The most important and interesting work of the Senate committees is done in executive session. These meetings are closed to all save the committee members, their staffs, and invited "insiders," representatives of executive agencies and private groups especially favored by the committee or its chairman. While hardly secret—"leaks" to interested reporters, lobbyists, other senators, congressmen, and administrative officials are part of the game and one of the bases of the committee member's influence—the semiprivacy of the executive session does encourage a free exchange of ideas and a disposition to compromise that would be difficult if not impossible to achieve under other circumstances.

Executive sessions, however, present an obvious barrier to the analysis of committee decision-making. Not all committee reports give even the final line-up of members for and against a measure, and none cast much light on the preliminary votes and give-and-take that make up the process of decision. "Leaks" to the public press and the recollection of committee participants are more illuminating but still tricky to evaluate and often misleading. Confidential committee records are not generally open to the general public or available to scholars. The student of legislative committee behavior must rely primarily on the public portions of the committee's work, the small fraction of the iceberg which stands exposed above the water line.[21]

It is possible to study the roll call voting of committee members on the Senate floor. Of course, a senator may behave one way in the semisecrecy of the committee room and in another on the floor of the chamber, but to vote very differently in committee and on the floor is not approved by the Senate folkways—senators are expected to honor their commitments, not to back down from a position taken early in the legislative process because of unanticipated pressure. A senator's effectiveness depends in no small measure on a reputation for keeping his word, and, except in the most extraordinary circumstances, once a senator takes a position in committee, he tries to stick with it when and if the bill comes up for floor debate and voting. It seems at least plausible that the roll call voting of committee members may tell us something about the internal operation of the committees themselves. Certainly it will tell us something about the effects of committee membership on the senators' public voting behavior.

21. For an excellent example of what may be learned about legislative behavior from a sophisticated study of published hearings, see R. K. Huitt, "The Congressional Committee: A Case Study," *American Political Science Review*, XXXXVIII (June, 1954), 340-65.

Committee members tend to be more nearly agreed on what should be done in their areas of policy than is the case with the Senate as a whole. In Figure 21, the percentage of all members of reporting committees favoring motions is compared with the percentage of all other senators voting "yea." In most cases, the senators who did not belong to the reporting committee were rather evenly divided, between 40 and 60 per cent of them voting "yea" on most roll calls. The committee members, on the other hand, were less frequently split down the middle.

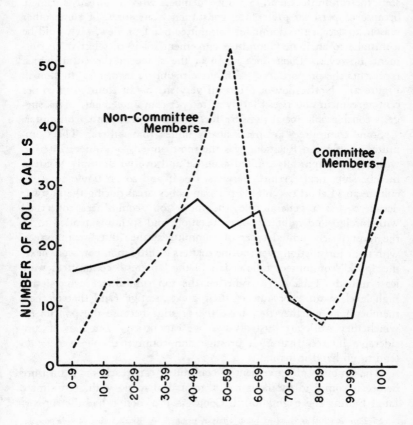

FIG. 21. Per Cent of Reporting Committee Voting Yea Compared with All Other Senators on All Roll Calls during 84th Congress

What causes this committee agreement? A number of factors no doubt enter into the process. Through years of committee service, friendships, "deals," and understandings develop which affect the members' voting. Furthermore, members of a committee are exposed to a constant and generally one-sided barrage of appeals from their committee's clientele; service on Foreign Relations, for example, is likely to lead to sympathy for the State Department's point of view, or membership on Agriculture, to the views of the Department of Agriculture and the major farm organizations. As we have earlier seen, the committees tend to attract members who are already inclined, because of personal preference, constituency pressures, or some other reason, to accept the dominant committee point of view. It would be a mistake to attribute committee agreement solely to selective recruitment, however. Look once again at the shape of the curve which represents the proportion of committee members favoring a motion in Figure 21. Notice how it drops off very sharply at from 70 to 99 per cent agreement and rises sharply at 100 per cent agreement. This suggests considerable social pressure for unanimity within the committee.

Some committees are more nearly united than others. The Committee on Foreign Relations was the most united committee; Interior, with its geographically limited clientele and overwhelmingly Western membership, next; Armed Services, third; and so on down to Agriculture and Labor, two highly partisan policy areas during the postwar decade.[22] As a general rule, the four "top" committees concerned with foreign and military policy, taxation, and spending tended to be the most nearly united types of committees; the "duty" committees, with their jurisdiction over routine matters of little moment, were next; the "pork" committees followed; and the "interest" committees were least united (Table 55). Whether the top committees achieve this high level of unity because of their great prestige (and that of their members) or whether they have the prestige because the policies on which they work are least divisive, we cannot say. But it is of considerable interest that high prestige and committee cohesiveness do tend to go hand in hand.

The amount of agreement a committee can reach on a measure before it comes to the floor has a great deal to do with its ultimate fate. During the Eighty-fourth Congress, if a motion had the support

22. This conclusion is based upon analysis using S. A. Rice's index of cohesion described in his *Quantitative Methods in Politics* (New York, Alfred A. Knopf, 1928), pp. 208-9. The index is merely the difference between the percentage for and the percentage against a given motion, a 50-50 split resulting in an index of zero and a unanimity receiving an index of 100. See Appendix D.

Table 55

MEAN INDEX OF COHESION OF TYPES OF COMMITTEES ON ROLL CALLS
PERTAINING TO BILLS WHICH THEY REPORT

(84th Congress)

Type of Committee	Number of Roll Calls	Mean Index of Cohesion
Top Committees	91	64.5
Duty Committees	5	53.2
Pork Committees	24	45.5
Interest Committees	92	40.7

of more than 80 per cent of the reporting committee's members, it passed the Senate every time (Figure 22). If from 60 to 79 per cent of the committee favored it in their roll call voting, it passed nine times out of ten. A sharp drop-off then ensues in the committee's batting average as the committee's internal agreement diminishes.

This again varies considerably from one committee to the next. In Table 56 the percentage of the time a majority of the reporting committee prevailed on floor roll calls during the Eighty-fourth Congress is presented for each type of committee. When this data is compared with the information contained in Table 55, it is apparent that more than just the cohesiveness of the committee shapes its influence on the floor. The top committees were both the most nearly united and the most effective in getting proposals they favored passed or those they opposed defeated by the Senate as a whole. The interest committees, while least united, were the second most successful in influencing the outcome of the floor votes. The duty committees, while almost as united as the top committees, were least successful in shaping the outcome of floor voting. The pork committees were in third place on both counts. Evidently, the over-all prestige of a committee, as well as its cohesiveness, affects its success or failure on the floor.[23]

PARTY, COMMITTEE POSITION, AND "EFFECTIVENESS"

In this and the previous chapter we have analyzed the two formal systems of power in the Senate: political parties and the standing committees. How do the senators' positions in these two structures influence their effectiveness as legislators?

23. The caveat should be made again that this analysis is based on roll call votes only. A study of *all* floor action, and not merely action on which a roll call was taken, might well change the picture.

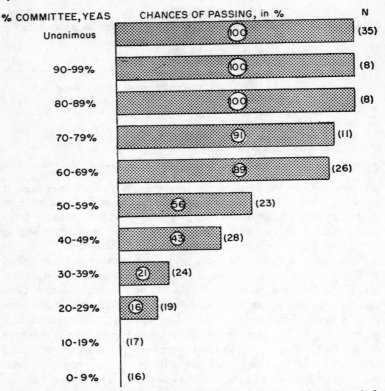

FIG. 22. Committee Agreement and Motions' Chances of Passing, 84th Congress

The senators' committee assignments are less closely related to their over-all legislative effectiveness than one might at first suppose. The effectiveness scores by committee of the senators serving during the Eighty-third and Eighty-fourth Congresses are presented in Figure 23. The Appropriations Committee contained the largest proportion of highly effective senators (22 per cent of its membership); Foreign Relations was next with 18 per cent; Finance, third with 17 per cent, and so on down the committee caste system. As a general rule, the lower the prestige of the committee, the smaller the proportion of its members ranking high in legislative effectiveness, but there is one surprising exception to the rule. The District of Columbia Committee, the most despised and lowly committee of them all, had a larger

Table 56

PERCENTAGE OF THE TIME A MAJORITY OF THE REPORTING COMMITTEE
PREVAILS ON FLOOR MOTIONS, BY TYPE OF COMMITTEE
(84th Congress)

Type of Committee	Number of Roll Calls	Percentage of Time Majority of Committee Prevails
Top	91	89%
Interest	92	78%
Pork	24	74%
Duty	5	60%

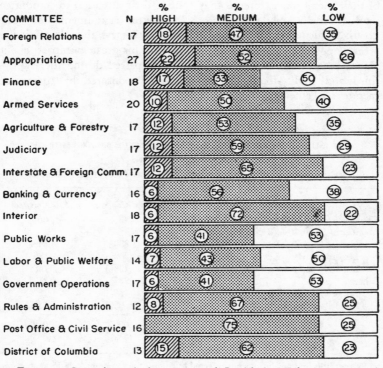

Fig. 23. Committee Assignments and Legislative Effectiveness, 83rd and 84th Congresses

proportion of highly effective senators than all but the elite committees. When one looks not just at the proportion of committee members possessing high scores but at the entire distribution of scores for each committee, it is obvious that some of the very high prestige committees have more ineffective members than the less important and less desirable committees.

One reason for this is that the high prestige committees provide the best Senate positions from which to build up a national following and attract far more than their share of presidential hopefuls. As we have seen in Chapter V, this type of senator usually does not conform to the chamber's folkways, sacrifices Senate esteem in favor of national publicity, and is not very effective as a legislator. Secondly, the often unimportant and sometimes trivial nature of the bills reported by the lesser committees probably contributes to the legislative effectiveness of their members, as long as they confine their attention to committee work. Finally, while a senator's committee assignments may not greatly influence his over-all legislative effectiveness, they do affect the areas of policy in which he is likely to have his greatest impact; about 70 per cent of all the bills and resolutions passed during the Eighty-third and Eighty-fourth Congresses were sponsored by committee members (Table 57).

Table 57
COMMITTEE POSITION, PARTY, AND SUCCESSFUL SPONSORSHIP OF BILLS AND RESOLUTIONS
(in percentage of all sponsored bills and resolutions passed)

Sponsor's Position	83rd Congress	84th Congress
Chairman of Committee Reporting Measure	43%	35%
Member of Committee Reporting Measure		
(except Chairman)	33%	34%
Majority party	(20%)	(18%)
Minority party	(13%)	(16%)
Others	23%	31%
Majority party	(14%)	(18%)
Minority party	(9%)	(13%)
	100%	100%
	(532)	(553)

NOTE: Bills and resolutions not referred to committee were omitted. First sponsors only were counted. Senator Morse, an Independent during the Eighty-third Congress, was omitted for that Congress.

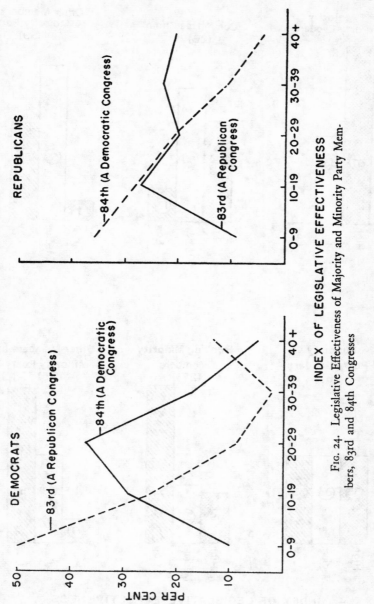

Fig. 24. Legislative Effectiveness of Majority and Minority Party Members, 83rd and 84th Congresses

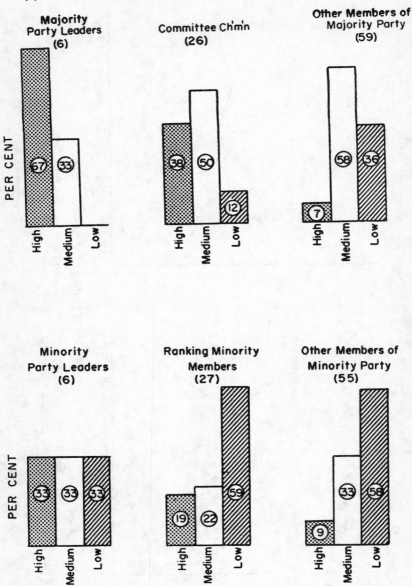

INDEX OF LEGISLATIVE EFFECTIVENESS

FIG. 25. Legislative Effectiveness of Party Leaders, Committee Chairmen, Ranking Minority Members, and Others, 83rd and 84th Congresses

Party affiliation appears to have a greater effect upon the senator's over-all legislative effectiveness, but it is not to which party a senator belongs but whether his party is in the majority that matters. In Figure 24 the effectiveness of Democrats and Republicans during the Eighty-third and Eighty-fourth Congresses is presented. The Democrats were far more effective in the Eighty-fourth (a Democratic) and the Republicans more effective in the Eighty-third (a Republican) Congress.

Even more important are party and committee offices. Elective party leaders were very effective during the Eighty-third and Eighty-fourth Congresses (Figure 25). While not nearly so effective as the party leaders, the committee chairmen were decidedly more successful in getting their bills and resolutions through the Senate than were the rank and file members. The same order of effectiveness—party leaders, committee chairmen, rank and file—held true within both the majority and minority parties. Thus the most effective groups in the Senate are the majority party leaders, followed by the committee chairmen and the minority party leaders. Some ranking minority members are highly effective but most of them are not. The rank and file of the majority party is considerably more effective than that of the minority, but neither group has much luck in getting bills and resolutions passed.

Clearly, the political party and committee structures greatly affect the legislative effectiveness of senators, but certainly they are not the only influential factors. Some rank and file minority party senators are more effective than committee chairmen. Even the party leaders vary in their ability to get legislative results. Some new and very green members of the District of Columbia Committee were, at least during the Eighty-third and Eighty-fourth Congresses, more effective than very senior senators of the Appropriations Committee. As a general rule, a strategic position in the party and committee structures tends to lend power, prestige, and effectiveness to a senator. But this, by itself, does not determine his effectiveness. Ability, intelligence, energy, integrity, "personality," and conformity to the folkways may lead to a high level of effectiveness for senators who do not possess important party or committee positions.

CHAPTER VIII

Senators and Lobbyists

A WASHINGTON LOBBYIST tells of a conversation he once overheard between two women in the Senate waiting room. One lady, evidently a Washingtonian, was pointing out the sights to her friend from afar.

"That's Senator ———," the Washingtonian said in a stage whisper, "and that"—indicating the man with whom the Senator was in earnest conversation—"is ———, the lobbyist for what's-its-name."

"O-o-oh!" responded the visitor in awed tones. "Is he bribing him now?"[1]

This attitude is not restricted to naïve tourists. The American public as a whole is aggressively suspicious of lobbyists and lobbying. Journalists have found a ready market for lurid accounts of the machinations of the "pressure boys." Politicians in search of a telling argument regularly charge that the opposition is backed by unseen and sinister "interests." Even the academics often view lobbying with alarm. The competition between interest groups is likened to "ignorant armies clashing by night."[2] To many others, the power of organized lobbies results in the triumph of organized greed over the public interest and rule by unseen and irresponsible minorities behind the facade of democracy.[3]

1. H. A. Bellows, "In Defense of Lobbying," in H. M. Bishop and S. Hendel, *Basic Issues of American Democracy* (2nd ed.; New York: Appleton-Century Crofts, 1951), p. 315.

2. S. K. Bailey in House Select Committee on Lobbying Activities, 81st Congress, 2nd Session, *Hearings*, I, 44.

3. See J. M. Burns, *Congress on Trial* (New York: Harper and Brothers, 1949); E. E. Schattschneider, *Party Government* (New York: Rinehart, 1942); W. Lippmann, *The Public Philosophy* (Boston: Little Brown, 1955), for variations on this theme.

Nevertheless, every sign indicates a rapid growth in the number, power, and ingenuity of lobbying groups. The depression and the New Deal, by committing the federal government to substantial intervention into the economy, made political influence worth striving for. World War II and the permanent crisis of the Cold War have intensified this trend. Today it is probably no exaggeration to say, as the recent House Select Committee on Lobbying Activities has, that lobbying is a "billion dollar industry."[4] Business is getting better every day. Political organization and lobbying by one group inspire counteractivity by another which persuades still a third group that they, too, must enter the pressure politics game.

SENATORS LOOK AT LOBBYING

Under these conditions, one might reasonably expect that senators, a major target of the lobbies, would be concerned and fearful. One would think, too, that they would be highly conscious of the snowballing pressures to which they are daily exposed. Neither expectation is true.

This does not mean that senators are unaware of lobbying. "Someone is lobbying for virtually every bill introduced—no matter how minor," according to one senator. Another says, "I've got to assume that everyone who comes to see me is a 'lobbyist,' although not always a paid one." Sometimes senators express resentment at the actions of a particular lobby in a particular situation, but there is little hostility on Capitol Hill to lobbying in general. Far more common is the attitude expressed by one senator that "lobbies are the most valuable instrument in the legislative process."

Personally, the senators do not perceive much of the lobbyist's action as lobbying. When asked how much "pressure" he actually felt, one well-known senator replied:

You know, that's an amazing thing. I hardly ever see a lobbyist. I don't know—maybe they think I'm a poor target but I seldom see them. During this entire natural-gas battle [in which he was a prominent figure] I was not approached by either side. Oh, I know that they are around and the union boys come in from time to time . . . . Of course, they stimulate a lot of mail. And they get people from back home to telegraph and call on the phone—it's amazing how they are able to find out who your friends are. But there are few threats, very few threats.

Moreover, when asked to identify the most active and effective lobbies in Washington, senators almost invariably name the groups

4. House Select Committee on Lobbying Activities, 81st Congress, 2nd Session, *General Interim Report*, p. 8.

with which they disagree. They are not entirely unaware of this tendency. One senator, for example, after a long account of the pressures he had experienced in the Senate added:

And then there are, of course, the lobbyists who agree with me. Now I believe in the fair trade laws. I was born over a [retail] store and raised in one. The [retailers] don't have to pressure me into seeing things their way. If anything, I'm lobbying them, telling them to get on the ball. And when their man comes around to see me, I don't think of him as a lobbyist with an ax to grind but as a man with sound judgment and good will.

A labor union lobbyist tells a story with a similar moral.

One time during the minimum wage battle, Senator ———— began to weaken on the $1.00 minimum. Someone had touched his sympathy with a picture of what the bill would do to the sawmills of the South. He told me that he was contemplating making an exception in their case. I said, "———— [first name], if you even hint that you might back down from your previous position, this place will be swarming with lobbyists!" "Lobbyists," he said, looking around him, "I don't see any lobbyists around here." Then he realized that I was one and laughed. Hell, we don't think of ourselves as *lobbyists!*

The senator's view of his relations with lobbyists depends, in large measure, on the relationship between what senator and lobbyist want. If the lobbyist and senator are in general agreement, the senator is unlikely to think of him as a lobbyist or to feel his efforts at influence as "pressure." But when a lobbyist tries to persuade or coerce a senator toward action that the senator does not relish, the psychological atmosphere is very different—the senator is likely to feel "lobbied" or "pressured."

Thus, the disparity between the "lobbying" that the objective observers see and the "pressure" that senators feel is substantial. Another reason for this is the nature of modern lobbying technique.

HOW TO INFLUENCE A SENATOR

Some lobbying is still done the old way—directly, personally, man-to-man, and face-to-face. The apprehensive lady tourist quoted at the beginning of this chapter was undoubtedly incorrect in the inferences she drew from the sight of a lobbyist talking to a senator. As one old-time lobbyist put it, "The green stuff doesn't change hands much anymore." But she was correct in realizing that strenuous efforts to influence senators were going on all about her—in the Senate waiting room, the dining room, the corridors, the offices, and hearing rooms scattered over the Hill.

Face-to-Face Lobbying

Most of the face-to-face discussion is innocuous. Senators probably see more lobbyists in the flesh at committee hearings than anywhere else. The lobbyist presents the case of his organization or clients, answers a few questions, and then retires from the witness chair to be replaced by another. But, as often as not, lobbyists prefer to work behind the scenes during committee hearings. "If I testify," one lobbyist explained, "I can give them the over-all picture. But if a member [of the lobbyist's organization] testifies, he can tell them what this bill will do to him and his business. This is more graphic—and more effective." On important bills, lobbyists often arrange to have an officer or an important member of their group appear before the committee. His statement is normally written and carefully rehearsed by the lobbyist, who may then try to insure a large turnout on the day "his witness" appears and even provide like-minded senators with lists of leading questions for the witness to answer. Such elaborate staging is desirable, for "some [amateur] witnesses get stage fright, others muff easy questions," and "hostile committee members can tie an inexperienced man in knots—they love to do that up there."[5]

But face-to-face lobbying is not just confined to formal appearances before committee sessions. At one time or another, most lobbyists wish to speak to senators privately.

Arranging an interview with a United States senator is not always an easy task. "In planning their schedules," one lobbyist remarked ruefully, "senators bow only to one other Being, and He is not on this earth." Persistence, however, almost always pays off. If a lobbyist is unable to obtain a personal appointment, simply waiting in the corridors of the Capitol or the Senate Office Building will generally produce a peripatetic interview. If the senator is "on the floor," a brief interview in the waiting room can often be obtained by sending in a card. Telephone conversations with a senator are, according to the lobbyists, relatively easy to obtain; even when the senator does not wish to talk to the lobbyist, his receptionist is not likely to know it. Finally, lobbyists are often willing to settle for an interview with the senator's administrative assistant or legislative assistant. "They have more time . . . they are more likely to hear you through." While there is great variation in the amount of influence they wield, often

5. This careful staging of a witness's testimony is done for another reason, too. The imported witness is generally an influential man within the lobbying group. To have him publicly embarrassed, or for him to be greeted with committee indifference and mass truancy, is a reflection on the lobbyist's competence.

"if you have persuaded the senator's assistant, you've won half the battle."

Partly because of these difficulties in obtaining access, lobbyists frequently farm out the job of private persuasion to an emissary. "If we can't see them," one powerful lobbyist said, "we know who can." Often these emissaries are chosen from among the influential joint constituents of the lobbyist and senator; or they can be hired from among the former senators, congressmen, and Congressional staffers who are in the law-lobbying business in Washington. "If I tried to see Harry Byrd," one able young lobbyist who regularly employs members of this group to do his personal lobbying explained, "I would get nowhere. But if a former colleague calls him up and says 'Harry, I've got something here I think you ought to see. Can I have half an hour?' he'll say, 'Yes,' even though he knows the former senator is a registered lobbyist."

Contacts and friendships not only gain access, they also help get results. All lobbyists agree that "friendships are a big help" and that "the more people you know personally [on the Hill], the better."

Most lobbyists work at developing these contacts, especially toward the beginning of their lobbying careers. "At first," one well-acquainted lobbyist says, "I pounded the corridors up there, calling on senators, catching them in the halls. But after a while I got to know them and they got to know me and I've been able to conduct a lot of business on the phone in recent years." Most groups do a certain amount of entertaining, too, although few admit that it has much impact. "I've always considered cocktail parties an expensive way to win friends and we don't throw any. We did have some lunches early in the session, but these were strictly good-will affairs." The ambivalence in this statement is fairly typical. "I wouldn't give a dime for the supposed 'influence' gained at these parties," another lobbyist said, while at the same time he admitted to having occasional dinners and fishing trips for congressmen and senators. Some lobbyists spend a great deal of time playing golf, so much time that some senators complain that "Burning Tree has been ruined by the lobbyists." A senator who celebrates a birthday or wedding anniversary, rejoices at the birth of a grandchild, who is ill, or who mourns a death in his family usually receives a number of appropriately worded notes from his thoughtful lobbyist friends.

Once made, a Capitol Hill friendship can take up a lot of a lobbyist's time. One business-group lobbyist explained why.

I do not attempt to contact a large number of congressmen and senators. I concentrate on a few men, strategically placed on the Appropriations committees. These men are economy minded and are generally in sympathy with our political outlook. I restrict my efforts for several reasons.

Over the years, I develop friendships with these men. You know they are all—well, almost all—exceptional men, the kind you would like to know even if you didn't have any business reason for doing so. To keep these friendships alive and genuine, I have to stop around to see them quite often just to say hello. For example, if I don't see ———— at least once a week, he'll say, "Where the hell have you been? You only stop around when you want something from us." Even a few contacts on the Hill demand a good deal of time and attention.

And when I stop around to see these men, they always ask me to do something for them—you know how overworked and understaffed most of them are. I can't afford to let them down.

Another lobbyist who works the other side of the political fence reports a similar experience.

We've discovered in this office that you can't do business indefinitely over the phone. Occasionally, they need to see you in the flesh, to see your face. After four or five conferences over the telephone we usually note some dropping off of cordiality and know it's time to make another personal call. When I stop by to see them I try *not* to have any specific business in mind. Of course, if they bring up something we are interested in, that's fine. But mostly, my calls are routine fence mending.

Many conversations between senators and lobbyists are ostensibly social in this manner. Many others are aimed not at persuading a senator to favor or oppose a policy but at bringing the group's problem into the harried senator's focus of attention. "They've got so many things on their minds that it's a good idea to remind them often that you are around." "There's not much point in talking to them much in advance of committee action. They'll forget about it, or if you give them memos, they may lose them." "We try," still another lobbyist said, "to remind them of our interest and arguments *just before* action is taken."

Some conversations between lobbyists and senators, however, are calculated to persuade and convince the latter. Rarely, if ever, do these conversations approach an argument. "Threats" or any line of argument that suggests that a senator can be "pressured" into a position regardless of his personal convictions are deeply resented by most senators and are avoided by experienced lobbyists. One Southern Democrat said, "Sometimes the labor unions say they would like to back me, but. . . ." More explicit suggestions of retaliation at the polls are not frequently made.

Most lobbyists believe that the best argument for most senators most of the time is advantage to the senator's state. "In the last analysis," one of the most powerful lobbyists in Washington said, "a senator won't go along with us because of friendship, or persuasiveness on our part, or even logic. The real argument is that the bill will do something worthwhile for his state. That's why someone from his own state is often the best person to approach him."

But, if he chooses to use it, the senator has an unanswerable counterargument that can be applied to almost any situation. The conflicting expectations of his constituents and the vagaries of the official definition of the democratic legislator's proper role—should he be a "leader" or a "representative?"—always provide him with a way out. One senator, for example, explained that he handled a "belligerent group of women" who threatened to vote against him if he did not support a bill prohibiting the advertising of alcoholic beverages on the Burkean ground that such a bill would, in his judgment, be unwise. Then, recounting another incident with lobbyists, he redefined his job completely: "A while back [the union lobbyists] tried to get me to vote for a bill which would forbid 'right-to-work' laws. I pointed out that the people of my state had voted overwhelmingly in favor of such a law. And I said if you really want to change the law, go to the people of —— and not to me. My job is to represent the opinions of the people of ——."

Backstopping Friendly Senators

The vast majority of all lobbying is directed at senators who are already convinced. "Mostly," one prominent senator says, "the 'pressure' is the pressure of arguments and facts." Most of these arguments and facts come from groups with which the senator is in general agreement.

The lobbyists themselves are the first to admit this. "Our principal activity," the chief lobbyist of one of the nation's most prominent farm organizations said, "is to provide factual material, speeches, and other services to the senators and congressmen who are already on our side." One of the lobbyists for a large and powerful business organization says, "The main thing we do is to bring our position to the attention of senators before a decision is made. . . . I seldom approach senators who are not in general sympathy with the [name of organization]."

The services a lobby can provide a friendly senator are substantial. Few senators could survive without them. First, they can perform much of the research and speech-writing chores of the senator's office. This service is especially attractive to the more publicity oriented senators. Members of the party that does not control the White House also find this service especially valuable, since they cannot draw upon the research services of the departments as much as can the other members. But most senators find this service at first a convenience and soon a necessity. "They can tell me in thirty minutes or less what it would take me hours to learn through reading and study," one of them remarked appreciatively.

Second, we have already seen that most senators specialize, that for a variety of reasons they give personal attention to only a relatively narrow range of public policy. Lobbyists, by keeping close track of what is going on in their area of policy can warn their friends in the Senate when something arises of possible interest outside the senators' focus of attention. This watchdog role is extremely valuable to the senators, for keeping track of what is going on on Capitol Hill is a tedious and time-consuming task. As one farm lobbyist said, "Doing this job is as demanding as operating a dairy farm—you can't goof off a day."

In addition to research, speech writing, and legislative watchdog services, a lobbying group provides friendly senators with a large array of other legislative aids: bills are drafted; advice on legislative tactics and help in building up support for measures among the public, the administration, interest groups, and other senators is freely given; and the appearance of effective witnesses at hearings is arranged, their statements written and rehearsed, if not given personally, by the lobbyist.

Much of this backstopping is requested by senators or their staffs. "They're being paid a big salary," one senator put the usual Capitol Hill attitude. "I might as well put them to work." This is the attitude that most lobby groups seek to encourage. "We try," one lobbyist said, "to get them habitually to draw upon our services." Another remarked, "If you make a congressman or senator look good, he'll come to *you* for help."

In order to establish such a relationship, a lobbyist or a lobby group must be "on the level" and not "double" the senator. Of course, the information and advice supplied by a lobbyist is slanted. This is understood by all concerned. But, if a lobbyist intentionally or even inadvertently misleads a senator or congressman, he is "doubling."

Once a lobbyist "doubles" a senator, he is through. On the other hand, "once you have established a reputation for reliability, you find it hard to keep up with all the business." As another one said, "It's about all we can do merely to keep up with requests. Of course this means we have lost the initiative, but I think it is worth it."

Grass-Roots Pressure

Not all lobbying is this benign. Sooner or later, most lobbies end up by attempting to apply real "pressure." The principal method of doing this is for the lobbyist to alert the senator's constituents concerning a piece of legislation and persuade them to write, wire, phone, or even visit their senator.

Senators' offices are, from time to time, deluged with petitions, chain letters, form letters, pamphlets, postcards, telegrams, and telephone calls ostensibly originating from their respective constituencies but in fact "inspired" by a lobbyist in his office a few blocks away. This "inspired" or "pressure" mail is usually very easy to spot. For one thing, it arrives suddenly at about the same time. Much of it is mimeographed or printed material which the constituent merely signs. Even when the letters, telegrams, and postcards are not mass-produced, they often share virtually identical wording. Look, for example, at this random selection of telegrams received by Senator Lehman, all from New York City and all dated May 9, 1956:[6]

Lehman's power bill deserves support.

Eraine L. Mantas

Lehman's power bill deserves support.

Bernard Segal

People are for Lehman's public power statute.

Joseph Marine

Urge support of Senator Lehman's public-power bill.

Madelaine Cole

Urge support of Senator Lehman's public-power bill.

Edward P. Tolley

Urge support of Senator Lehman's public-power bill.

Fred Hill

People for Lehman's public-power statute.

J. Van H. Whipple

Lehman's power bill deserves support.

Hyman Rosenblum

Lehman's public-power bill should pass.

Charles Hunt Picaid

Urge support of Lehman's public power bill.

Hyman Abrams

Lehman's power bill deserves support.

Veronica Keane

People are for Lehman's public power statute.

Ben Pincus

6. *Congressional Record* (Daily Edition), May 15, 1956, p. 7317.

People are for Lehman's public power statute.

Anthony Trezini

The public favors public power keep up the good work.

Harry Kendell

The public favors public power keep up the good work.

Murray Zwang

Your public power bill crowns a great career.

Matthew Intner

Your public power bill crowns a great career.

Albert Levy

Congratulations on your fine visionary public power plan.

James Rosenthal

Your public power bill crowns a great career.

Stephen Botsford

Your public power bill crowns a great career.

Leon Rabbin

Your public power bill crowns a great career.

Frank McNabb

Press passage of your public power bill.

Milton Seltzer

We want Lehman's power proposal.

Adolf Summerfield

We want Lehman's power proposal.

Irving Smith

Lehman's power bill deserves support.

Jacob Bobbins

We want Lehman's power proposal.

Una Hadley

We want Lehman's power proposal.

Ben Rader

Press passage of your public-power bill.

Edward Stockvis

Press passage of your public-power bill.

Everett Hall

Lehman's power bill deserves support.

Mrs. W. A. Carson

Press passage of your public-power bill.

Frances Schwartz

We want Lehman's power proposal.

H. M. Sachs

Hope your public-power law passes.

Norman Natko

People are for Lehman's public power statute.

Seymour B. Thaler

Lehman's public power bill should pass.

Louis Glassbert

Hope your public power law passes.

Eugene Young

Hope your public power law passes.

Louis Mangini

Lehman's public power bill should pass.

Raphael Fuentes

Hope your public power law passes.

Richard Mass

The public favors public power. Keep up the good work.

Mary J. Grissom

Your public power proposal is a very good one and should become law.

William V. Purcell

Your public power proposal is a very good one and should become law.

Jack Holtzberg

This kind of thing fools nobody. It is expected, quickly recognized, and heavily discounted by the senators and their staffs. "Right now," one senator said, "a veteran's bill which I oppose has passed the House. I know damn well what will happen. The minute that bill hits the floor, my phone will begin to ring and the telegrams will pour in from every damned Legion post in the state of ———." In most senators' offices, the "inspired" pressure mail is segregated from the "genuine" legislative mail, perhaps tabulated pro and con, and acknowledged with a form letter reply.

This device, perhaps the biggest weapon in the lobbyist's arsenal, suffers from several inherent limitations. "This stuff [pressure mail]," one lobbyist said, "seldom gets past the administrative assistant anyway. Like everybody else, he has interests of his own and pet projects. He selects out of the mail what he wants the boss to know." Many lobbying groups, perhaps most of them, do not have a large enough membership or a membership spread widely enough throughout the country to make this a fruitful approach to legislative influence. There is a limit to how often a lobbyist can expect his members to write, telegraph, or call their senators. "This is not the kind of thing you can do every day. We go to our members with a plea for them to write their congressmen or senators only two or three times during a typical session." These restrictions are most keenly felt by groups with an interest in a wide range of policies—such as the AFL-CIO and the Chamber of Commerce—and these are generally the groups otherwise best equipped to perform this kind of operation. Counterbalancing this, to some degree at least, is the fact that a group able to stage a mass pressure campaign may therefore find it unnecessary. Rather than tie up their staffs with a vast quantity of extra work and to suffer through a campaign of mass nagging, a senator who does not feel strongly about an issue may find it easier to "go along." At least one lobbyist tells of a time when a senator whom his clients had been deluging with mail called him on the phone and said, "If you'll get those ——— off my neck, I'll do anything you want."

But many lobbyists believe that mass-mailing campaigns are too crude, and have too many limitations, to be really effective. A limited number of phone calls, personal visits, and letters from among the senator's personal friends and political supporters, including campaign contributors, are likely to be more manageable and effective.

Lobbying Coalitions

Most bills, at least major bills, are backed by one coalition of interest groups and opposed by another. Committee hearings serve as a means by which both senators and lobbyists can "smoke out" those both pro and con. The subsequent pooling of resources by a number of groups may be either highly formalized or very informal, but in either case this procedure tends to enhance the power of the lobbyists vis-à-vis the senators. A coalition tends to have a larger and more widely distributed membership, more time and more money to invest in the campaign. It is possible, too, for a coalition's face-to-face lobbying to be more effective than that of a single group. "Then we divided up the doubtful senators," one lobbyist explained, "each group taking the one they were most likely to be effective with. Their lobbyist may be a friend of the senator or his assistant, they may have a larger membership in his state, they recently may have done a favor for him like preparing a memo for a speech. Of course, there are likely to be a few left over. . . . Sometimes we can get a friendly senator to approach these in exchange for lobbying someone else on another matter."

A full-scale lobbying campaign planned and executed by a tight-knit coalition of lobbies can be an awesome thing indeed, but the full potential of the lobbying coalition is seldom if ever achieved. A broad-based lobbying coalition is likely to be shot through with conflicts of interest and opinion. A homogeneous coalition of groups may suffer from fewer internal strains but will also be less effective. Their membership and other resources are generally smaller, and their contacts all with the same senators. In either case, the in-fighting between lobbyists is likely to be substantial.

Usually, natural lobbying allies are in competition with one another to represent the same clientele. As a result, some groups hesitate to enter into any formal coalition. "We are friendly with other like-minded groups. The members of the boards, for example, will sometimes get together," one lobbyist said. "Our staffs will sometimes have bull sessions. But there is never any formal cooperation. After all we are in competition with each other and want to protect our trade secrets." Moreover, groups concerned with holding or expanding their memberships often try to get some credit for lobbying triumphs by getting in on the campaign early and doing no work. "A well-financed outfit working on a single bill or issue can really do a job, compared with one like this interested in hundreds of bills. When I find out that we are in agreement with such a group, I try to get us tied up with them, let them do the real work, and just jump when I'm kicked in the rear. We receive credit for wide activity and accomplishment that way." Understandably, the stronger groups are often reluctant to go along with this procedure. When asked about cooperation with other groups, the lobbyist for one of the most powerful lobbies in Washington said, "Yes, we consult with those groups who agree with our position. . . . They call up and say, 'What are you going to do?' And I say, 'I don't know yet. What are you going to do?' And they say, 'I don't know either.' A lot of that goes on. They want the prestige of our name."

Most lobbying coalitions, therefore, present a somewhat deceptive front to the world. Generally, there are a few groups who compose the hard core of the coalition and who do the real work. Then there are the "hitchhikers," who lend their names and little else to the cause. "On Wednesday," one inveterate hitchhiker explained, "I'm testifying on a bill in which we are interested but not enough to launch an all-out effort of our own. My statement is being written by Harry Truman's former ghost writer! But," he added, "this works the other way, too. We were very interested in the social-security bill. One man in our office wrote statements for eight or nine different groups on that one. When we feel strongly about something, we do our work ourselves—and perhaps for several other groups, too."

HOW TO INFLUENCE A LOBBYIST

The orthodox discussion of lobbying stops right here. Most student of politics have been far more interested in probing the way lobbyists influence senators than vice versa. Yet this preoccupation has resulted in a major distortion of the relationship between lobbyists and senators. Influence seldom if ever flows in a single direction. Let us examine how senators influence the lobbyists.

Noncooperation

The first, and most potent, way in which senators influence lobbyists is simply by the threat of noncooperation. The senators have what the lobbyists want—a vote, prestige, access to national publicity, and the legislative "inside dope." Moreover, the lobbyist wants this not just once but many times over a number of years. The senators are in a position to bargain. They need not give these things away.

Of course, some lobbying groups are so powerful in a senator's state that to vote wrong may have serious electoral consequences. But Senate terms are long and constituencies large and heterogeneous. Senators are seldom without discretion in the matter. Moreover, a "cooperative" senator does far more than just vote right. He can be extremely helpful to a lobbyist in many ways, and this kind of cooperation can be turned off or on without the senator's constituents being any the wiser. At any rate, lobbyists are highly aware of this possibility and sensitive to the wishes, demands, and interests of the men they are paid to influence.

The Friendship Ploy

It is true, as one senator expressed it, that "friendship with a lobbyist creates an atmosphere that predisposes us in his favor." But the friendships between lobbyists and senators, so often feared by the man in the street, also serve as a means by which a senator protects himself from lobbying.

"It is possible," one lobbyist said, "to become too friendly with a senator. You become a part of him. You began to think, 'Should he say this?' 'Should he do this?' 'Will it benefit him?' It's not that you don't take his problems into account at other times, but it's different. You just can't pressure a friend." The senators are clearly aware of this tendency and actively seek some lobbyists as friends. "Whenever I get a call from a senator who says 'Hello, Johnny-boy, come on up for lunch today,'" one lobbyist explained, "I know that he's going to do something we won't like."

Obviously, friendship with a lobbyist can be as beneficial to a senator as to a lobbyist. It makes the lobbyist indebted to him, more sensitive to his political problems, less willing to apply "pressure," a more trustworthy ally.

Building up "Credit"

As we have already seen, lobbyists attempt to build up "credit" with senators by doing part of the senators' jobs for them. The same thing also happens in reverse.

Few lobbyists could survive without sources of inside information on the Hill. The legislative process is, as the respondents of this study so often pointed out, like an iceberg—most of it is not open to public view. "Leaks" from the senators and their staffs are indispensable if a lobbyist is to be effective. Exact information concerning the views of their colleagues can also be obtained from senators. Some highly valuable canvassing is regularly done by the senators and their staffs for lobbies.

Perhaps the most effective way in which a senator can build up "credit" is by helping the lobbyist satisfy the lobbyist's constituents. This can be done in a number of ways.

A senator who delivers a ghost-written speech, or who merely has it inserted in the *Record,* thus gives the group a free publicity break, and "there are a lot of groups that have no other way of getting their message across to the people." Such an arrangement is highly advantageous all around. The group gets publicity; so does the senator; it impresses the lobbyist's constituents.

Senators have it in their power to make lobbyists "look good" in other ways. Many hearings on Capitol Hill are, as one committee staffer has said,"weird dances of witnesses heatedly testifying for and against measures that will not pass—and everyone knows it." At least some of these hearings are held to help out the lobbyists concerned. "They come up here, testify, and the bill is defeated. They have won a great 'victory' and earned their keep."

The senators, too, spend a good deal of time helping out friendly lobbyists in membership, financial, or publicity drives. The groups benefit mightily from some of these efforts, of course, but at a cost. They are, as a consequence, indebted to the senator. The senator may build up such popularity and support within the group that he assures himself of its support regardless of his votes or the opinion of him entertained by the group's leadership.

Some of these services may be provided in exchange for an explicit *quid pro quo,* but more often, this type of behavior is merely a means by which a senator builds up generalized "credit" and good will that can be drawn upon as the future demands.

Attack

The final means by which senators influence lobbyists is through attack and the threat thereof. Lobbyists are sitting ducks—their public reputation is so low that public attack is bound to be damaging. To invite public attack, or even worse a Congressional investigation, is, from the lobbyists' point of view, clearly undesirable. Here, then, is the shotgun in the closet. Its recoil may be substantial—efforts to punish lobbyists by publicity often decrease the prestige of the Senate as well as the lobbies—but then, the mere fact of its existence means that it need seldom be used. "We've always got to be prepared," one lobbyist said, "to be investigated."

THE EFFECTS OF LOBBYING

It is a mistake, then, to think of lobbying in terms of a one-way flow of influence from the lobbyist to the senator. Lobbying is a matter of bargaining. The senator is far from a passive puppet manipulated from afar.

This does not mean, however, that lobbying is without effect—far from it. It does mean that the effects of lobbying are less clear and simple than is generally assumed.

Reinforcement

Lobbying changes relatively few votes. Indeed, not much lobbying is intended to do so. The principal effect of lobbying is not conversion but reinforcement.

Certainly the elaborate "backstopping" efforts of most lobbies serve chiefly to keep group supporters in line and to provide them with acceptable rationalizations for an already established position. "A while back a senator called me," a lobbyist explained, "and said, 'I'm in favor of free trade and against subsidies. I would like to vote for your cause. But there are 3,000 beet growers in my state. If I voted for you I'd be taking money away from them. What can I say to them? What arguments can I use?' We gave him the arguments and he went along." Moreover, a good backstopping job makes a senator dependent, to some extent, upon the group. It makes it more difficult for him to change his mind. "Over the years," one lobbyist said, "a senator develops a set of sources of information. Once they are established, they are hard to change. I know of one senator who changed sides [on agricultural policy] recently. Of course, he lost all his old sources, and he didn't have sufficient experience with them to trust his new ones. It was a tough situation."

Political collaboration far more often leads to friendship than the other way around. Once established, senator-lobbyist friendships also tend to reinforce the senator's commitment to a particular group and line of policy. Perhaps on minor bills, friendships are more important. "You can't go far on friendship alone. Oh, maybe once a senator would push a little bill for you because you were his friend. But a senator is like a well—you can only draw on it so many times. And if he does something for you on that basis that proves to be politically unwise, he won't do it again. Chances are he won't do *anything* for you again."

Finally, much of the "inspired" pressure from back home is directed at those who would vote right anyway. A group with enough active members in a state to launch a successful mass-mailing campaign is quite likely to find their senators already favorably inclined. Moreover, some lobbyists believe that it is a good idea to pressure their regular supporters in the Senate. "Why," one lobbyist said of a consistent supporter, "Senator ———— would begin to wonder what had happened to us if he didn't get any mail from us." Another one commented that "friendly senators need to be reassured that they will receive credit for their position . . . that they are not forgotten." There is another reason why much of the pressure mail is aimed at the already

convinced—it's an important way for the lobbyist to impress his constituents with the fact that he is a jim-dandy lobbyist well worth his
keep. "In the office here," one business group lobbyist said, "we don't
think mass mailings are very effective. About twice a year we do have
mass mailings but it's mostly to keep the membership happy. Some
of our members are conscientious businessmen sold on our program.
They want to do something—so we get them to write their congressmen and senators."

Activation

Much lobbying is a struggle for the senator's time and attention.
Most senators and their staffs are vastly overworked and can be active
and informed on only a small portion of the legislative output of the
Senate. Moreover, as we have already seen, this sort of specialization
is encouraged by the chamber's folkways.

The choice that confronts a senator when an issue comes before the
Senate is not merely to cast a "yea" or "nay" vote. Rather there are
a wide range of actions open to him. He may decide merely to vote
one way or the other or to abstain. He may decide actively to campaign in support of his views both on and off the Senate floor, or he
may decide to become an active leader in favor of, or in opposition
to, the bill in question. These alternatives might be roughly dia-
grammed in the following fashion:

PRO			NEUTRAL				CON	
Lead, Pro Campaign	Participate, Pro Campaign	Inactive, Vote Pro	Inactive, Pair Pro	Abstain	Inactive, Pair Con	Inactive, Vote Con	Participate, Con Campaign	Lead, Con Campaign

A large part of all lobbying is aimed at persuading the senator to devote more of his limited time and energy to a specific bill or policy area, to activate him.

All of the ordinary lobbying techniques, when directed against "friendly" senators, can have this effect. A large part of all face-to-face lobbying is calculated to result in such activation. "Backstopping," by making it easier for a senator to be active on a wider range of issues, leads quite often toward greater legislative activity and involvement where the group wants it. Even the most obviously inspired mail is likely to force a senator to commit himself and lead to increased activity on his part.

As one lobbyist said:

Ninety per cent of what goes on here during a session is decided on the previous election day. The main drift of legislation is decided then: it is out of our control. There is simply no substitute for electing the right folks and defeating the wrong folks.

Our job is a little like that of a football coach. Our material is given. By careful coaching we can sometimes improve the effectiveness of the material.

Conversion

Relatively few senators are actually changed by lobbying from a hostile or neutral position to a friendly one. Perhaps a few on every major issue are converted and this handful of votes may carry the day. But quantitatively, the conversion effect is relatively small.

Of course, as we have seen, only a small part of all lobbying activity is calculated to change votes. Face-to-face lobbying and "backstopping" are primarily calculated to reinforce and activate the already convinced senators. The pressure a lobbyist can "inspire" from back home is more likely to change votes than any other form of lobbying, but much of this comes too late in the legislative process to change votes.

The most effective mail and telephone calls are those which arrive before the senator has made up his mind and announced a position. Most senators have made up their minds a great deal earlier in the legislative process than most people realize. On some matters a senator's mind is made up before he is elected. No amount of pressure is likely to alter Harry Byrd's economy-mindedness or Paul Douglas' belief in welfare programs. Even on specific bills, a good many senators' minds are made up before the bill is introduced. Some bills come up session after session in almost identical form; a man who has served in the Senate for any length of time is likely to have an established, public position on such a measure which it is not "good politics" to abandon. The common practice of co-sponsorship in the Senate results in many senators announcing a position on the bill before it is even introduced; a senator who backs down from such a commitment in the face of unanticipated pressure from back home is likely to lose considerable prestige and effectiveness in the Senate. Committee consideration of the bill commits committee members to either favoring or opposing the bill. The result is that by the time an important bill reaches the Senate floor, most senators have already made—and announced—a position. Yet it is during floor debate that most of the "pressure" is applied.[7] Moreover, it is rare that a mass campaign is not recognized as such.

Yet, on Capitol Hill there is less tendency to dismiss this pressure as ineffective than there is among lobbyists. Everyone realizes that "pressure mail" is a most untrustworthy manifestation of public opinion. Most senators will vote against the weight of "inspired" pressure mail quite often, far more often than the literature on pressure politics would indicate, but even so, it is not without its impact. "If a senator gets enough mail on a subject," one administrative assistant said, "even if it is obviously inspired, he begins to worry some." A flood of mail, as one senator said, makes the issue "one of those on which you begin to count the mail, pro and con."

Boomerang

Not all lobbying works out the way the lobbyist planned. Lobbying can, and fairly often does, boomerang.

Lobbying is most likely to have the boomerang effect when a senator is pressured in a direction that he does not wish to go. As we have already seen, it is under these conditions that he is most likely to feel pressured and lobbied.

The lobbyists are quite aware of this and go to considerable length to avoid pressuring an opposition stalwart. Thus we find that the first thing knowledgeable lobbyists do, in entering a fight for a bill, is to determine just where a senator stands on the matter. Very often, this can be predicted with a high degree of accuracy on the basis of past voting records. If this is not possible, informal discussions with the senator's assistants (or a "leaked" copy of the form letter used by

7. In some cases this poor timing may be the fault of the lobbyist. Some so-called lobbyists spend most of their time on other matters and are surprisingly ignorant of the legislative process. In most cases, however, the lobbyist seems unable to persuade his members to take action until the bill emerges into the publicity limelight. The political inactivity and ignorance of the lobbyist's constituents is a major problem for him, too.

the senator in answering his mail on the issue) will generally do the trick. Once a list of probable supporters and opponents is developed, most lobbyists try to focus their pressure on the undecided senators and avoid those deeply committed to either side. "We knew," one lobbyist in the natural-gas fight of 1956 said, "who was with us, who was against us, and who was doubtful. We narrowed it to less than twenty doubtful senators, and we really put the pressure on them from back home. The other side was doing the same thing. We never went near the senators who were red hot for the bill. And we went near the senators who were on our side only to see if they needed material for speeches."[8]

These efforts to focus pressure where it will do the most good with the least possibility of harm are never entirely successful. Voting projections may be inaccurate, the group's membership may be in the wrong states, the lobbyist may give in to sentiment within his constituency and apply pressure where it is likely to be harmful. The result is that on almost every major bill a few senators feel overlobbied, and that feeling is, from the lobbyist's point of view, quite dangerous. It may completely alienate the senator so far as voting "right" on that issue is concerned. (In all likelihood, he would not vote their way on the issue in any event.) It is also likely to diminish the group's effectiveness with him on other issues in the future, and there is always the possibility of a damaging public attack or investigation. The lobbyist's fear of this kind of boomerang effect makes conversion relatively rare. It is far safer to "work your side of the fence" and those who are still undecided than to attempt to win votes away from the opposition.

We began with the query: why is it that senators are less frightened by lobbying than either the public or academic students of politics? The answer to this question should now be clear.

First of all, much lobbying is not perceived as pressure by senators: an important distinction must be drawn between objective pressure (what the outside, objective observer conceives to be efforts at influence) and subjective pressure (efforts at influence perceived as such by the senators). There is far less of the latter than of the former for a number of reasons. Because of the general feeling against lobbying, few senators perceive the efforts of their supporters as lobbying or pressure. Moreover, the essence of "good" lobbying is to disguise the efforts at influence as something else: friendship, expert advice, and

8. *Wall Street Journal*, March 12, 1956.

genuine and spontaneous manifestations of public opinion. Moreover, the vast majority of all lobbying is directed at senators who are already convinced and least likely to think of it as lobbying.

Most analyses of lobbying—both journalistic and academic—obscure the fact that lobbying is a political process, that the relation between lobbyists and legislators is essentially one of bargaining. As a result, most "realistic" analyses of lobbying are misleading.

The basic reason for this error is simple. Traditional analyses of lobbying assume that the legislator has far less maneuverability than, in fact, he has. The present study shows that a senator, when confronted with a bill, has a wide range of actions open to him. Voting "yea" or "nay" are only two of these possibilities, and lobbyists are very interested in what he does in addition to voting. When confronted by pressure from lobbyists, a senator need not meekly acquiesce to their wishes. He may bargain the possibility of future "right" votes for a "wrong" one now, or he may refuse to cooperate altogether. Of course, following either of these alternatives may sometimes have unfortunate electoral consequences, but modes of cooperation and noncooperation other than voting are not likely to affect future election returns. A senator can be helpful enough to a lobbyist in ways other than voting—as a source of "leaks," as an amateur lobbyist, as an aid to the lobbyist in grappling with constituency problems—that he thereby increases his maneuverability in the voting situation. Lobbyists are not likely to bring about the defeat of a valuable contact, even if his voting record is not perfect. Finally, the senator has it within his power to trigger a damaging Congressional investigation if the lobbyist persists in insulting his self-esteem through pressure without persuasion, or if he blatantly violates the rules of the game, as in "doubling."

It is the threat of and use of these countermeasures which help explain why so little lobbying is aimed at conversion. A lobbyist minimizes the risk of his job, the cause which he serves, and his ego by staying away from those senators clearly against him and his program. For, of all types of lobbying, attempts at conversion are most likely to boomerang. As a result of this, along with the inherent limitations of lobbying devices, the major effects of lobbying are reinforcement and activation.

Lobbying is important. The Senate could not possibly operate in the mid-twentieth century without it. But the effects of lobbying are not what most observers have assumed them to be.

CHAPTER IX

Senators and Reporters

IN THE GOOD old days of short Congressional sessions and long adjournments, lightly populated constituencies, convention nominations, and machine politics, the typical senator's dependence upon the mass media of communications was not great. Today, newspapers and magazines, radio, and television are the major links between senators and their present and potential constituents. As a result, the modern senator's relations with the Washington press corps are close. Sometimes his relations with reporters are more intimate, and more important, than those with his Senate colleagues.

To reporters, on the other hand, the Senate is a "cockpit of drama," a "huge pipe-organ of publicity" with all the stops pulled out, a "rich source of everything a reporter considers news."[1] True, the growth in power and energy of the executive has made the White House and the departments far more important sources of news than in the tranquil days of Harding and Coolidge. Even when the president dominates the nation's headlines—and the postwar exploits of such senators as Taft, Vandenberg, McCarthy, Kefauver, George, McClellan, Johnson, and Knowland indicate that neither President Truman nor President Eisenhower was always able to seize the news initiative—the Senate remains a lush source of news. Most newsworthy political happenings have repercussions there, and many times things which happen at the White House, in the "downtown" departments, or on

1. The first and last descriptions of the Senate may be found in D. Cater, "To Make All Laws Which Shall Be Necessary and Proper," *Reporter*, February 7, 1957, p. 45. The "pipe-organ" image is from an interview with a wire-service reporter.

the other side of the globe can be followed better from the Senate than on the spot. When it adjourns, many a reporter starts "looking under rocks for news."[2] The relations between senators and Washington reporters are, therefore, of vital importance to the parties concerned.

These relations should be of considerable interest to students of politics and consumers of political news as well. Oddly enough, the subject has largely escaped popular and scholarly attention.[3] Very few Capitol Hill reporters have cared to disclose their trade secrets. Professional students of the legislative process have yet to give senator-reporter relationships their serious and systematic attention. Yet the interaction of senators and reporters shapes, to a very considerable extent, both the behavior of senators and the character of Capitol Hill news.

"COVERING" THE SENATE

In a typical postwar year, more than a thousand newsmen were accredited members of the Senate press galleries. This group was not a homogeneous one. Some reporters represented small out-of-town papers, while others were employed by the Washington newspapers or belonged to one of the large Washington bureaus maintained by the *New York Times, St. Louis Post Dispatch, Chicago Tribune,* and other metropolitan dailies. Some were reporters for the three wire services—the Associated Press, United Press, and International News Service[4]—while still others wrote for news magazines. A few were columnists and radio-TV news commentators. These different kinds of reporters were interested in different types of news, and this fact influences both the frequency and the nature of their dealings with senators.

The Two Levels of Reporting

Most Washington reporters work for small out-of-town newspapers and seldom cover national news. Rather they specialize largely in stories with a local slant—the appointment of postmasters, the letting of federal contracts to local concerns, and the like—leaving the coverage of "top" news to the wire services to which their papers subscribe.[5]

2. F. C. Othman, " 'A Fond Farewell' to Congress," Raleigh (N.C.) *News and Observer,* September 2, 1957.

3. A major exception is L. C. Rosten, *The Washington Correspondents* (New York, Harcourt, Brace and Company, 1937). D. Cater's fine, *The Fourth Branch of Government* (Boston: Houghton-Mifflin, 1959), appeared in print after these pages were written.

4. Since the decade studied here, the United Press and the International News Service have merged into a single wire service, United Press International.

5. "I worked for a small Southern paper for awhile," one reporter said. "They wanted me to relate everything to the local congressmen and senators. Of course, there

Such a division of labor makes a great deal of sense. The wire services maintain sizeable staffs in the House and Senate galleries, in the White House, and in the executive departments. The Washington bureaus of most out-of-town papers are very small (often a single reporter), and they must try to cover the entire town. The wire services, by working in shifts, can cover news events continuously. Their stories are transmitted over their leased wires more quickly than other reporters can wire in their stories.

But wire-service reporting has its limitations. Despite the fact that they maintain regional services specializing in news of interest to specific regions of the country, wire services cannot possibly provide locally slanted news for all of their subscribers. Moreover, wire-service news stories are written close after the event for transmission to scores of widely scattered subscribers with different needs and political persuasions. They tend to be severely factual, lacking in background and interpretation, and scrupulously objective. In order to overcome these limitations, a few metropolitan newspapers with large Washington bureaus, the Washington dailies, and the news magazines cover top news for themselves.

Thus Senate news is covered on two different levels. The vast bulk of the reporters for out-of-town papers (plus the regional reporters for the wire services) spend only part of their time on the Hill and are concerned with locally slanted news stories. A small number of the wire-service reporters and men from the Washington newspapers, large metropolitan dailies, and news magazines spend all their time on Capitol Hill covering top news.

The Reporter's Limited News Sources

No matter which level of news he seeks, the reporter's important news sources in the Senate are likely to be few in number.

This is most obvious in the case of reporters writing locally slanted stories. Within the Senate, only the two senators from their paper's state are likely to know of or care about the news they report. These two offices, however, are extremely fertile sources of the news such reporters need. The two senators, if they are of the president's party, play a major role in the making of federal appointments to local citizens. Usually they and their staffs have actively advocated the granting of contracts, franchises, and other forms of federal largess to

was no real relationship much of the time, but that made no difference to them. There are a very large number of correspondents in Washington who file nothing but this kind of story." For a more extended treatment of the differences to be found within the Washington press corps see Cater, *The Fourth Branch of Government*, Chs. 1, 5.

their constituents. Most executive agencies, after making decisions
on such matters, automatically notify the senators before making the
news public.[6] Also, senators who have served for any length of time
have built up informal information machines among political de-
pendents scattered all over town. They are likely, again especially after
they have some seniority, to serve on Senate committees of particular
importance to the folks back home. Rather than making a daily
canvass of the scores of departments, agencies, bureaus, commissions,
and committees making decisions of local interest, reporters can, by
maintaining close liaison with their senators and representatives, obtain
the same information more quickly and easily.[7] But this short cut
has its price. As one such reporter said, "The stress on the local angle
makes us very dependent upon the senators and representatives from
————— and their staffs."

The relatively few full-time Capitol Hill reporters writing top news
have many more potential news sources. Indeed, this is one of the
attractions of Congressional reporting. "In the White House," one
prominent reporter explained, "you sit around until someone gives
you a hand-out and then you write a story on the basis of it. That's
not *reporting,* that's *stenography*." In the executive departments,
especially in the State and Defense Departments, "they can really
punish a critical or unfriendly reporter who needs more than routine
hand-outs to meet his obligations to his paper. Up here we can be a
lot more independent." In actual practice, however, most top news
reporters on Capitol Hill develop a limited number of news sources
and lean on them heavily.

In part, this is the result of the time pressure under which most
Washington correspondents work. "You just can't go around and
talk with all of them, so you tend to fall back on the ones that you
know are most helpful to you." For the wire-service reporters, especially, this is important. Yet this is not the only reason that the reporters of national news each have close regular contact with few
members of the Senate. "If I had all the time in the world," one
reporter for a weekly news magazine said, "there are some senators
I wouldn't bother to see."

Correspondents also desire off-the-record background information
and interpretation. "If what you want is background information not
for quotation, it takes a fairly lengthy and close relationship before they

6. Except in such nonpartisan areas as national defense, members of the president's
party are usually notified *first* so that they can receive the greatest publicity "mileage"
out of breaking the news.

7. Cf., Rosten, *Washington Correspondents,* p. 78.

will be completely open with you," and "a senator naturally talks more freely off-the-record when he knows you and has learned to rely upon your discretion." Even when such a confidential relationship is well established, the reporter must know his informant well enough to read between the lines. "I don't mean 'getting to know' in the sense of knowing where to reach them but really and intimately knowing them as persons. You've got to be able to distinguish between what they mean and what they say. For example, I talked to Senator ———— the other day about his stand favoring an additional cut in foreign aid. Now he didn't say so in so many words but I carried away the impression that 99 per cent of this was for [home state] consumption so I played the whole thing down."[8]

Still another factor encouraging the reporter's reliance upon a relatively few news sources in the Senate is the chamber's internal patterns of influence. "I don't talk about this for obvious diplomatic reasons," one reporter for a nationally known paper said, "but there's not too much use in talking to more than five or six senators. After you've talked to them, you know what is going on." Another top news reporter elaborated on the point. "Take ———— or ————, for example, they have big hearts but no real influence. Much of the time they don't have a good idea about what is going on, or what will happen in the future. I could ask ———— how many votes a bill will get on final passage and he probably would tell me. But it wouldn't be as good an estimate as that of a more influential senator. ———— is just not a member of 'the club.' "

Finally, as still another reporter said, "Some senators have a good news sense—they are good reporters. If we call them off the floor they can summarize developments briefly in newsworthy form."

For all these reasons, then, it is no exaggeration to say, "Every newspaperman on Capitol Hill must have a sponsor. We all have three or four congressmen and senators with whom we are intimate and from whom we get most of our news."

Influence on the Reporter's Sources

What factors determine the specific "sponsors" or "sources" a reporter has on the Senate side of the Hill?

First of all, the newspaper or organization for which he works shapes the reporter's access to senators. "Senators like to see their

8. This same reporter is said to have once written a front-page story on the basis of a senator's shrug of the shoulders. In a car full of reporters, a senator pointed to the day's headlines and shrugged. The reporter assumed that the senator was trying to tip him off and thought he knew what the shrug meant. As it turned out, he was wrong.

names in the Washington papers—it's funny, even after a lifetime in politics they like knowing that their colleagues are reading about them over their breakfast coffee. They also like publicity in their hometown papers and in the *New York Times* and *Herald Tribune*. Reporters from these papers plus the wire services have the best access." Other factors also enter in. "Congressional reporting is a big and lucrative field and reporters work hard at developing contacts and news sources on the Hill." All reporters agree that "if they like you it helps a great deal." "I used to take quite a kidding about my terrific 'in' with ————," a reporter for a nationally important paper said. "I don't know quite why I had it—I disagreed strongly with most of his policies. Of course being with the [newspaper] helped a great deal. This is a stuffy way to put it, but we had respect for each other. And we liked each other." Ideology also affects a reporter's contacts and sources. Reporters who are liberals, or who represent liberal papers, tend to work with liberal senators and vice versa. "During the McCarthy exposures a whole new group of reporters arose who worked closely with him and his staff." This is especially the case with columnists, commentators, and interpretive reporters, for "by the time they have been around here long enough to write a column, their political views are pretty well known and they have easy access to the senators who agree with them."

This does not mean that reporters talk only to senators whose political position is similar to their own or that of their employer. Relations between political opponents here, as in the Senate itself, are generally cordial. It does mean, however, that reporters are seldom able to establish a confidential relationship with a senator over too wide an ideological chasm. If they want completely frank and uninhibited opinions or information from a senator to whom, for this or some other reason, they are not close, reporters are likely to get it from some other member of the press corps who enjoys greater access to the senator concerned. "A good bit of the time, reporters cover the Senate by talking to each other."

The way in which the Washington reporters go about covering Senate news causes wide variations in the frequency with which individual senators are in contact with reporters and differences in the types of reporters they normally see. All senators are in close and frequent communication with the bureaus of their home-state newspapers, but, since most of this news is routine, the actual contacts are usually handled by their staffs. The frequency of a senator's contact with national news reporters depends largely upon his influence within the chamber. The floor leaders, committee chairmen, and elder states-men are often in daily communion with these men, while the ordinary senators see them much less often. Senators with a sense of national news are also in demand. The particular top news reporters a senator sees depends, of course, on all sorts of factors, but, as a general rule, senators see top reporters who work for papers in which they wish to receive publicity, whose political position is similar to their own, or who are personal friends.

THE POLITICAL ROLE OF THE REPORTER

According to the "Fourth Estate myth," reporters are neutral ob-servers entirely divorced from the situation on which they report. No matter how laudible this myth may be, one need not spend much time on Capitol Hill to observe that it departs drastically from Con-gressional realities. In fact, reporters play an important role in the operation of the Senate and profoundly shape the behavior of its members.

The Reporter's Definition of News and Senatorial Behavior

In order to survive, most senators must make "news" by the re-porters' definition of the term. To advance to even greater political heights (i.e., the White House) a senator must become a national celebrity. Thus much senatorial behavior is shaped by the senator's perceptions of the reporters' notion of news.

Some senators try harder to anticipate press reaction to their be-havior than do others. As we have already seen in Chapter V, a few senators take the view that "no one knows how you vote but everyone remembers what you say" and avoid publicity as much as possible. Others define the role of the senator largely in terms of public "educa-tion" or propaganda and expend a larger amount of their time and energy on seeking publicity than doing anything else. Most senators fall somewhere between.

Even so, most of what is said on the floor of the Senate is aimed at "making news" via the press galleries. Congressional investigations, too, are more often calculated to affect tomorrow's headlines than the statute books. The types of bills a senator introduces, the committee assignments he cherishes, how he votes on roll calls, and what he de-fines as an "issue" are influenced by anticipated press reactions.

Over the years, most senators develop a "sense of news"; that is, they are able accurately to anticipate what events will be considered "news" by which reporters. This is more complicated than it sounds, for different types of reporters seek different types of news. The

Washington reporters for a senator's home-state papers may give a big "play" to a story which the regular wire services will ignore. To send the same kinds of stories to reporters operating on the two different levels of reporting can result in loss of confidence by both kinds of reporters in the senator's news sense and the downgrading of the importance attached to all future releases. "Why, ——— has no news sense at all," one reporter complained. "If the President of the United States dropped dead before his eyes it would not occur to him that this was news." If a senator wishes to receive favorable publicity, he had better not earn this kind of reputation. Most of them do not. Most of them learn what is "news" and how to make it. In other words, they behave in accordance with the reporters' expectations.

Reporters as Informal Advisors

Reporters do not always wait for the senators to learn by themselves how the press wishes them to behave. The preparation of a senator's routine news releases is, especially for relatively new members, often a joint endeavor of the senator's staff and the home-state bureaus. If the relationship between senator and reporter matures into one of close collaboration and respect, the reporter is very likely to become an informal advisor to his Senate news source. For example, Richard Nixon, while a member of the House Un-American Activities Committee, first seriously investigated Whittaker Chambers' "pumpkin papers" on the advice and insistence of Bert Andrews of the *New York Herald Tribune.* An alert newspaper reporter first suggested the televising of Senator Kefauver's crime investigation.[9]

"Pressuring" Senatorial Action

This kind of relationship shades imperceptibly into the reporters' forcing action they desire from apathetic or reluctant senators through their influence over the news.

One good example of this was Senator Fulbright's recent investigation of the stock market. Upon becoming chairman of the Banking and Currency Committee, Fulbright was asked by a reporter what the committee would be doing during the next session of Congress. The senator from Arkansas said he did not know for certain, plans were still indefinite. The reporter persisted: would the committee be looking into the housing situation, the policy of the Federal Reserve Board, the recent rise in stock market prices? The senator replied, yes, probably they would. The next day the reporter broke the sensational

9. B. Moody, "The United States Senate," *Holiday,* February, 1954, pp. 90-91.

news that the committee would investigate the stock-market boom. In this manner the investigation got under way.[10]

Another example of "pressuring" is the explosive investigation of Secretary of the Air Force Harold Talbott by the Permanent Investigating Subcommittee. Charles Bartlett, the Washington correspondent for the *Chattanooga Times,* received a tip from a businessman acquaintance that Talbott was conducting private business from his office in the Pentagon. Bartlett took the tip to the staff director of the committee, a personal friend, and they agreed to look into the matter. Five months later, both Bartlett and the committee staff believed that they had obtained sufficient information to merit a public investigation. The night before the committee was told of the results of the staff investigation, Bartlett, fearful either that the story might leak out or that the committee would not take action on the matter, published his story. The committee had no choice but to proceed.[11]

Almost endless examples of this sort of thing could be repeated here. A reporter for the *Washington Post* helped trigger the recent investigation of the natural-gas lobby; the Teapot Dome scandals were initially uncovered by a newspaper. So, too, were the "five-percenter" inquiries during the Truman administration.

The truth of the matter would seem to be that while newspapermen make news, they cannot—with the exception of a few columnists—admit it. "When we find some newsworthy item, we take it and 'bounce it off' some news source. For example, if we discover a scandal in an executive agency we generally take it to a senator or congressman and try to get an investigation, or at least his comments. Then it becomes news."

The Press, External and Internal Communication

A major source of the senators' information on the outside world is the public press. They do not, unlike the members of the executive, possess a far-flung information and intelligence network of their own. While the normal senator has great (and sometimes misguided) faith in personal observation and experience, it is clearly impossible for him personally to gather more than a tiny fraction of all the facts and ideas he needs.[12] Most senators are avid newspaper readers, for their busy schedules and personal inclinations do not seem to permit the ex-

10. C. Seib and A. Otten, "Fulbright: Arkansas Paradox," *Harpers,* June, 1956, p. 61.
11. *Congressional Record* (Daily Edition), May 9, 1956, p. 6950.
12. For analyses of the Congress which place considerable stress upon this point see R. A. Dahl, *Congress and Foreign Policy* (New York: Harcourt, Brace and Company, 1950) and L. Dexter, "Congressmen and the People They Listen To" (unpublished MS, 1955).

tensive reading of books. Most of them read the Washington papers, the *New York Times* or *Herald Tribune* (sometimes both), plus several leading home-state papers every day. (Their staffs usually either clip or mark news items of interest to them in other papers in the home state.) The Senate cloakrooms contain the wire-service tickers and they are regularly consulted by all the senators. The *Congressional Record* contains, each day, a large number of news articles and interpretative columns inserted by the members for the possible edification of their colleagues. The basic themes of many a Senate speech have clearly been stimulated by, or borrowed from, the latest efforts of Krock, Reston, Lippmann, and their local equivalents.

This is obvious. Yet it is not so well known that the senators often find out what is going on in the Senate by reading the papers. Senators are incredibly busy people. Most of them have specialized legislative interests. Most important legislative events take place in the myriad committee and subcommittee meetings occurring all over the Hill. Senators have neither the time nor energy to keep tab on this hundred-ring circus. The newspapers help immeasurably in the senators' never-ending struggle to keep track of what is going on in the Senate. It is ironic but still true that the members of so small a legislative body should find it necessary to communicate with each other via public print, but often they do.

It is a great deal easier to say that reporters play an important political role in the Senate than to document precisely what that role is. The reporters' influence is so all pervasive that it is hard to isolate it from other factors. Even so, we have suggested a number of ways in which the reporters shape the behavior of senators. Their definition of "news" influences how the senators act and what the "issues" are, they sometimes serve as informal advisors to the senators with whom they work closely, they can and do "pressure" senators into taking action merely by the way they "play" a story, and they serve as an essential link between senators and the outside world and as a means of communication within the chamber. These factors must have been in the mind of one Senate staff member who, when queried concerning the role of reporters in the Senate, answered, "Hell, they run the place." But the blatant subservience of most senators to reporters is not solely a manifestation of the latter's power. It is also, as we shall see, one way in which senators try to control reporters.

THE TACTICS OF THE PUBLICITY HOUND

Reporters influence the behavior of senators, but senators possess considerable leverage over the reporters as well. For one thing, the senators vary in the amount of publicity they need in order to survive. A senior senator, thoroughly entrenched in his constituency, without presidential ambitions or a thirst for fame, can say, "When you've got the votes, you don't have to talk,"[13] and largely ignore the press corps. This immediately increases his attractiveness to the reporters, although most senators who adopt this stance are in such powerful legislative positions that they would be hotly sought after news sources in any event. The more usual situation is one of extreme senatorial sensitivity to publicity. "You ought to see a senator read the papers the day after he has made important news," one reporter said. "The *implications* he can read into every word!" The appearance of still photographers or TV cameramen regularly touches off vigorous senatorial jostling and elbowing contests. "They all want to be in the middle of the picture, standing next to the big man. I'll bet that sometimes they go home at night with real bruises."

Even the senators who, through personal choice or political necessity, are publicity hounds can influence what the reporters write about them and how often. Nor need they, in an effort to maximize the favorable publicity they receive, invariably knuckle under to the reporters' demand that they make news, by the reporters' definition. They can also manipulate the men who report the news.

The tactics of the publicity hound are few and highly standardized. They seldom fool anyone, but, within limits, they still work.

Overcooperation

Senators, their staffs, and (indirectly) the American taxpayer provide all kinds of services and special privileges to the press corps. The Senate press galleries—larger, more cheerful, more comfortable than perhaps any other in town, "a good place to run into friends and catch up on the latest gossip"—are the most tangible of these services and help explain why the Senate and senators are such favored sources of news.

But the senators' staffs also provide home-state bureaus, wire-service men, and the press galleries with press releases as a matter of routine, written in the proper form and appropriately timed to suit the reporter's convenience. "I try to be fair in writing up these stories," one senator's press assistant said, "but you can be sure that the boss's name is right up there in the story." Interested reporters are notified in advance by the senator's staff whenever he is scheduled to make a floor

13. The quotation is from Senator Carl Hayden. AP dispatch printed in *Hampshire Gazette* (Northampton, Mass.), Nov. 8, 1956.

speech or a presentation to a committee. The texts of his speeches and statements are dispatched to the proper people at the proper time.[14] The Washington press corps is so dependent upon this prefabricated material (which most of them gladly make their own) that extemporaneous speeches, the give and take of debate, and the flow of committee questioning of witnesses are seldom adequately covered in newspaper accounts of Senate proceedings. Another consequence of this practice is that the senators gain more control over the content of news dispatches than they otherwise would have.

Most senators are easily accessible to reporters—at least those they wish to please—at almost any time. "They are the only ones who can go into his office without any preliminary rigmarole," one legislative assistant said of his boss. "Why, if he were having dinner with the Queen of England and [name of reporter] wanted to see him, he could and right away. When they call, everything else in the office stops." One enterprising young newspaperman confesses that he obtains most of his interviews with senators by telephoning them at home in the evening, obtaining their unlisted numbers from Washington's Social List. He reports that his annual $15.00 investment in "the green book" is money well spent and that "they are always delighted to talk."

A senator can provide many other services to a reporter as well. "Why, [senator's first name] is practically another member of our bureau," one reporter explained. "If I am unable to get some information from an executive agency that I need for a story, I call ——— about it. Within thirty minutes I get a phone call from some big wheel in the agency with the information. ——— will do that even if the story will not include his name; it pays off in a better press." Thus the basic gambit of the senator-publicity hound is overcooperation. It results not only in good will but in a sense of indebtedness on the part of the reporter as well, and at least some control is exerted over the reporter's stories. After all he, or more likely a member of his staff, wrote some of the stories in the first place.

Off-the-Record Interviews, Leaks, and Exclusives

Off-the-record interviews, leaks, and exclusive stories are variants on this same technique with one important difference; they are not "across-the-board" policies applied to many reporters but special favors granted to a select few.

14. A few unusually influential senators do *not* send advance copies of their important speeches to the press galleries, thus forcing the reporters to attend the session and to hang on their every word. See W. S. White, "Inquiry Into the Art of Politics," *New York Times Magazine*, June 8, 1952, p. 37. This is a variation on the policy of publicity via abnegation mentioned above.

Reporters, as we have already seen, are dependent upon access to confidential and unauthorized information. Once they have found senator-sources of such information, they understandably wish to "keep their sources open" for the future. Moreover, the reporter is likely to feel beholden to his source. "Suppose," one radio-TV news analyst explained, "that ———— came up to me at a party and said, '————, you're doing a wonderful job. Now there are a couple of things I think you ought to know' and then proceeded to give me some valuable inside information. I darn well wouldn't lambast him on the program that night." Indeed, the warm glow of the experience might even result in his saying something nice.

Sometimes a reporter's flattery of a senator is coldly calculated. "My critics have sometimes accused me of getting news by buttering-up certain officials, referring to them as 'able' Senator So-and-so, or the 'astute' Secretary of So-and-so. That was once true. I think I can even fix the date when I swore off."[15] In many interpretative and behind-the-scene news stories originating on Capitol Hill (including those written by the man who allegedly has sworn off), the reporter's confidential sources are as clearly identifiable as the "good guys" in a grade-B Western movie. Whether or not this is the reporter's conscious policy, is, from the senator's point of view, irrelevant. He has obtained a better news break than he otherwise would have received.[16]

According to one senator's press secretary, "There's such a thing as being too cooperative with the press. If what you want is publicity, I'm convinced that often the best way to get it is to withhold stuff from the press, treat it as a 'secret document,' and then leak it out a little at a time. The word will get around and then they all will be calling here to find out the inside information." In this day of the mimeographed hand-out, press agents, and press conferences, the Washington reporters are hungry for "exclusive" stories. "If a senator calls me in and gives me the story as an exclusive, rather than calling a press conference, I'll give it a bigger 'play' and so will the paper— there's no doubt about that." After all, it makes both the paper and the reporter look good.

15. Drew Pearson, "Confessions of 'an S.O.B.,'" *Saturday Evening Post,* November 3, 1956, p. 91.

16. A number of New Dealish columnists were very kind to the Eisenhower Administration during its early months. According to Capitol Hill insiders, most of these reporters' old news sources had disappeared and their amazingly gentle treatment of the new administration was a necessary part of their efforts to develop new ones. If this is true, it suggests that the honeymoon period of an administration of a party different from its predecessor is likely to be unusually warm and prolonged.

In this manner competition within the press corps works in the senators' favor. They can, by the judicious use of off-the-record interviews, leaks, and exclusives, build up the reputations of friendly reporters and papers and even win themselves a few new journalistic friends. This gambit, it should be added, works not only within each of the media but between them as well. One Democratic senator, confronted by an unusually hostile press in his home state, suddenly began breaking news stories over his weekly radio program before releasing them to the newspapers. Just as suddenly, his newspaper coverage improved.

The Friendship Ploy

Many a reporter has found that his best stories are obtained at Washington parties. At social occasions the senators' usual loquacity is "intensified by the lulling warmth of the liquor, the geniality of the group, the camaraderie of the occasion, and the absence of those inhibitions against confidential speech which are found in the formal press conference, the presence of a stenographer, or the vigilant portrait of George Washington on the wall."[17] As one old-time reporter has put it, "The most important news usually comes out after the second highball."[18] As a result, some reporters do a good deal of entertaining, and in turn are entertained by members of the Senate.

It is difficult to determine who gains the most from such commercial friendships. The reporters pick up tips and inside stories, but the senators gain protection. As one powerful columnist has written: "The more you go out to dinner, the more friends you make and the more you diminish the number of people you can write about without qualms of conscience or rebukes from your wife."[19] A member of a small Washington bureau put the same point a little differently. "I've found it not a good idea to be too friendly with senators from my paper's state," he said. "It complicates matters too much; if you have to clobber them they are liable to get mad . . . it's best to keep your relationships [with home state senators] on a strictly professional basis." "Take Drew Pearson," still another reporter said, "I'm sure that many members of the Senate thoroughly despise the man, yet they do business with him. And, at social occasions, I've seen them flock around him. It's a form of self-protection, I suppose."

17. Rosten, *Washington Correspondents*, p. 105.
18. The aphorism is that of the late Charlie Michelson. Quoted in Pearson, "Confessions," *Sat. Eve. Post*, Nov. 3, 1956, p. 88.
19. *Ibid.*, p. 87.

Just as in their relationships with lobbyists, constituents, and Senate colleagues, the senators find, in their dealings with reporters, that at least the semblance of friendship pays off.

Noncooperation and Attack

The basic tactic of the publicity hound is to provide services and special favors to reporters which then may be withdrawn in the event the newsmen do not live up to their end of the bargain—i.e., render favorable coverage. The bargain, it should hastily be added, is invariably implicit and perhaps not even recognized as such by either side, but that makes it no less a bargain.

When a reporter does not live up to his end of the deal, his relations with the senator involved cool; the senator understandably loses some respect for the reporter's judgment and may take his inside dope, leaks, and exclusives elsewhere. The seriousness of this situation, from the reporter's standpoint, depends largely on which level of news he writes. The local-story reporter, with many fewer *potential* sources and less prestige on the Hill, can be hurt a great deal more than the top news reporter with a wider group of potential news sources. Neither kind of reporter, however, is likely to bring on such a situation needlessly or without considerable prior thought.

Very rarely one hears of a senator boycotting a reporter. Senator Morse of Oregon was recently so infuriated by an AP story that he banned all AP reporters from his office and press conferences for about a year. More often, but still also rarely, a senator will publicly attack a member of the press corps. A few years back, for instance, Senator McKellar of Tennessee became so angry with Drew Pearson (who had written that he possessed an uncontrollable temper!) that he took the Senate floor and said of the capital's number one peeper into political keyholes:

He is an ignorant liar, a pusillanimous liar, a peewee liar. . . . That statement is a wilful, deliberate, malicious, dishonest, intensely cowardly, low, degrading, filthy lie.

When a man is a natural-born liar, a liar during his manhood, a liar by profession, a liar for a living, a liar in the daytime, a congenital liar, a liar in the nighttime, it's remarkable how he can lie.

. . . .

A revolting liar! It suits Pearson exactly. . . . Gentlemen, I am not angry. I am just sorry that this great nation of ours, this nation of honest men, has within its borders any person so low and despicable, so corrupt, so groveling, as this low-down, low-lived, corrupt and dishonest Pearson. . . . The animal called a skunk cannot change his smell. This human skunk cannot change his smell. He will always be just a low-life skunk. Mr. President, if I have been guilty of exhibition of temper, I hope the senators will forgive me.[20]

The same reporter was once physically assaulted by Senator McCarthy.

Several recent Congressional investigations have been ill-concealed efforts to punish hostile news media. Senator Bricker of Ohio, for example, recently cast himself in the unlikely role of trust-buster in an investigation of the broadcasting industry. The radio and TV news commentators had, almost to a man, panned the proposed Bricker Amendment a short while before.[21] And Senator Eastland spearheaded a Senate exposé of "Communists" on the *New York Times* staff after the paper had repeatedly and vigorously disagreed with his policies.[22]

The trouble with these sanctions is that they do not work. A senator who boycotts a reporter, paper, or news service usually does himself more harm than good—the AP survived the Morse boycott with considerably greater ease than did the senator—nor are public tongue-lashings of reporters likely to result in a better press in the future. To punish the publicity media via publicity is a difficult trick, even when utilizing that awesome instrument for doing so, the Senate investigation. To the reporters, efforts to use such extreme sanctions against them merely indicate that the senators "just don't understand our business and are not likely to be good sources, anyway."

CONFLICT, COOPERATION, AND THE NEWS

The potential sources of conflict in the relations of senators and reporters are almost infinite. The reporters want news, and the senators desire favorable publicity for themselves and their programs; the two are by no means identical concepts. The newspapers and magazines for which most reporters work are identified with policy preferences which, be they "liberal," "conservative," or between, are always repugnant to some members of the chamber. The columnists and interpretative reporters, of course, face this problem in an extreme form. It is often unclear whether a reporter's discussion with a senator is "on" or "off" the record, and the reporter's use of information is a

20. *Ibid.*, Nov. 24, 1956, p. 148.
21. *Washington Post and Times Herald*, June 10, 1956.
22. *Ibid.*, January 29, 1956, and April 20, 1956; *New York Times*, March 23, 1957.

potential source of considerable strain.[23]   Given the conditions of the journalist's work, some inaccuracies are inevitable in Congressional reporting, and senators can be extraordinarily sensitive about small errors.   There are, too, some things that senators would prefer not to expose to the bright glare of publicity.   It is certainly to the senators' advantage to maintain large areas of semisecrecy about which reporters can learn only through leaks which place the reporters in their debt.   The reporters, on the other hand, have a vested interest in free access to information, softened, to be sure, by their understandable desire for "beats" and "exclusives" which the present type of semisecrecy makes possible.

The Infrequency of Senator-Reporter Conflict

It is not surprising, therefore, that animosities, hurt feelings, and ill will often characterize the relations between senators and reporters. In the process of covering Washington political news, many reporters develop a thorough-going distaste for politicians, including senators. "When I first started reporting I was told to treat 98 per cent of all public officials with contempt. I propose no change to this rule— except to up the percentage to 99." They complain that "to some politicians, lying just comes naturally"[24] and develop a profound distaste for "the monumental pomposity of most senators."

The senators and their staffs, on the other hand, complain fairly often of violated confidences; of inaccurate, distorted or misleading reporting; that "while reporters talk about freedom of information, all they really want is a public-relations man to write their stories for them"; and that the reporters, by playing up "side shows" and personal conflict, paint a distorted picture of the Senate and senators.

Yet the surprising thing to the outside observer is that these animosities seldom break the surface. Given the potential sources of conflict, the relations between senators and reporters are remarkably free of friction.

One reason for this is that, through close and regular contact and despite the cynical talk, many reporters and senators begin to identify with each other and to understand each other's problems. For example, one publicity-oriented senator has bitterly complained for years of the lack of coverage he receives in his home-town newspapers. The reporters for the papers, it seems, have been able to "get off the hook"

23. According to one reporter, "Usually a senator doesn't even have to say 'this is off the record.' You are supposed to know what is and what is not given to you in confidence."

24. Pearson, "Confessions," *Sat. Eve. Post*, Nov. 24, 1956, p. 148.

by showing him copies of all the stories about him that they have filed but which have not been printed, thereby re-directing the senator's wrath toward their employers. Many senators excuse the reporters in their preoccupation with scoops and sensations on the grounds that this is what the reporters' editors and readers want.

At the same time, the reporters of top news who spend full time on the Hill tend to become socialized into the Senate folkways and to develop a sympathetic understanding of the senators' plight. "Up here," one of these reporters said, "we tend to become identified with the Senate. It's a little like being a war correspondent; you really become a part of the outfit you are covering."[25]

More than sentiment softens reporter-senator conflicts. Rational calculation does as well. Few groups are more dependent upon each other than senators and Washington reporters. They need each other so badly that the use by either side of sanctions stronger than non-cooperation is not rational policy. The inevitable hostilities and frustrations of such a dependent relationship usually remain unexpressed or disappear rapidly: "If I write an unfavorable story about a senator, our relations may be a little cool for a few weeks, but it won't last long."

Senator-Reporter Cooperation and the News

Both senators and reporters have it in their power to build each other up. A senator, by giving a reporter preferential treatment, can enhance newsmen's prestige among the press corps, his standing with his employers and readers, and his earning power. A reporter, by giving the senator a good break, can contribute substantially to the success of the senator's career. This kind of "back scratching" is far more profitable to both sides than conflict.

In local-story reporting, "it pretty much happens across the board." The mutual build-up is less common in national news reporting, but even in this kind of reporting "back scratching" is not unknown and the pay-offs in fame, power, and Pulitzer prizes are great. We have already mentioned the close collaboration of Richard Nixon and Bert Andrews (of the *New York Herald Tribune*) on the Hiss-Chambers case. At least partly as a result of their joint endeavors, Nixon became a national figure almost overnight and quickly won election to the Senate and the vice-presidency, and Andrews won a Pulitzer prize.

25. Probably the most rhapsodic book ever written about the Senate was produced by the chief Congressional correspondent of the *New York Times*. See William S. White, *Citadel: The Story of the U.S. Senate* (New York: Harper and Brothers, 1956), a fine book but also an embarrassingly public love affair.

Arthur Vandenberg and James Reston (of the *New York Times*) are another example of a senator-reporter team which, through intimate collaboration, rapidly "built each other up" in their respective worlds. William S. White, then of the *Times,* had impressive "ins" with Robert A. Taft and the Southern patriarchs in the Senate. As a result of this arrangement, both Taft and the Southern leaders gained sympathetic national publicity, and White, a well-earned Pulitzer prize. And so it goes.

Senator-reporter "back scratching" has a decided influence on Capitol Hill news. The national news reporters' best sources receive a better press than their actions merit. The chamber as a whole escapes the searching criticism that some members of the press corps would like to give it, if they dared.[26]

At the same time, one must be careful not to push this conclusion too far. There is a limit beyond which a reporter cannot go. He cannot suppress a really newsworthy story. "There are few secrets in the press corps. We all love to come up with exclusive stories but we don't succeed very often. If I held back on something fairly newsworthy, some other paper would most certainly pick it up." But the reporters are their own judges of newsworthiness, and their standards may easily vary from one situation to the next. In a marginal case, this judgment of newsworthiness may well be influenced by the reporter's desire not to "go out of my way to embarrass a reliable source." For instance, reporters admit to *not* writing stories concerning senators who took mid-session Florida vacations, had brushes with traffic policemen, were drunk and disorderly at Washington parties, and failed to return to their constituencies during summer recess. These are certainly not world-shaking events, but they might conceivably be viewed as "news."

Generally speaking, however, it is *how* a story is written, and not whether it is written, that is influenced by reporter-senator "back scratching." Let the reader beware.

Reporters, the Folkways, and Intra-Senate Conflict

While relations between senators and reporters are amazingly smooth, this very fact tends to stimulate conflict within the Senate.

26. Another reason for the relatively good press the Senate receives is that there is no "sounding board" for the reporters to use for their unfavorable stories concerning it. The Congress performs this function eagerly and well for the executive branch—a reporter who uncovers a scandal in the executive branch need only take it to a member of Congress to make it news. There is no comparable "sounding board" to be used against Congress.

The senator's locally oriented publicity is far less conducive to intra-Senate conflicts than are his efforts at making national news. Other members of the Senate are generally ignorant of the kind and amount of publicity a senator receives back home. They all know it is essential, and besides it does not affect them in any way. There is, however, one important exception to this rule: the other senator from the same state. Each senator watches the publicity of his colleague very closely indeed, and many a feud has been touched off by the fact that one senator seemed to be getting better publicity than the other. Sometimes full-scale "publicity battles" will break out between the two senators. In one case, a senator made a practice of arriving at work each morning armed with a personal count of the number of times his colleague's name appeared in the paper that morning compared with the number of times that his own name had been printed. These comparisons were invariably invidious, despite the best efforts of a succession of administrative assistants, until his colleague was defeated for re-election.

Even when such a battle does not break out, the kind and amount of publicity one senator seeks is generally affected by what his colleague is doing. One Midwestern senator, for example, had served with quiet efficiency in the Senate for some years when an ambitious, young, publicity-oriented man won the other seat. "At first," an assistant to the older man has said recently, "we thought we could go on as before and that the contrast between ———'s and ———'s styles would be to our benefit. But we pretty quickly changed our minds. One thing [the younger man] has done is to educate a lot of people about what is going on here. Now we get out as many, indeed a few more, press releases for home consumption than he does! The people in the Iowa offices do a lot less than we do and their state is about the same size and type as ours. But they don't have ——— to contend with." The relations between two senators from the same state are almost always strained, and their competition for publicity in the same arena seems to be one reason for this coolness.

Competition for national publicity, however, is even more disruptive to intra-Senate harmony. One way to make national news is to play a significant part in the making of important legislation. This is not a role that can be played by all senators simultaneously and, given the present structure and folkways of the Senate, is most often and easily played by those senators with the least need for publicity. The ordinary senator can usually make national news only through such frowned upon practices as "grandstanding"—making sensational speeches, engaging in "personalities," excessive partisanship, and other forms of behavior calculated to get his name in the headlines without legislative accomplishment—or through such "side shows" as Senate investigations of war profiteers, grafters, criminals, and Communists. If enough senators do not voluntarily engage in such activities, the reporters, especially those from the wire services, try to stimulate conflict. "They often call up my boss," one legislative assistant explained, "and say 'Senator so-and-so just made this statement. Do you want to attack it?' If he makes a tough enough statement they print it. Their attitude is 'Want to fight? I'll hold your coat.'" The reporters' desire for controversy-laden national news and the relatively uninfluential senator's desire to make it are highly subversive to the Senate folkways.

CHAPTER X

Senators and Their Constituents

THE LATE Vice-President Alben Barkley's favorite story was about Farmer Jones. Barkley began doing favors for Jones when he started out in 1905 as prosecuting attorney of McCracken County, Kentucky, and continued doing favors for him as a judge, United States representative, and senator. Barkley, so the story goes, visited Farmer Jones in a hospital in France during World War I to console him; he interceded with General Pershing to get him home quickly after the armistice; he intervened with the Veterans' Bureau to speed up his disability compensation; he helped him get loans from the Farm Credit Administration. On top of all this, he got Farmer Jones a federal disaster loan to rebuild his farm after a flood had struck, and he also got Mrs. Jones an appointment as a postmistress. Then, in 1938, Barkley found himself in a close primary fight. To his astonishment, he learned that the man he had so often befriended, Farmer Jones, was going to vote for his opponent. He hurried to see Jones and reminded him of his many labors in his behalf.

"Surely," Barkley said, "you remember all these things I have done for you?"

"Yeah," said Farmer Jones sullenly. "But what in hell have you done for me lately?"[1]

The moral is clear. To an elective politican, constituents often appear unpredictable, arbitrary, ungrateful. Their support can never be assumed.

1. *Washington Post and Times Herald*, May 1, 1956.

The United States senator faces the usual risks of the elective official, along with others that are more or less unique. His electoral fortunes may be affected by forces over which he has no control. Depressions, wars, scandals, a dramatic shift in the popularity of the president and his administration, the emergence of new issues can result in electoral tides which sweep highly competent and popular men out of office. He has little if any control over who his rivals are, and yet his popularity is measured not absolutely but in comparison with that of opponents in party primaries and general elections. The senator's constituency is very large. Only the president and vice-president represent more people than the senators from the larger states, and the president has greater prestige, easier access to the mass media, and the assistance of millions of subordinates to ease the burden. The senator's job physically separates him from his constituents most of the year. Some governors and other state officials may have equally large constituencies, but at least they are "on the ground."

These problems, of course, are more acute for some senators than others. Senators from two-party states face greater risks than those lacking vigorous partisan politics. Those from states with large, urban populations have constituency problems which, quantitatively and qualitatively, dwarf the problems of senators from the sparsely settled rural states. A few senators come from states so near Washington, D.C., that their geographical separation from "home" is relatively insignificant. Yet for all senators, constituents pose major problems. How they attempt to solve them—sometimes successfully and sometimes not—is the subject of this chapter.

THE MAIL

The mail provides the most regular and important means of personal communication between senators and their constituents. It arrives in appalling and ever-increasing volume. Old-timers around the Senate can remember when twenty letters in one day was "big mail." Today, the average senator on a more or less typical day receives several hundred letters.

This increase in the senators' mail is not just the result of population growth. "Until the turn of this century, national legislation touched the daily lives of Americans only briefly, if at all. As late as the 1920's, President Calvin Coolidge said the federal government could cease to operate and the average citizen wouldn't know the difference for three months." Now, after several decades of rapid expansion of federal government activities and services, the average citizen is in intimate contact with the federal government every day. The transmission of news by television, radio, newspapers, and magazines has been speeded up and increased in volume. The typewriter, telephone, mimeograph, improved telegraph, and speedier printing have also contributed to the flood of communications which pours into the Capitol every day.[2]

Of course, the volume of mail varies from time to time and from senator to senator. Those senators from the larger states receive proportionately more mail, and those from the small states, proportionately less. (There is at least one important exception to this rule; the Southern senators receive less mail proportional to population than the others. The region's large Negro minority, low levels of education, and the greater political security of their senators appear to account for this.) The mail is heavier for all senators during the legislative session than during recess, and it tends to go up when important or emotional issues are debated on the floor.

The senators consider their mail of very great importance. Most of them insist that every letter from a constituent be answered— if possible on the day that it is received. Most also agree that "Your votes and speeches may make you well known and give you a reputation, but it's the way you handle the mail that determines your re-election."[3]

How the Mail Is Handled

No senator has the time to read, let alone answer, all of his own mail. As a matter of fact, most senators see little of it. As a general rule the mail is opened by a clerk who routes the routine (in *her* eyes) letters to various members of the senator's staff.

Letters concerning pending legislation, perhaps half to two-thirds of the usual haul, are referred to the senator's legislative assistant, who prepares replies for mailing over the senator's signature. Since the members regularly receive hundreds of letters on the same issues, many of these replies are form letters written by the legislative assistant, approved by the senator and then individually typed, over and over again, by automatic typewriters.

The rest of the mail, from one-third to one-half of the typical day's haul, requests some kind of service or favor from the senator. Some of these requests are trifling affairs. Will the senator secure theater

2. E. Kefauver and J. Levin, *A Twentieth-Century Congress* (New York: Duell, Sloan and Pearce, 1947), pp. 171-72.
3. *Ibid.*, p. 171. Senator Kefauver was told this by Speaker Bankhead when first elected to the House.

tickets or hotel reservations for a constituent? Buy an outsized pair of over-alls for an elephantine voter? Send research materials to the high school debating team? Mail a copy of *Child Care* to a new mother? Senators are regularly asked for help by mental cases, unwed mothers, sufferers from venereal diseases—all kinds of lost and bewildered people who do not know where else to turn. "Dear Senator," one of these letters began, "I am complaining about my feet that are flat and badly callused and stay like they are on ice all the time."[4] But most of the requests which come to a senator ask assistance in dealing with the executive branch of the federal government. A constituent "wants his son out of the Army; he wants to get his delayed crop check; he wants to get a contract to construct an Army building; he wants to disagree with a ruling of the Interstate Commerce Commission," will the senator please help?[5] This vast miscellany of requests is, in the argot of Capitol Hill, called "cases."

In almost every office, a girl specializes in military and veterans cases, another in immigration cases, and so on. These case workers, who have often previously been employed by the departments or agencies with which they deal, are very familiar with the organization (both formal and informal) and the procedures of the relevant agencies.[6] Only the more complex cases, ones which involve personal friends and important supporters, or ones which involve large classes of constituents are handled by the administrative assistant or the senator himself.

Legislative Mail and Constituency Opinion

Most senators believe that their mail provides them with the best single indication of constituent attitudes on legislative issues.[7] In most offices, the number of letters received on each issue is tabulated— sometimes daily or weekly, in other offices only intermittently—along

4. *Washington Post and Times Herald,* February 12, 1956.

5. D. P. Griswold, "A Freshman Senator Makes a Report," *New York Times Magazine,* March 8, 1953, p. 17.

6. "Ideally," one widely respected administrative assistant said, "we like a girl from our state who is already down here and has had some government background. We want girls with government backgrounds, not political backgrounds—we'll take care of the political end of the job. A knowledge of government operations and contacts in the departments are what we need. For example, we have one girl who has been with the senator for eleven years. She knows someone by his or her first name in virtually every department we deal with. That's the kind of girl we want." There is, according to this same informant, one important exception to this rule. "The receptionist really ought to be from your state. After signing the guest book, all the visitors ask, 'And where are you from in ———?' "

7. Cf. M. Kriesberg, "What Congressmen and Administrators Think of the Polls," *Public Opinion Quarterly,* IX (Fall, 1945), 334.

with how they divide, pro and con, but the senators feel, quite correctly, that these figures are often misleading.

For one thing, nearly half of the legislative mail a senator receives is "inspired" or "pressure" mail. An experienced mail clerk can spot these quickly. These letters, while not without effect, are heavily discounted as manifestations of public opinion. In some offices, for example, this "pressure mail" is entirely excluded from the mail count. In others, it is counted separately.

Even the "genuine" or "spontaneous" legislative mail has severe limits as an index of constituency sentiment. Only a small minority of the American people ever write their congressmen and senators, and the letter writers are far from a representative sample of all voters.[8] The mail tends to overrepresent the views of the better educated, the well-to-do, the leisured, the politically articulate segments of the senator's constituency. Some people are chronic writers of letters to public officials. It seems to give them an experience of power, a sense of importance and social responsibility.[9] "You'd be surprised," one staff man said, "how often a person writes the senator just because he wants to get a reply from him that he can carry around in his pocket." Moreover, Americans "seem to be more ardent in opposition than in advocacy"; the people who fear that their side is going to lose a legislative skirmish are far more likely to write than those who feel reasonably assured of winning.[10] Finally, constituents tend to write senators with whom they agree, "people lend support to the man who holds their viewpoint rather than trying to change the opinion of an opponent."[11] For these reasons, perhaps along with other factors as well, the mail can give sensationally false pictures of mass sentiment.[12]

8. J. L. Woodward and E. Roper, "Political Activity of American Citizens," *American Political Science Review*, XLIV (December, 1950), 872-85, found that 20 per cent of a sample of the national electorate *said* that they had talked to a congressman *or other public official* to give them their opinion on a public issue during the preceding year.

9. R. Wyant, "Voting via the Senate Mailbag (I)," *Public Opinion Quarterly*, V (Fall, 1941), 359-82, and R. Wyant and Herta Herzog, "Voting via the Senate Mailbag (II)," *Public Opinion Quarterly*, V (Winter, 1941), 590-624, analyze this phenomenon well. Almost twenty years after they were written, these two articles are still among the best on this subject.

10. The language is from P. Douglas, "The Gap Between Congress and Main Street," *New York Times Magazine*, September 16, 1951, p. 56.

11. Wyant, "Voting" (I), *POQ*, p. 365.

12. One famous example of this occurred during the 1939 special session called by President Roosevelt to repeal the arms-embargo act. "The mail of House members, it has been estimated on the basis of samples, ran five to one *against* repeal; that of senators, even higher. Yet in a public opinion poll taken at that time 56 per cent of the sample favored repeal. . . ." A year later, "the situation repeated itself with selective service.

Why, then, do the senators have such great respect for the mail? One reason, and perhaps the most important, is the dearth of more reliable evidence. The sample survey is certainly the best means for determining mass attitudes, but it is far too expensive for the senators to use. The commercial polls by Gallup, Roper, and others publish national, not state-by-state, sounding.[13] Press comments, visits from constituents, and trips back home certainly provide evidence of public sentiment but can be just as misleading as the mail.

The senators' faith in the mail also reflects the fact that they are not just interested in the proportion of people who are for or against a measure; they are also interested in the intensity with which these opinions are held and the organizational strength of the antagonists. Constituents who feel very strongly about an issue are far more likely to remember it when the senator next comes up for re-election, usually some years in the future, and senators must concern themselves not just with votes, but with other sinews of political battle—money, volunteer labor, organization, loyalty, and enthusiasm. The mail tends to isolate, to identify, and to overrepresent the views of groups and individuals who feel strongly about a matter and who are best organized to do something about it.

These preoccupations are clearly indicated by the types of mail which influence senators most. Telegrams, they virtually all say, have less effect than any other kind of communication. They take very little time or trouble to send. Why did the sender not make his wishes known earlier and in more detail? Mimeographed and printed postcards supplied by an interest group are the next easiest way to communicate with senators—generally one need but supply a signature and drop it in the nearest mailbox. Next to telegrams, they carry the least weight. Identical letters also indicate that the senders were supplied with the contents of the letter and gave the matter relatively little thought, time, and attention. They are discounted as "pressure mail." Letters which show individual thought and initiative, especially if

---

Once again the 'isolationists' dominated the mail. In a sample of 35,000 letters to fourteen senators of different views, 90 per cent of the writers opposed the measure. Nevertheless, 70 per cent of a public opinion sample favored the proposed bill." Robert A. Dahl, *Congress and Foreign Policy* (New York: Harcourt, Brace and Company, 1950), p. 34.

13. Polls are taken by members of the House, apparently in increasing numbers. Most of these, however, are public relations gimmicks. The "sampling" is sloppy, the questions loaded, and the data on public attitudes obtained are of very dubious value. Cf. Harry Alpert, Carl Hawver, Frank E. Cantwell, Philip M. DeVany, and M. Kriesberg, "Congressional Use of Polls: A Symposium," *Public Opinion Quarterly*, XVIII (Summer, 1954), 121-42.

they are handwritten or are from a personal or political friend, usually are given the most weight.[14]

When the senators "vote against their mail," which they do far more often than outsiders realize, these qualitative considerations are often the reason. But these are not the only ones. Senators, like the rest of us, are captives of their own pasts. Once they have a clear and well-publicized stance on an issue, they are loath to abandon it even in the face of "pressure." They have their share, perhaps even more than their share of the normal ability to rationalize expedient behavior, but there is a limit to every senator's flexibility. To appear to be a man without principle, a "politician" who will favor anything that is popular, is not "good politics" in America. Moreover, senators often make commitments to party leaders, committee colleagues, and Senate friends which restrict their maneuverability. Most of the mail, as we have already seen, comes in toward the end of the legislative process, when bills receive the greatest publicity. By then, senators are often committed and rarely dare to back down. To do so often would not only destroy their self-respect but also their standing in the eyes of their colleagues. This can hamper their effectiveness in serving their constituents in the future.

Mail, while it may be the best single indication of the distribution and intensity of constituent opinion, often supplies this indication too late to be of much use. Much of the time—and this is especially the case in the area of his committee work—the senator must make up his mind before many of the letters have arrived. Even more often, there is no appreciable public reaction at all. Finally, when an issue does evoke a sizeable response from the senator's constituents, its meaning often is highly ambiguous. "Anyone who tells you that they know what public opinion is on an issue is crazy," one senator remarked. "You are never quite sure."[15]

"Cases": The Mail That Really Matters

Perhaps one-third of the average senator's mail presents "cases," the precise proportion varying from one senator to another. Some senators are extremely responsive to requests for favors, others less so. The

14. Cf. Kefauver and Levin, *Twentieth-Century Congress,* pp. 172 ff., R. E. Baldwin, *Let's Go Into Politics* (New York: Macmillan, 1952), pp. 154-55; J. Voorhis, *Confessions of a Congressman* (New York: Doubleday, 1947), pp. 53-54.

15. Another senator said, "Look—if you try to figure out what your constituents want on each issue and vote accordingly, you will soon have grey hair and be a one-termer, too."

word gets around and influences the character of the mail they receive.[16]

These requests for favors are received with a mixture of resentment and glee. Handling cases is tedious and time-consuming work, and a large majority of the time and energy of every senator's staff is devoted to this never-ending task. The more important and complex cases cannot be entirely delegated. The senator's personal participation in case work is a heavy burden; almost all senators complain that they do not have time to devote to the "important" part of their job— legislating. "If only the people would leave us alone," they say wistfully, "we could do our job the way it ought to be done." Moreover, the requests imply a certain disrespect for the senator and the dignity and importance of his office. The constituent's attitude often seems to be, "We pay him, why not use him."[17] Even some of the most hard-bitten Professional Politicians in the Senate profess shock at the outrageous, unethical, or clearly illegal actions which their constituents occasionally ask them to perform.

Case work involves the regular, day-to-day intervention by the senators and their staffs in the administrative process. This tends to reinforce the institutionalized suspicion which administrators have for legislators and vice versa. To the bureaucrats, the senators and their staffs appear as special pleaders for the narrow interests of their constituents even when these conflict with the "national welfare," which bureaucrats tend to equate with the over-all rules and programs of their agency or department to which the senators so often seek exception. To the senators and their staffs, the bureaucrats appear arbitrary, patronizing, and compulsively attached to formal rules and procedures even to the detriment of "justice." Witness this exchange between a former Assistant Secretary of Agriculture and a senator:

MR. APPELBY. I think perhaps the principal source of troubles with members of Congress is that they do not recognize how powerful they are.

SENATOR DOUGLAS. They feel very impotent and very helpless indeed with the civil service.

MR. APPELBY. So do the bureaucrats with members of Congress.

SENATOR DOUGLAS. We are completely ineffective.

MR. APPELBY. Representations from members of Congress weigh much more than members of Congress know, and that is the reason why I think

16. This is another area in which the behavior of one senator from a state influences the other: if one senator does not emphasize case work, the case burden of his colleague is increased.

17. Senator Fulbright in Subcommittee to Study Senate Concurrent Resolution 21 of the Senate Committee on Labor and Public Welfare, 82nd Congress, 1st Session, *Hearings*, p. 266.

they sometimes go overboard. They are trying to be effective and they speak with more force than is necessary for them in their position.

.   .   .   .

MR. DOUGLAS. I am struck with this air of excessive purity with which people in Washington who are not exposed to the rigors of winning elections put on about politicians . . . it always reminds me of the superior feeling that staff officers around headquarters had for the foot soldiers out in the field who did the dying.[18]

The costs of case work, measured in terms of lost time, dignity, and self-respect, are heavy.

Nonetheless, case work, properly done, has even greater political rewards. "The world's greatest publicity organ is still the human mouth," one senator's assistant said. "When you get somebody $25.00 from the Social Security Administration, he talks to his friends and neighbors about it. After a while the story grows until you've single-handedly obtained $2,500 for a constituent who was on the brink of starvation." The support gained in this fashion cuts across normal party and factional lines. It is a following, too, which is not likely to be affected by how the senator votes on issues. Good case work can contribute to the senator's maneuverability on matters of policy.

Over a six-year period most senators do a tremendous number of favors. "During the last year and a half," one senator from a large Eastern state said, "I have done favors for about 3,000 persons. When you consider the word-of-mouth spread, this amounts to a substantial number of voters." In the better-organized offices, a card file is kept on the cases in which the favors have been significantly large. This file can often be of great value later.[19]

Moreover, the constituents who turn to their senators for help are often "little people," small businessmen who do not belong to trade associations, for example.[20] To aid in the humanization of Big Gov-

18. *Ibid.,* pp. 175-76, 299-300.

19. "When we get a positive action of some significance in our case work," the administrative assistant to one Southern senator explained, "we add the man's name and address plus a report on what we have done for him to our card file of friends. The last time —— ran for re-election, we sent this file down to his campaign manager. His manager then wrote a personal letter to every person on that list, informing him that —— was facing opposition in the primary and would he help out. The response was amazing—75 to 80 per cent must have volunteered to help."

20. Even businesses with trade associations find that their Washington offices are quite reluctant to "run errands" for them. To do this for some members means that they might have to do it for all. Their staffs are seldom large enough to handle this burden. Moreover, many cases concern competition within a single industry for government contracts, etc. The trade association executive cannot afford to handle these matters. Thus, many trade associations and lobbies in Washington refer all the cases they receive to the sender's congressman and senators.

ernment is a worthy and satisfying job. "A senator can set a business back on its feet, saving a whole town from being parched of its only payroll. Sometimes, by a telephone call with muscle in it, he can see that personal justice is done and change the whole course of a family's life. A little problem? Not to the family—and being able to do that sort of thing brings one of the greatest inner rewards of public service."[21] Such gratification is especially welcome during the early years of service when opportunities for exercising legislative leadership are few.[22]

While all senators recognize the political importance of cases, they vary in the effectiveness with which they handle them. Some—in particular, the Professional Politicians with insecure seats—devote a large share of their own time and attention to pursuing cases. In other offices—the senior, the secure, the Amateur—these chores are most often delegated. Up to a point, the more personal attention a senator pays to his case work, the more likely he is to get prompt and favorable action from the executive branch. "Sometimes," one administrative assistant said, "we think that they [the bureaucrats] must all be sent to a school where they teach them that if a senator's office sends over a case with a 'buck slip' [routine note of referral] they can safely forget it; if the request is contained in a letter from the senator this demands more attention; if there is a call from the senator's staff, it's still more important; and if the senator calls himself, do it." But there is a point of diminishing returns. A senator who plays too active a personal role in case work is likely to expend his "credit" on relatively unimportant things and to diminish, through overuse, his influence on larger executive decisions. He is likely, too, to develop heavy political debts and, when a vote comes up in which the administration is interested, to be reminded of them. Then, too, excessive personal attention paid to case work detracts from the amount of time and energy a senator can devote to the legislative side of his job. A senator who goes too far in this direction violates the folkways, loses respect in the Senate, and is likely to lose some effectiveness as well.

A senator's committee assignments also influence the extent and locus of his influence on administrative decisions. Appropriations Committee members possess a type of leverage over the departments and agencies which is likely to be reflected in especial responsiveness "downtown." Members of other Senate committees seem to have the

21. B. Moody, "The United States Senate," *Holiday,* February 1954, p. 87.

22. Cf. L. Dexter, "Congressmen and the People They Listen To," (unpublished manuscript, 1955), Ch. VII, p. 5.

most luck with departments within the jurisdiction of their committees. A department's special friends and leading enemies in the Senate receive a little more than the usual treatment. ("You can be sure that the State Department used to think twice before turning down a request from Senator McCarthy.") Finally, a senator's party also seems to have some impact on his effectiveness as a case worker. Routine cases are handled by career civil servants in the departments and little, if any, party favoritism is likely to be shown, but a good many cases involve policy implications. Decisions on these are made at the politically sensitive higher level of department and agency management. For this type of case it helps to be a member of the president's party.

MENDING FENCES

Any inhabitant of Capitol Hill, from elevator operator to vice-president, will tell you that "the most effective kind of campaigning is done between elections." The incumbent senator who campaigns during the political off-season has no opponent. In the absence of an electoral fight, the voters are likely to perceive the senator as a senator rather than as a candidate or "politician." The prestige of the office is at its peak between elections; its incumbent gains stature and persuasiveness then, too.

Virtually all senators make brief visits back home during the session, as well as more extended trips during adjournment, to take advantage of this favorable atmosphere. The frequency and length of these trips vary, of course, according to the proximity of the senator's state, the security of the senator's seat and the nearness of the next election, the extent of the senator's Washington responsibilities, and his conception of his role. All senators are quite aware of the political potency of these visits. "I didn't go back and I got beat," is a frequent lament of the many former senators in the city.

These fence-mending trips are both exhilarating and exasperating experiences. They give the senators a sense that they have re-established personal rapport with the voters. "If you really want to know what they are thinking," there is no substitute for putting your own ear firmly to the ground. Fence-mending trips help in regaining perspective. "Ninety-nine per cent of what happens on Capitol Hill doesn't create a ripple back home," and all senators desperately need, from time to time, to relearn this lesson. A senator's well-publicized presence in the home state symbolizes that he has not forgotten the people who put him in power. These trips also provide an opportunity to give some attention to personal and business affairs.

But fence-mending is also "damned onorous." For one thing, trips back home conflict with the proper performance of legislative responsibilities. "I've seen many very good senators defeated because they wouldn't go home," mused a staff member of one of the senatorial campaign committees. "—— was a good example. I went around to see him a number of times and told him that he was in trouble and that he'd better get out there. But he, like all the others, said that he was too busy, that he had too many subcommittee meetings to attend." The pressure for conformity to Senate folkways is a major cause of constituency neglect.

Moreover, the trips are hard work. While at home, it is hard for a senator to insulate himself from constituent demands on his time and attention. As one senator said, "It's a little different there—people aren't satisfied by seeing one of the girls. They want to see *me*. Its difficult to get rid of them." Most of those who press for an audience are interested in cases. "You may have received thousands of letters from your constituents, many of them asking you to do something for them. When you go home they all want to know how their project is coming along. I can assure you that when they ask, I don't say, 'I can't remember your request and haven't the faintest idea how it's progressing.' How effective would that be? So you learn to equivocate."

Nor to the outside observer do these fence-mending trips appear to be reliable ways of probing constituent sentiment on issues. Without the most stubborn and conscientious efforts, a senator is almost certain to see and talk mostly with friends and supporters on such a trip. Since both categories are likely to be in general agreement with him, the image of constituency opinion he brings back to Washington is usually distorted in favor of his own views. This is, no doubt, a gratifying consequence of such visits. But the spurious support they provide to the senator's own patterns of thought can be dangerous.

A less arduous means of campaigning between elections is provided by radio and television. More than half of the postwar senators make regular weekly or bi-weekly broadcasts to the people back home. These shows, ostensibly "nonpolitical" reports to constituents, are usually fifteen-minute panel discussions filmed or taped at the government-owned Radio-Television Facility in the basement of the Capitol Building. The senator pays the costs of production and ships the films and tapes to stations in his state. These in turn, usually run them free of charge as a public service.[23]

23. A brief description of the Radio-Television Facility may be found in "Some Votes Are Made that Way—" *U.S. News and World Report*, July 15, 1955, pp. 70-71.

Both media are demanding and few senators are really first-rate performers. The audience they receive in competition with commercial programs is small. Yet, "even if they turn you off, they know that you are interested enough in them to make the report." Moreover, they can and do serve as a valuable antidote to a hostile or inaccurate newspaper press.

As primary time rolls around, the senator's reliance on radio and television declines. For one thing, when he becomes an official candidate, the stations will no longer broadcast his programs without charge. The costs of purchasing the time he received free of charge between electoral seasons is generally prohibitive. The nature of the programs changes, too. From "nonpolitical" panel shows, the trend is toward longer "documentaries" on the life and accomplishments of the senator and short "spot" announcements to be inserted in the stations' regular programming at peak audience hours.

The newsletter is another means by which the senator can reach his constituents without leaving Washington. "Usually two or three mimeographed sheets of 'news' chosen to show the writer as the parliamentary peer of Sir Winston Churchill," the newsletter's primary target is the rural weekly and semi-weekly press. Often, these newsletters are the only Washington news these papers receive. "Hundreds print them, gratefully, without changing a word."[24]

The rest of a senator's mailing list presents more of a problem. It may take years for a senator to develop a good list, and mailing lists become outdated rapidly. Most senators attempt to break their lists down into small homogeneous categories—lawyers, party officials, teachers, farmers—so that the proper form letters, reprints of speeches, and other materials may be sent to the appropriate persons. As a result, without constant attention, some people receive material which does not interest them, while others are likely to receive several franked copies of the same publication. This can and does make people mad.

As the burdens of office increase, the senators have placed increasing reliance on communication with their constituents through the mails, radio, and television. None of them finds this an adequate substitute for dealing with their constituents in person, but there seems to be no alternative.

CONSTITUENCY AND ROLL CALL VOTES

So far we have merely attempted to describe the stream of communications flowing from constituents to the senators and back again.

24. Russell Baker, " 'My Dear Constituents . . . ,' " *New York Times Magazine*, May 1, 1955, p. 14.

How much effect does this have on the senators? In previous chapters we have attempted to show how a senator's constituency affects his conformity to Senate folkways and "effectiveness," his committee preferences, and his working relations with lobbyists and reporters. Now we shall try to show how, and how much, his constituents affect his votes on Senate roll calls.

The United States Senate provides an unusual opportunity to explore this relationship since each constituency is represented by two men. If constituency "pressure" is all important, then the two men elected from each state should agree on virtually every issue. If a senator's constituency is unrelated to his voting, then we should find that the two senators from the same state vote together only by chance.

Figure 26 shows the frequency with which pairs of senators from the same state voted together on all the roll calls in 1951.[25] Eight of the forty-seven pairs for whom we have information voted on the same side of more than 90 per cent of the roll calls, seventeen voted together from 80 to 89 per cent of the time, and nine pairs voted together from 70 to 79 per cent of the time. Obviously, there is a decided tendency for the two senators from the same state to vote together,[26] but Figure 26 also shows that some pairs of senators regularly vote on opposite sides of the same issue. For example, during 1951, three pairs of senators voted together from 30 to 39 per cent of the time, four pairs voted together from 40 to 49 per cent of the time, and another pair voted together from 50 to 59 per cent of the time.

The principal reason for this disagreement appears to be party affiliation. The typical pair of senators from the same state and same party voted together over 80 per cent of the time in 1951. The "typi-

25. These figures were obtained from the *Congressional Quarterly Weekly Report*, January 4, 1952, pp. 16-17.

26. This does not necessarily mean that they do so entirely, or even partially, as a result of constituency "pressure" as usually conceived. We have already demonstrated in Chapters II and III that different types of constituencies tend to send different types of men to the Senate. States in which the union movement is very strong tend to elect men to the Senate who would be "liberals" *even if they were not in the Senate*, while states in which the preponderant view on race relations is segregationist tend to elect men who, as private citizens, are segregationists, and so on. There may be, therefore, a considerable congruence between the senator's private views (his "conscience") and the demands he hears from his constituents. Of course this "natural" harmony between the views of the senator and his constituents is never complete. A senator's constituencey is very large and often quite complex. He cannot possibly agree with everyone on everything or share their views with equal intensity, and we have argued earlier that service in the Senate tends to widen the gaps in perspective between the senators and their home-state supporters. Nonetheless, selective recruitment seems to explain much of the correspondence between senatorial voting and expressed constituency preferences.

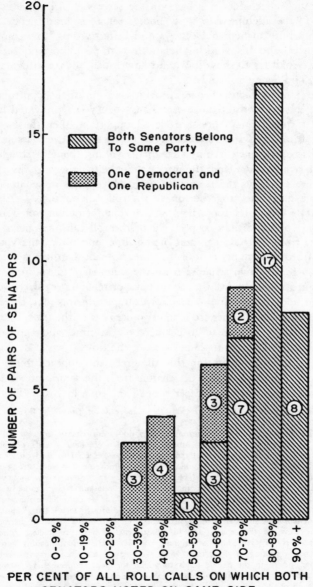

Fig. 26. Agreement of Pairs of Senators from Same State on All Roll Calls in 1951

cal" pair of senators from the same state but of different parties voted together slightly less than half of the time. Evidently, a senator's political party affiliation influences which groups in his constituency he chooses to "represent," since he cannot possibly represent them all. When the two senators from the same state belong to the same party, they tend to identify with similar groups and to have similar voting records. When they are of different parties, their electoral followings may be radically different even though contained within the confines of the same state.

The importance of a senator's party in defining his constituency varies in different state party systems. In one-party states, a single party includes almost the entire ideological spectrum. The significant political contests take place within the dominant party's primary and there is no single way in which all Democrats or all Republicans seek to build electoral majorities. The state party organizations, having little to do with the senator's election, have little leverage on them in office, so pairs of senators from one-party or modified one-party states are far more likely to diverge in their voting than those from the same party in the two-party states (Table 58).

Table 58

AGREEMENT OF PAIRS FROM SAME STATE AND PARTY ON ALL ROLL CALLS
IN 1951, BY TYPE OF STATE PARTY SYSTEM

Percentage of All Roll Calls Two Senators from Same State Voted Together	Type of State Party System		
	Two-Party	Modified One-Party	One-Party
90% plus	33%	9%	20%
80%-89%	60	36	40
70%-79%	7	27	30
60%-69%	0	18	10
50%-59%	0	9	0
	100%	100%	100%
	(15 pairs)	(11 pairs)	(10 pairs)

The degree of social and economic heterogeneity found within the state also shapes the extent to which its two senators vote together. Senators from the same party vote together more often if their state is either highly urban or highly rural than if it is a state containing substantial numbers of both urban and rural voters (Table 59).

Table 59

AGREEMENT OF PAIRS FROM THE SAME STATE AND PARTY ON ALL ROLL CALLS
IN 1951, BY URBAN-RURAL CHARACTER OF THE STATE

Percentage of All Roll Calls Two Senators From Same State Voted Together	Type of State		
	Rural (20%-39% Pop. Urban)	Mixed (40%-59% Pop. Urban)	Urban (60% Plus Pop. Urban)
80% plus	78%	56%	82%
70%-79%	11	31	9
60%-69%	11	6	9
50%-59%	0	6	0
	100% (9 pairs)	100% (16 pairs)	100% (11 pairs)

NOTE: The same relationship holds true, in slightly diluted form, when type of state party system is controlled.

While every state has two senators, they are not elected at the same time. Some are elected in presidential years, others in off-year elections. The balance of forces within a state may be appreciably different in these two circumstances. Moreover, the climate of political opinion changes. Men elected from the same state at different times may have run on quite different issues. In 1946, for example, popular desire for "normalcy" plus frustration with wartime regulations over consumer goods were the salient and winning issues in many senatorial campaigns. The sizeable number of conservatives elected that year were called, without too much exaggeration, "meat-rationing senators." In 1948, President Truman and his Democratic colleagues were able to re-establish the primacy of pocketbook issues in the minds of many voters. As a result, many economic liberals were elected to the Senate. In 1950, the issue was "communism." A number of men were elected to the Senate largely, if not entirely, because of their skillful exploitation of this issue.

The importance of the senator's initial "mandate"—partially self-defined, partially reflecting popular sentiment—is hard to overestimate. Senators, once in office, establish working relationships with like-minded senators and understandings and friendships with sympathetic lobbyists, administrators, and reporters that are difficult to change. They quickly make a public record, and it is often unwise to alter it drastically.

This phenomenon is suggested graphically in Figure 27. In the figure, the distribution of conservatism-liberalism scores is presented for the entire Senate during the Eightieth through the Eighty-fourth Congresses. There were sizeable shifts in the ideological make-up of the Senate during this ten-year period, but this was not the result, for the most part, of incumbent senators shifting their positions. Note that "the class of 1947" maintains very much the same ideological complexion during the entire ten-year period. The "class of 1949" has its ideological center of gravity well to the left during the entire period. Nor apparently has there been much change in the over-all stance on issues of those elected in 1950. A senator's initial "mandate," therefore, may be a major influence on his voting many years after it was received.[27] Since the two senators from the same state were elected at different times, they may interpret the wants and needs of their state quite differently.

United States senators are not ciphers, they are "not equivalent to the steel ball in a pinball game, bumping passively from post to post down an inclined plane."[28] They are complicated human beings. They bring with them into the Senate their own sets of interests, biases, and predispositions. These are reflected in their roll call votes. Figure 28 demonstrates this point pretty clearly. The average conservatism-liberalism scores for all the senators serving during the Eighty-first Congress have been plotted on the graph, by party and type of constituency. We see that the Democrats from Northern, urban states are the most liberal; Northern Democrats from rural states, next most liberal; and so on down to the most conservative group, the Republicans from urban, interior states. The average conservatism-liberalism scores of senators with four different types of backgrounds and careers have also been plotted: the Amateurs with intellectual backgrounds, the Professional Politicians with urban-ethnic group backgrounds, the Professional Politicians with rural backgrounds, and the Amateurs with business backgrounds. Their mean conservatism-liberalism lines tend to slope downward from left to right. This suggests that regard-

27. Figure 27 by itself does not conclusively demonstrate this point. It is possible that the similar ideological make-up of the Senate "classes" in different Congresses could exist despite considerable fluctuations in the conservatism-liberalism scores of individual members. Such, however, is not the case. The individual senators show marked consistency in their ideological positions from one Congress to the next. Cf. D. R. Brimhall and A. S. Otis, "Consistency in Congressional Voting," *Journal of Applied Psychology,* XXXII (February, 1948), pp. 1-14.

28. D. B. Truman, *The Governmental Process* (New York: Alfred A. Knopf, 1951), p. 332.

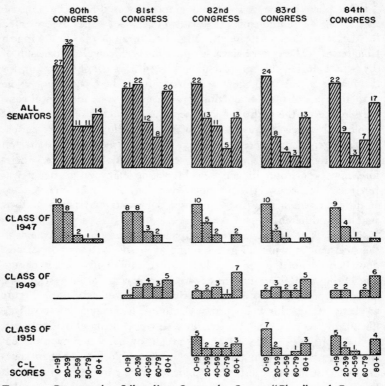

FIG. 27.   Conservatism-Liberalism Scores, by Senate "Class" and Congress

less of the senators' personal backgrounds, men from liberal areas tend
to be liberal, those from conservative areas tend to be conservative.

But, and this is the important point for present purposes, the intel-
lectual-Amateurs have a consistently more liberal record, and the rural-
Professionals, a consistently more conservative one than the average
senator regardless of their party or the nature of their constituency.
The situation with regard to the other career types is a little more
complex.   The urban-ethnic Professionals are certainly a liberal group
in the Senate, but they become senators only under the most liberal
circumstances—in the Democratic party in the North.   For Northern
Democrats they are less liberal than the average.   The very few busi-
nessmen-Amateur Democrats are very liberal, and the Republicans
with the same career types are very conservative.   Evidently, a busi-

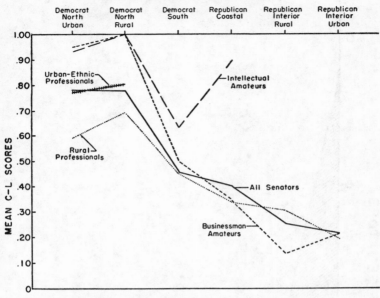

FIG. 28.   Mean Conservatism-Liberalism Scores of Types of Senators, by Party and Type of Constituency, 81st Congress

ness background combined with political inexperience is associated among senators with an extremist rather than with either a left or right position.   At any rate, this analysis shows that the senators' personal backgrounds are related to their over-all position on issues, independent of the effects of party affiliation and constituency pressures.

What then does this all add up to?   What does the analysis contained in this section tell us about the effects of the senators' constituents upon their roll call voting?

First of all, it suggests that a constituency as large as a state can be "represented" in many different ways.   Up to some point, the senators are free to choose which groups and interests within their formal constituency they will champion.   The senators' party, in two-party states, largely commits them to one approach in satisfying their constituents, yet this is not the case for the men from one-party or modified one-party areas, where apparently each senator has greater discretion in defining his own constituency.   Senators from socially and economically heterogeneous states also enjoy greater maneuverability, along

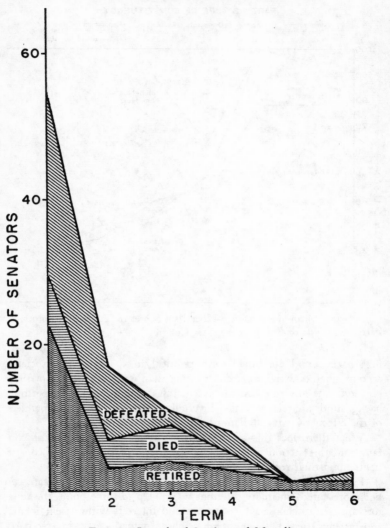

Fig. 29. Length of Service and Mortality

with greater risks. The senators' initial mandates provide them with a political "set" which survives for quite a long time. Since senators are elected at different times, when political conditions and moods are different, they sometimes see things differently even when they share identical formal constituencies. Finally, senators have different back-grounds, careers, values, and group identifications which do not vanish when they become legislators. These, too, affect how they define their constituencies.

THE POLITICAL LIFE-CYCLE OF THE SENATOR

"Most of them could make this a lifetime job, if they handled it right," remarked one senatorial campaign manager a few years ago. Other members of this hard-headed craft agreed. Most senators do not succeed in doing so. Figure 29 presents the outlines of the story. During the postwar decade, 180 men and women served in the Senate. Of these, fifty-five served for one term or less. Only seven of these "single-termers" died in office. The remainder were either defeated or, what is fairly often the same thing, "voluntarily" retired. Senate mortality declines very sharply thereafter. Only seventeen dropped out during their second term, and ten of these were defeated in pri-maries or general elections. From then on, political defeat became even rarer. Death and retirement accounted for most of the Senate mortality beyond the third term. To look at the figures in a slightly different way, 61 per cent of all the defeats suffered by postwar incum-bent senators occurred during their first six years of service.

What kinds of senators survive? What kinds are most often de-feated?

First of all, the extent of the senators' pre-Senate political experience is related to their lasting power in the institution (Table 60). Of the sixty-two Amateur Politicians among the senators studied, 41 per cent had been defeated in a primary or general election by January of 1957, 24 per cent had retired, and 13 per cent had died. The Agitators had the second highest mortality rate; 22 per cent of them were beaten in electoral contests and 33 per cent retired. The most experienced poli-

Table 60

MORTALITY AND CAREER TYPE

Pre-Senate Career Type	Defeated	Retired	Died	Total Mortality	
Amateurs	41%	24%	13%	78%	(62)
Professionals	21%	15%	11%	47%	(96)
Patricians	15%	15%	8%	38%	(13)
Agitators	22%	33%	0%	55%	(9)

NOTE: Mortality figured until January, 1957.

ticians upon their first election—the Professionals and Patricians—displayed the greatest staying power. Only 21 per cent of the Professionals and 15 per cent of the Patricians were defeated, and only 15 per cent of each type retired.

The manner in which they first became senators also shapes their chances during the critical first re-election bid. Men who were initially appointed to the Senate did less well than those who first became senators after an electoral contest. Only 39 per cent of the senators who were appointed to the office won re-election, while 75 per cent of those initially elected did. This is the case partly because many men appointed to the Senate to fill vacancies were "seat-warmers," men who were chosen by their state governors precisely because they had no chance of election to the post and no desire to hold it permanently, and who would retire from the scene after relatively short service. Over a third of the men initially appointed to the Senate retired, more or less gracefully, at the end of their first period of service, while only 7 per cent of the elected senators did.

Even when one discounts for this factor, the elected senators did better in their first re-election efforts. Eighty-one per cent of the initially elected senators who sought re-election won; only 59 per cent of the appointed senators who sought re-election achieved it. The several reasons for this seem obvious. Men who are appointed to the Senate to fill a vacancy often serve very brief periods of time, perhaps only a year or so, before they must run in their own right. This often does not provide the time for an adequate "build-up" before election day. The elected men, who are generally elected to a full six-year term, usually have a longer period of time in which to make preparations for the critical first re-election contest. Moreover, they have the added advantage of a long publicity build-up during their initial campaign. Too, they have shown potential rivals and political contributors that they have sufficient popularity to win the office once, while the appointed senator is often an unknown quantity.

A third factor, of greater long-range significance, is the degree of party competition in the senators' states (Table 61). Twenty-three senators from one-party states ran for initial re-election, and all twenty-three of them won. Those from the stronger party in modified one-party states were considerably less successful in their first effort at re-election; only 77 per cent of them won. Seventy-five per cent of the senators from two-party states won in their first try at re-election, while only one-third of the senators from the weaker party in modified one-party states were successful in gaining re-election.

Table 61

THE ELECTORAL RISKS OF INCUMBENTS, BY STATE PARTY SYSTEMS

		Percentage of Time Incumbent Won			
Number of Re-election Bid	*One-Party*	*Modified One-Party, Senator in Stronger Party*	*Two-Party*	*Modified One-Party, Senator in Weaker Party*	*All Senators*
1st	100% (23)	77% (35)	75% (77)	33% (6)	80% (141)
2nd	100% (19)	78% (14)	81% (30)	50% (2)	84% (65)
3rd	86% (7)	83% (6)	92% (12)	0% (0)	88% (25)
4th plus	67% (6)	50% (4)	60% (5)	0% (0)	57% (15)

This is not surprising. The intriguing figures in the table are those on electoral risks for subsequent re-election contests. The one-party state senators not only won all of their first re-election bids but all of their second re-election bids as well. They did noticeably less well from then on. Eighty-six per cent won in third re-election campaigns, and only 67 per cent won in all re-election campaigns beyond the third. Evidently, the risk of defeat begins to increase significantly for one-party-state senators after about twelve years of service.

A different pattern of risks prevails for the senators from modified one-party and two-party states. Their chances of winning their first re-election are significantly lower than are those from one-party areas. Yet if they survive this crisis, their chances for electoral survival tend to increase. By the time they are ready to run for a third re-election (and not many of them survive that long), their chances of success are as good as those from one-party states. Beyond that point, however, their re-election chances, as those for men from one-party states, decline very sharply.

The most hopeless situation is possessed by the senators from the weaker party in modified one-party areas. Apparently, in most cases, their initial election was the result of a serious division within the stronger party. At any rate, only one in three was successful in winning a second term. Once past that hurdle, however, their electoral chances went up somewhat; they won bids for a third term exactly half of the time.

These figures suggest that the senators, in their relations with their constituents, go through what might be called a political life-cycle. Not all of them go through the entire cycle, yet some of them do.

Once seated, a senator is hard to beat under most circumstances;

the prestige of the office rubs off, even on very ordinary senatorial timber. The senator's influence on the distribution of federal patronage helps him to build a personal "machine" quickly and to insure that the state party organization is loyal. Aggressively pursued case work provides him with a larger circle of friends. He has the publicity edge on almost any challenger. His seniority and legislative know-how are valuable to his constituents, and many of them know it.

If the senator survives the first challenge to his position, then he becomes more secure than before. All the advantages he possessed at his first re-election bid are even more compelling now. But with greater seniority and security go additional legislative responsibilities. By the end of his second term, he is, in all likelihood, a senior member of major committees. He is well on the way to becoming an important national figure, increasingly concerned with pressing national and international problems. In the vocabulary of social psychology, his "reference groups" change, he becomes more concerned with Senate, national, and international problems, and devotes less time and attention to the folks back home. The press of legislative duties becomes ever harder to escape. Advancing years make fence-mending trips increasingly onerous. Senility, real or apparent, may become a political problem. Yet "once you are in [the Senate], you can't quit voluntarily. In order to do so you have to break with your friends. They are terrified at the slightest hint that you might retire."

Meanwhile, there have been changes in the character of his state, and it is difficult to alter publicly staked-out positions and group relationships formed when circumstances were different. "I had been away from the state for twenty-eight years," one former senator explained. "A whole new generation of voters had come along and a lot of them thought I was too old. I didn't get back to the state as often as I used to. I couldn't, I was working too hard. Most of my old friends had passed away." Thus, as a senator's power and prominence approaches a peak, his electoral support is crumbling. Beyond a third term, the senior senator has less chance of gaining re-election than a freshman! The cycle reaches its bitter end when a Herman Talmadge runs rough-shod over a Walter George, a Price Daniel frightens a Tom Connally out of a Texas primary fight, a Mike Monroney bowls over an Elmer Thomas, an Albert Gore defeats a Kenneth McKellar, a John M. Butler beats a Millard Tydings, a Frank Barrett upsets a Joe O'Mahoney. Not many senators survive to the end of this political life-cycle, but for the few who do, defeat suffered at the peak of their careers provides a cruel reminder of their constituents' power.

CHAPTER XI

Action on the Floor

NEAR THE CLOSE of the 1951 session, Senator Matthew Neely of West Virginia rose to his feet, pointed to a hundred-pound stack of *Congressional Records* upon his desk which recorded the session's proceedings, and accused his colleagues of being "irrepressible windbags." Comparing the Senate to the Tower of Babel, he beseeched all senators with speeches in their bosoms to deliver them during recess "in highly secluded places . . . where the only auditors will be hoot owls, turkey buzzards, and shitepokes. These, when vexed, as they certainly would be, could take the wings of the morning, noon or night and fly far, far away."[1]

Senator Neely expressed his views in a style—as encrusted with verbal flourishes and biblical allusions as Victorian mansions are with cupolas and stained-glass windows—which has now largely passed from the Senate scene. But his sentiments were up-to-date. Most senators are appalled and bored by the outpouring of words in the chamber. Perhaps no point of view is more universally popular among them than that most of this talk is meaningless.

THE NATURE OF "DEBATE"

A debate, as this author understands it, is a face-to-face contest between two or more speakers before a common audience. This situation occurs infrequently in the Senate. Most of the time senators do not debate; they talk.

1. *Washington Post and Times Herald,* January 19, 1958.

During the morning hour, which usually extends from noon until
2:00 P.M., senators are free to insert materials in the *Record* by unanimous consent, to make short speeches on any subject, and to conduct
other routine business. Almost all of this activity is "strictly for home
consumption," and the half-dozen or so senators awaiting their turns
in the chamber rarely pay much attention to what their colleagues are
saying. Almost never do they rise to challenge a point or object to
the insertion of materials in the *Record* no matter how repugnant it
may be. Reciprocity rules the day.[2]

At the close of the morning hour, the Senate turns its attention to
pending business. Here one might reasonably expect real debate.
Most of the time he does not find it.

"Debate" on a bill tends to go through a number of stages. The
first speeches are made by the floor managers—the leading protagonists
and antagonists of the measure. Usually, as the bill's sponsor, committee or subcommittee chairmen, or senior members of the committee
reporting the bill, these men are experts in their fields. If the bill is
both important and controversial, their addresses are likely to be long,
set speeches, delivered from a manuscript. Usually prepared, at least
in part, by experts on committee staffs, in the executive departments,
or employed by interested lobbying groups, these speeches tend to
be dispassionate, technical, and factual. A handful of the speaker's
friends and supporters listen, largely as a matter of courtesy.[3] Sometimes they will ask the speaker to yield for a question. More often
than not, the questioning goes like this:

2. Sometimes a freshman learns this the hard way. Witness this story in the *New
York Times,* March 18, 1957: "Last Tuesday Senator Styles Bridges, Republican of
New Hampshire, rose to make a few remarks about the proxy battle being waged by
the Penn-Texas Corporation to get control of Fairbanks, Morse and Co. Mr. Bridges
said that he had made a speech in the Senate fifteen years ago about the 'questionable
activities' of Fairbanks-Morse, he thought it still pertinent, and he asked unanimous
consent, etc.

" 'I object,' someone cried.

"The president's gavel halted in midair. The clock stopped. A hush fell over the
chamber.

"The objector was the freshman senator from Ohio, Frank J. Lausche. He explained that he did not think the august halls of Congress should be used to air views
in a proxy fight.

"Mr. Bridges desired to say, 'If Senators are going to start objecting to requests, I
will return the compliment manifold.' "

Majority leader Johnson intervened as peacemaker and Lausche's objection was withdrawn.

3. The attendance of like-minded members is not an accident. Aides of the senator
giving a speech often ask the assistants of like-minded senators to get their bosses on
the floor.

MR. MANSFIELD: Mr. President, will the Senator yield?

MR. SMITH of New Jersey. I yield.

MR. MANSFIELD. Is it not a fact that the amendment could create serious difficulties in our relations with Japan and that the impact on Japan of the amendment might tend to push Japan toward the Communist orbit?

MR. SMITH of New Jersey. I agree with the Senator from Montana.

MR. MANSFIELD. Does the Senator from New Jersey believe that if Japan loses some of its markets in this country, ways and means would be found by which to take up the slack, perhaps in Red China; and that perhaps the opening of the market would be sufficiently important to us to recognize the significance of the position which Japan occupies in the world today?

MR. SMITH of New Jersey. That is a problem which we discussed in the Committee on Foreign Relations, and I am glad that the Senator from Montana has called attention to it. We do not wish to push Japan into a horse trade with Communist countries. Japan must find some way of solving its problems. Japan is willing to find a solution of the problem which will be satisfactory to the United States and to our industries, and it is willing to agree to a proper distribution of its textile exports.

MR. MANSFIELD. Mr. President, will the Senator yield further?[4]

When the opposition takes the floor, usually with an equally long and scholarly speech, there is heavy turnover in the Senate audience. A few of the opposition speaker's friends and colleagues appear, while most adherents of the other side quietly slip away to the cloakrooms or their offices. The "debate" remains, for the most part, an exchange of mutually agreeable remarks.[5]

After the principal antagonists have had their say—and this can sometimes consume several days—other committee members and specialists on the bill speak, again usually to small, friendly audiences. As the "debate" progresses towards resolution, however, its character also changes. The chamber's acknowledged experts have had their say, the less well informed take the floor. By now, the party leaders have very likely negotiated a unanimous-consent agreement limiting debate to a specified number of hours for each side. This means that the speeches are not only less well informed but also shorter. All the major arguments have been made many times before. The temptation to score debater's points and to resort to flamboyant language is therefore increased. As time for the vote approaches, the chamber gradually begins to fill. The audience becomes larger and more heterogeneous. Hostile questioning becomes common. The final minutes,

---

4. *Congressional Record* (Daily Edition), June 28, 1956, p. 10183.

5. The similarity of this situation to grass-roots political discussion during presidential campaigns should be noted. See B. Berelson, P. F. Lazarsfeld, and W. N. McPhee, *Voting* (Chigaco: University of Chicago Press, 1954), p. 106.

devoted to a hurried reiteration of the arguments of both sides, are debate in the ordinary sense of the word.

Actually, of course, the talk is not as neat as this sounds. The senators giving the longer speeches are constantly interrupted by quorum calls, by other senators seeking to say a few words on another matter or belatedly attempting to insert material in the Appendix of the *Record*. The floor leaders may wish to announce the next day's schedule or the terms of a unanimous-consent agreement or to seek quick passage of a noncontroversial measure. Technically, the speaker need not yield for these purposes, but the spirit of reciprocity suggests permissiveness. All senators can, and sometimes do, waste many hours waiting around the chamber to obtain the chair's recognition in order to conduct relatively minor matters. If a speaker freely yields to the convenience of others, he can expect similar treatment for himself.

Most of the time, Senate debate lacks drama and excitement. Since most members have already made up their minds, the audience is pitifully small and often inattentive.[6] Moreover, the senators tend to listen to the speakers with whom they agree and to absent themselves when the opposition takes the floor. The debate is not sharply focused but skips from one subject to the next in an apparently chaotic manner. "I wonder," one old reporter once said, "if in the whole history of the Senate two speeches in a row ever were made on the same subject."[7] Usually the talk lacks the literary grace, wit, and adversary character of debate in the British House of Commons or other parliamentary bodies patterned after this splendid model. Yet it is far more informed than the House of Commons' debate, especially during the early stages. To hear a Clinton Anderson expound on atomic energy, a Hubert Humphrey on agricultural problems, a Mike Mansfield on foreign policy, a Eugene Millikin on taxation, a Robert Taft on labor, or a Joseph O'Mahoney on antitrust legislation is to be impressed by their mastery of highly complex and technical fields. It may not be debate, but it is political talk of a very high order.

Still, it changes few votes. Why do the senators engage in this seemingly futile exercise?

6. Of course a senator need not attend the debate to be exposed to the argument, since a more or less verbatim account of what transpires will be contained in the next morning's *Congressional Record*. While this substantially increases the size of the Senate audience for the debates, it does not alter the basic point made here. Senators read the *Record*, as they attend the debate, selectively, and tend to pay more attention to arguments that agree with their biases or conclusions than to opposition arguments.

7. Arthur Edson in an Associated Press column, *Washington Post and Times Herald*, June 16, 1959.

THE FUNCTIONS OF "DEBATE"

Some members, as Senator Neely so quaintly suggested, "just get a bang out of hearing themselves talk."[8] Fortunately, most of those who are tempted to "feed their egos" at the expense of their colleagues' time and patience are discouraged by the not so subtle social pressures described in Chapter V. A handful persist in their highly vocal ways to the obvious irritation of their colleagues and at the expense of their own effectiveness.

The most frequent motivation for taking the Senate floor, manuscript in hand, is something different. The speech is expected to pay off politically. It will please some constituents back home. It may help build up the senator nationally. Perhaps it will settle a political debt to, or build up credit with, Senate colleagues—personal friends, the party leader, the committee chairman. A speech can serve the same end in a senator's dealings with lobbyists, journalists, and the administration.

But motivations must not be confused with functions. The reasons for senators talking on the floor are one thing; the contribution made by this talk to the operation of the Senate is quite another. Viewed in this light, Senate debate takes on a new importance.

In the first place, debate in the Senate, while it does not change many votes, does serve as an important means of communication between advocates. Bills that reach the floor are backed by a coalition of senators, congressmen, staff assistants, lobbyists, voters, and administrators and, if the bill is at all controversial, are opposed by a similar coalition. Communication between advocates is not always simple and "signals passing between leaders and followers are by no means always given behind the scenes. Floor statements are often the quickest and most effective method of passing the word around. . . ."[9] Moreover, the arguments made over and over again in debate tend to reinforce the commitments of supporters, to whip up enthusiasm among the group, and to activate the latent predispositions of those whose over-all

8. The former staff aide to one such senator describes his boss in the following words: ". . . he is inclined to speech-making both in public and in private. He will enter his office in the morning after a forty-five minute drive full of ideas acquired in the forty-five minutes of privacy. He immediately begins talking, or dictating, trying out ideas—they seem to have no validity until he has spoken them and got them in the best phrasing he can. This is part of his technique of persuasion, and he practices it on himself as well as on others. . . . It is a necessity for him to have someone to talk with. . . ." C. E. Gilbert, "Problems of a Senator," (Ph.D. dissertation, Northwestern University, 1955), pp. 52, 58.

9. B. M. Gross, *The Legislative Struggle* (New York: McGraw-Hill, 1953), p. 366. Gross's analysis was particularly helpful in writing this section.

policy positions are congenial but who remain uncommitted. Debate serves an important function for the senators as individuals, too. Making a "yes" or "no" decision on most policy matters is very difficult and always involves an element of rather arbitrary judgment. Debate is a means by which senators can express the intensity of their approval of, or opposition to, a measure; in effect it permits them to vote 65 per cent "yes" or 90 per cent "no." They are aware that a few bad decisions—sometimes one will do the trick—can end their political careers. Doubts and second thoughts are inevitable. Participation in debate can and does put many of these fears to rest. "He really didn't feel strongly about it at first," one staff member remarked about his boss and his floor leadership of a highly controversial bill. "Only as the fight progressed and he had to argue for the bill and defend it from attacks, did he become convinced that it should pass." In addition to quieting doubts, the debate provides ready-made justifications—rationalizations, if you wish—to be used in the event that his vote becomes the subject of controversy back home.

Debate is also a means of delaying the final vote. Usually, this is done so as to permit more time for intra-Senate negotiations and cloakroom lobbying. At other times, by delaying the vote, one side hopes to enlarge the group of citizens aware of the issue and thereby favorably to alter the balance of forces on the bill. Several days' delay, accompanied by massive publicity and heroic efforts to stimulate mail, telegrams, and telephone calls by the senators' lobbyist allies, can sometimes pick up a few votes that otherwise might not have materialized. Those who engage in this tactic, and almost all senators do at one time or another, often argue that such purposely prolonged debate is intended to be "educational," that it sticks to the merits or demerits of the bill in question, while a filibuster is pure parliamentary obstruction. This dividing line is very hard to draw, nor is it particularly important to do so.[10]   Delay through debate can be used, not only to give additional time for "public opinion" to make itself felt, but also as a means of wringing concessions from the opposition or even the defeat of a bill regardless of popular sentiment. This does not happen very often. The point is that it always could happen, and the threat of a filibuster can sometimes be more effective than the real thing.

10. Perhaps one reason for the frequency with which an effort is made to draw this distinction is that Senate liberals—ideologically committed to the notion of strict majority rule and opposed to filibustering—so often find it necessary to resort to prolonged debate in order to arouse their broad, often unorganized and inattentive, followings.

Debate lays a basis for future campaigns. Embalming all of the facts and arguments in the *Record* can assure the losers that their positions will not be forgotten the next time a similar measure comes before Congress. The losers can, through building a substantial opposition record, demonstrate and symbolize the lack of consensus on the measure. "For the winning side, [speeches] help in the task of keeping the campaign alive until victory is won in the other house, in the conference committee, or at the stage of presidential signature. For either side, when a bill is due to become law, they help prepare the ground for carrying on the contest in the administrative and judicial arenas. An innocent-sounding explanation of a section or clause, totally ignored by most members of Congress when first made, may later be used as proof of 'congressional intent' and become highly important in administrative or judicial decisions."[11]

Finally, despite much folklore to the contrary, Senate speeches *do* influence votes. Most of the time, as we have already argued, they reinforce or activate votes, not change them. On almost every bill, there are a few members who are unable to make up their minds until the last minute, and when floor amendments raise new and unanticipated questions, a sizeable number of senators may be susceptible to a skillful speechmaker who provides them with a simple, appealing, and defensible justification for voting his way.

THE PROCESS OF DECISION

In earlier chapters we have shown that the senator's voting is affected by a number of different factors—his own personal background and beliefs, pressures from his constituents and lobbies, his party affiliation and leadership, committee recommendations, and the like—but we have not as yet attempted to describe the process by which senators make up their minds. This is an incredibly difficult thing to do. Nonetheless, a few generalizations can be made on the process of decision which not only are of interest in and of themselves, but which provide at least some clues to the relative importance of the various factors.

Specialization and Time of Decision

Most senators specialize. That is, as we have already seen, they tend to focus their attention upon a relatively narrow range of public policy. The reasons for this are several and compelling: the bulk and diversity of legislative measures, the pressure of nonlegislative tasks, the desire to maximize their legislative impact, pressure from their

11. Gross, *Legislative Struggle*, p. 367.

colleagues, and fear of retaliation if they upset someone else's apple cart. These factors tend to encourage this narrowing of attention.

At least three considerations enter into the senator's choice of specialty. One of these is his personal background. If he is a former economist or Secretary of Agriculture, for example, he is likely to want to focus his energies on the subject in which he possesses some skill. Moreover, his colleagues will very likely turn to him for advice on such matters, thus forcing a specialty upon him whether he wants it or not. Another factor, more important in most cases, is the senator's perceptions of the interests of his present and possible future constituents. Most senators try to specialize in areas of policy of particular interest to the folks back home. Yet in most states, the interests of his constituents are sufficiently varied to permit considerable range of choice, hence the importance of the perceptual element. Finally, the area of policy in which a senator specializes depends upon his committee assignments.

Of course, over the long run, there is a tendency for these factors to converge. And the senator's personal background is likely to reflect, to some extent, the interests of his constituents. Senators try hard to get on committees that concern the folks back home. But the seniority rule, the limited supply of seats on committees with jurisdiction over especially popular policy areas, and the complexity of their constituencies insure that the senators are not always on the committee that handles the bills of special interest and importance to them and their constituents. While the informal division of attention and skill in the Senate is closely related to the formal committee structure, it is by no means identical.

The specialists generally make up their minds on bills within their focus of attention very early in the legislative process. They are, after all, personally and politically interested in the subject. They have, especially if they have served in the Senate for any length of time, committed themselves to one side or the other in previous years. Both their interests and biases are known by other senators and lobbyists, who do their best to get early and favorable public decisions from them. Many of the specialists have sat through the committee hearings on the bill and have been forced to take a position by committee proceedings. They may even have sponsored (or co-sponsored)[12] the matter under consideration.

12. The Senate practice of co-sponsorship is, in the eyes of a number of senators, "getting to be a racket." It forces senators to enter into premature or casual commitments which can sometimes prove to be highly embarrassing. "If a senator is able to peddle his bill around among other senators, either by mail or in person, until

Making up his mind at the committee stage or earlier, the specialist is confronted with a very different political situation from that of the nonspecialist. The chances are, for instance, that he has experienced very little "pressure" from the bulk of his constituents before he makes a decision—most of the mail, telegrams, and delegations pour in after the bill has hit the floor and the headlines. The organized interests have, of course, made their positions abundantly clear in committee hearings and through direct, personal lobbying, but a specialist-senator is usually in the unhappy position of having to anticipate the reactions of broader publics on the basis of little evidence. Of course, the lobbyists can be of some help here, but once a senator has established a reputation as being for or against certain policies he is seldom approached by unfriendly lobbyists. Thus the estimates of the electoral consequences that he hears are overwhelmingly one-sided. Finally, the specialist knows that even though he must take a stand early in the game he is expected to stick with it. To back down under pressure is to lose esteem in the eyes of his colleagues.

The voting situation of the nonspecialist is very different. His personal interests lie elsewhere and, often, so do those of his constituents. He makes up his mind later in the legislative process and is less likely to have a fixed position on such matters. He is more susceptible to "pressure" from party leaders, lobbyists, and constituents. Lacking other clear-cut cues, he will very often fall back on the advice of one or more of his specialist colleagues.

Patterns of Advice Giving and Advice Taking

"I try, and I think most other senators try," one senator said, "to read the report on a bill before voting on it, but I must admit that I have voted on many hundreds of bills solely on the basis of what other senators told me about them." Another senator—this one a Southern Democrat—said: "If Senator George tells me that he has studied a bill and that it's good legislation, I'll vote for it without knowing a damned thing about it. And so will a lot of other senators." Advice giving and advice taking is, therefore, a vital part of the Senate in operation. But what factors determine which colleagues a senator consults? Which specialist does he choose to follow and why?

---

he obtains a majority of the Senate, and they become committed to the bill by joint introduction, of what value is it to have committees?" Senator Alben Barkley, *Congressional Record* (Daily Edition), April 25, 1956, pp. 6214-15. One of Senator Barkley's last official acts was the introduction of a joint resolution prohibiting the practice of co-sponsorship. The resolution did not emerge from the Rules Committee.

First of all, it takes some time for the senator to learn who knows what. Until he does, the freshman is likely to fall back on the other sources of advice. One such source is his own personal staff. (Since they are also often green and, in any case, do not have time to do a thorough and independent research job on all bills outside their boss's span of attention, they are likely to seek advice from members of committee staffs. The advice giving and advice taking occur at a different level, but they still take place.) The senior senator from his own state, especially if he is of the same party, is an easily available source of advice and assistance to the new senator, and during the early months of service the almost inevitable competition between the two usually has not reached serious proportions. Brand-new senators are often disproportionately influenced by the party leadership, as well.

As his seniority increases, the senator fits more neatly into the existing patterns of advice giving and advice taking. What then determines which of the competing specialists a senator decides to follow?

One important factor is the specialists' intra-Senate prestige. One former senator made the point quite well: "If I were not on the Agriculture Committee and had to vote on the farm bill under consideration right now, I would go to Senator ———— or some other member of the committee and ask him about it. If he were a *higher-type senator like* ————, he would give me a straight story." The advice seeker is most likely to approach a man he respects and trusts, a man who will give a fair and considered answer to the query: "What will it do to my state?" The relationship between the two senators' voting records also has substantial impact on who consults whom. One knowledgeable administrative assistant to a New England Republican explained his boss's choice of specialists on agricultural legislation in the following fashion: "The farm bill coming up is a highly technical matter of little concern to our state. The senator, who knows very little about it, will follow the advice of Senator ————. The senator respects ————. They have very similar political positions, and ———— will look at it from a New England point of view. Probably, he will have come to the same conclusion that my boss would have reached if he had had time to study it." Sometimes on relatively unpartisan issues the lines of consultation cross party lines. Some of the very senior Southern Democrats have substantial followings among Republicans, while some Republicans have influence among Democrats, but the normal pattern on most issues is for advice giving and advice taking to stop at the center aisle. Personal friendships are another factor affecting patterns of consultation. All other things being equal, senators with wide acquaintanceships and warm relations with numerous colleagues are sought out for advice more often than the others, and advice giving and taking tend to flow along lines drawn by social compatibility. This is not as nonrational as it at first appears to be. Friendship is a means of assuring oneself that the other fellow has your interests at heart. Just as the lobbyists complain that they "can't pressure a friend," so senators are not likely to "double" a colleague whom they enjoy having around.

The Senate should not be visualized as a homogeneous body, but as a cluster of specialists, each with his own following. Within their areas of competence these specialists possess considerable influence, but the area of competence of most senators is limited to one or a few policy areas. In most areas of policy, the senators can choose between several competing specialists with somewhat different points of view. Much advice giving and advice taking is reciprocal: Senator "A" advises Senator "B" on labor bills while "B" advises "A" on agricultural matters. Thus are many of the senators bound together in an endless web of interdependence.

All of this does not mean that some senators are not more powerful than others. Occasionally a senator possesses such prestige that his advice is sought on all kinds of issues, as for example was the case with Taft and George toward the end of their Senate careers. Some specialists have far larger followings than others. On some highly esoteric and relatively unimportant matters, virtually the entire Senate may rely upon the judgment of one or two men, while in others—agriculture is a good example—specialists abound.

Nor does it mean that the formal organization of the Senate, in particular its party and committee organization, is insignificant. If the senators' informal but intricate patterns of advice giving and advice taking were mapped in all their fascinating detail, we would find a very considerable correspondence between them and the lines of formal authority. On the whole, the findings of this book agree with David Truman's conclusion that the "real" leaders of the Senate are, for the most part, those in positions of formal authority.[13] But a look at patterns of advice giving and advice taking in the Senate suggests the processes by which formal authority is translated into actual influence and how these processes are perceived by the actors themselves. It

13. D. B. Truman, *The Congressional Party: A Case Study* (New York: John Wiley and Sons, 1959), p. 285 and *passim*.

also helps explain how and why and in what directions departures from the formal lines of authority occur.

Probable Outcomes and the Vote

Occasionally the result of a roll call is a surprise, but usually the predictions made by floor managers and party leaders are quite accurate. Moreover, if a senator is in doubt concerning the likely outcome of a roll call, he need merely withhold his vote the first time his name is called, quickly tally the votes of his colleagues, and then finally cast his vote when his name is called a second time. Even from the galleries a reasonably astute observer cannot help but see members of the Senate do this on important and reasonably close roll calls. In this way, senators frequently know the probable outcome of the roll call before they cast their votes.

This fact has a very real impact on how senators vote, especially the late-deciding nonspecialists. If the conclusion of a vote is foreordained, an uncommitted senator is more likely to vote what he conceives to be the expedient way than when he believes that his vote might make a difference in the legislative outcome. When caught, for example, between the blandishments of his floor leader and the demands of a fairly significant group in his constituency, a senator will often make a conditional commitment to one side or the other: "If you need my vote to win, I'll vote with you." The same kind of "deal" can be made with him when his personal preferences diverge from the apparently politically profitable course.

The fact that the probable outcome of most votes is known has another, and sometimes countervailing, consequence. Senate folkways, as we have already seen, discourage "grandstanding" actions purely for their political effects. One manifestation of grandstanding is an uncompromising attitude on issues, an unwillingness to "go along." As a result, there is a decided bandwagon effect in Senate voting. Look, for example, at Figure 30, which shows the number of senators voting on the losing side in all nonunanimous roll calls held during the Eighty-third and Eighty-fourth Congresses. Obviously most nonunanimous roll calls are won by relatively slim margins; the losing side is usually quite large. Roll calls in which a small number of senators hold out against the preferences of the overwhelming majority of their colleagues are relatively infrequent occurrences.

Some senators obviously do vote against the preferences of a vast majority of their colleagues from time to time. The frequency with which individual senators do this varies widely. In Figure 31, the

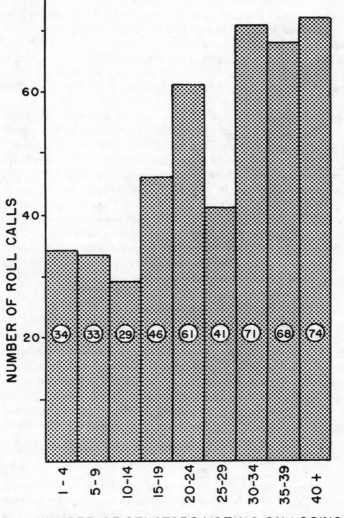

FIG. 30. Number Voting on Losing Side, All Non-Unanimous Roll Calls, 83rd and 84th Congresses

number of times individual senators voted with small minorities against the rest of their colleagues is presented. More than half of the senators who served during the entire four-year period did not once vote with a minority of five or less. On the other hand, Senator Langer (Rep., N.D.) held out against the overwhelming sentiment of the chamber nine times. Senator Malone (Rep., Nev.) voted with small minorities seven times; Senators Lehman (Dem., N.Y.) and Morse (Dem., Ore.), five times; Senators McCarthy (Rep., Wisc.), Williams (Rep., Del.), and McCarran (Dem., Nev.) four times. The bandwagon effect obviously is more compelling to some senators than to others.

What characterizes the senators who do not jump on the bandwagon as often as the ordinary senator? Party affiliation, ideological position, constituency characteristics, apparently are not much involved. Personality factors may have a great deal to do with it, but we are unable to examine the possibility with sufficient rigor to be sure. The most reasonable conjecture is that those least affected by the bandwagon psychology place an unusually low value on the approval of their legislative peers. If this is true, we would expect that those senators who frequently vote with small minorities fail to conform to the Senate folkways. Table 62 shows, rather conclusively, that this is indeed the case. Those who frequently vote with small minorities speak more on the Senate floor and specialize less. They are far less "effective" as legislators.

Thus, to recapitulate briefly, the senators' estimates of the probable outcome of roll call votes sometimes affect their voting decision. If the vote is expected to be very close, their own beliefs as to what is right are likely to be more important than when the vote is obviously going to be very lopsided. For the thoroughly socialized senator, the bandwagon effect takes over at some point as the probable vote becomes more uneven, and he votes on the winning side at least in part because everyone else has. The bandwagon effect, however, does not influence the nonconformist senator as much as those who respect and live up to the Senate folkways.

FOUR BELLS 'TIL JANUARY

As midsummer approaches, the temper and tempo of the Senate changes. After six or seven months of regular sessions, the senators begin to lose patience with one another and with the almost endless frustrations, pressures, and insecurities of their job. Tired, they begin to hanker for travel, or for the seashore, a lake, a mountainside. In

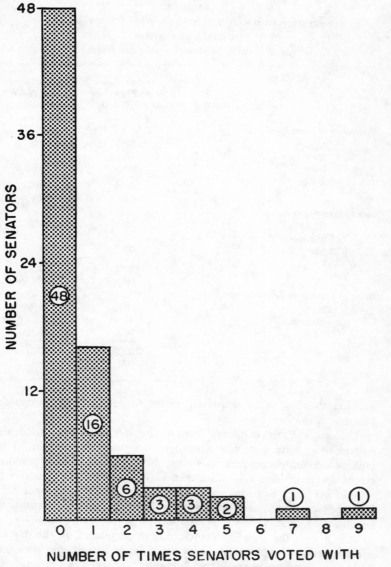

FIG. 31. Frequency Individual Senators Voted in Small Minorities (5 or Less), 83rd and 84th Congresses

Table 62

CONFORMITY TO SENATE FOLKWAYS AND FREQUENCY OF VOTING
IN SMALL MINORITIES

(all roll calls, 83rd and 84th Congresses)

	Senators Voting More Than Once With Minority of 5 or Less	Senators Voting Once or Never With Minority of 5 or Less
Frequency of Floor Speaking		
High	33%	9%
Medium	47	36
Low	20	55
	100%	100%
	(15)	(66)
Index of Specialization		
High	7%	19%
Medium	33	36
Low	60	45
	100%	100%
	(15)	(66)
Index of Legislative Effectiveness		
High	0%	14%
Medium	47	60
Low	53	26
	100%	100%
	(15)	(66)

an election year, many desperately want to get home to campaign before it is too late.

Under these circumstances, compromise is easier. Bills suddenly emerge from committees where they have languished for months. The bulk of the committee work now over, the convening of daily sessions creeps up from noon to 11 A.M., then to 10 A.M., and often runs well into the evening. Saturday sessions are held with increasing regularity. Bills are passed with ever more speed. The preadjournment rush has begun.

Along with the speed-up comes endless speculation on the day of adjournment. Finally, the majority leader, after consultation with the senators, the speaker of the House, and others, announces a target date.

As the final days arrive, the senators' efforts to get everything done become almost frantic. Some of those who fear that their pet projects may be overlooked in the rush hint that they will "talk at some length" if the matter is not attended to. Then come the inevitable congratulatory and sentimental close-of-session speeches. On the last night, there is likely to be a little horseplay. Finally, most often in the small hours of the morning, it is over. The Senate bell—used to summon members to the chamber for the beginning of daily sessions, quorum calls, roll calls, and the like—rings out four times. The Senate has adjourned *sine die*. Within a few days, virtually all of the senators will have gone. If it is an election year, not all of them will return, at least not as senators.

But the following January the Capitol, abandoned for several months to the tourists, comes to life again. The senators reappear. Along with them come the throngs of journalists, lobbyists, staff assistants, and administrators who live on the fringe of power. Desks, filing cabinets, chairs, and other pieces of office equipment are busily reshuffled in the Senate Office Building as the defeated move out, the old timers move up to better offices, and the newcomers move into whatever is left. The bell rings again. The Senate goes on.

APPENDIX A

United States Senators, January 3, 1947, to January 3, 1957

	Period of Service				
	80th Congress 1947-49	81st Congress 1949-51	82nd Congress 1951-53	83rd Congress 1953-55	84th Congress 1955-57
Alabama					
Hill, Lister (Dem.)	x	x	x	x	x
Sparkman, John J. (Dem.)	x	x	x	x	x
Arizona					
Hayden, Carl (Dem.)	x	x	x	x	x
McFarland, Ernest W. (Dem.)	x	x	x		
Goldwater, Barry (Rep.)				x	x
Arkansas					
McClellan, John L. (Dem.)	x	x	x	x	x
Fulbright, J. W. (Dem.)	x	x	x	x	x
California					
Downey, Sheridan (Dem.)	x	x			
Knowland, William F. (Rep.)	x	x	x	x	x
Nixon, Richard M. (Rep.)			x		
Kuchel, Thomas H. (Rep.)				x	x
Colorado					
Johnson, Edwin C. (Dem.)	x	x	x	x	
Millikin, Eugene D. (Rep.)	x	x	x	x	x
Allott, Gordon (Rep.)					x
Connecticut					
McMahon, Brien (Dem.)	x	x	x		
Baldwin, Raymond E. (Rep.)	x	x			
Benton, William (Dem.)		x	x		

	Period of Service				
	80th Congress *1947-49*	*81st* Congress *1949-51*	*82nd* Congress *1951-53*	*83rd* Congress *1953-55*	*84th* Congress *1955-57*
Bush, Prescott (Rep.)				x	x
Purtell, William A. (Rep.)				x	x
Delaware					
Buck, C. Douglass (Rep.)	x				
Williams, John J. (Rep.)	x	x	x	x	x
Frear, J. Allen, Jr. (Dem.)		x	x	x	x
Florida					
Pepper, Claude (Dem.)	x	x			
Holland, Spessard L. (Dem.)	x	x	x	x	x
Smathers, George A. (Dem.)			x	x	x
Georgia					
George, Walter F. (Dem.)	x	x	x	x	x
Russell, Richard B. (Dem.)	x	x	x	x	x
Idaho					
Taylor, Glen H. (Dem.)	x	x			
Dworshak, Henry C. (Rep.)	x	x	x	x	x
Miller, Bert H. (Dem.)		x			
Welker, Herman (Rep.)			x	x	x
Illinois					
Brooks, C. Wayland (Rep.)	x				
Lucas, Scott W. (Dem.)	x	x			
Douglas, Paul H. (Dem.)		x	x	x	x
Dirksen, Everett M. (Rep.)			x	x	x
Indiana					
Capehart, Homer E. (Rep.)	x	x	x	x	x
Jenner, William E. (Rep.)	x	x	x	x	x
Iowa					
Wilson, George A. (Rep.)	x				
Hickenlooper, Bourke B. (Rep.)	x	x	x	x	x
Gillette, Guy M. (Dem.)		x	x	x	
Martin, Thomas, E. (Rep.)					x
Kansas					
Capper, Arthur (Rep.)	x				
Reed, Clyde M. (Rep.)	x	x			
Schoeppel, Andrew F. (Rep.)		x	x	x	x
Darby, Harry (Rep.)		x			
Carlson, Frank (Rep.)			x	x	x
Kentucky					
Barkley, Alben W. (Dem.)	x				x
Cooper, John Sherman (Rep.)	x			x	
Withers, Garrett L. (Dem.)		x			
Chapman, Virgil (Dem.)		x			
Clements, Earle C. (Dem.)			x	x	x
Underwood, Thomas R. (Dem.)			x		
Humphreys, Robert (Dem.)					x

	80th Congress 1947-49	81st Congress 1949-51	82nd Congress 1951-53	83rd Congress 1953-55	84th Congress 1955-57
Louisiana					
Ellender, Allen J., Sr. (Dem.)	x	x	x	x	x
Overton, John H. (Dem.)	x				
Feazel, William C. (Dem.)	x				
Long, Russell B. (Dem.)		x	x	x	x
Maine					
White, Wallace H. (Rep.)	x				
Brewster, Owen (Rep.)	x	x	x		
Smith, Margaret Chase (Rep.)		x	x	x	x
Payne, Frederick G. (Rep.)				x	x
Maryland					
Tydings, Millard E. (Dem.)	x	x			
O'Conor, Herbert R. (Dem.)	x	x	x		
Butler, John Marshall (Rep.)			x	x	x
Beall, J. Glenn (Rep.)				x	x
Massachusetts					
Saltonstall, Leverett (Rep.)	x	x	x	x	x
Lodge, Henry Cabot, Jr. (Rep.)	x	x	x		
Kennedy, John F. (Dem.)				x	x
Michigan					
Vandenberg, Arthur H. (Rep.)	x	x	x		
Ferguson, Homer (Rep.)	x	x	x	x	
Moody, Blair (Dem.)			x		
Potter, Charles E. (Rep.)				x	x
McNamara, Patrick (Dem.)					x
Minnesota					
Ball, Joseph H. (Rep.)	x				
Thye, Edward J. (Rep.)	x	x	x	x	x
Humphrey, Hubert H. (Dem.)		x	x	x	x
Mississippi					
Bilbo, Theodore G. (Dem.)	x				
Eastland, James O. (Dem.)	x	x	x	x	x
Stennis, John (Dem.)	x	x	x	x	x
Missouri					
Donnell, Forest C. (Rep.)	x	x			
Kem, James P. (Rep.)	x	x	x		
Hennings, Thomas C., Jr. (Dem.)			x	x	x
Symington, Stuart (Dem.)				x	x
Montana					
Murray, James E. (Dem.)	x	x	x	x	x
Ecton, Zales N. (Rep.)	x	x	x		
Mansfield, Mike (Dem.)				x	x
Nebraska					
Butler, Hugh (Rep.)	x	x	x	x	
Wherry, Kenneth S. (Rep.)	x	x	x		

	Period of Service				
	80th Congress 1947-49	81st Congress 1949-51	82nd Congress 1951-53	83rd Congress 1953-55	84th Congress 1955-57
Seaton, Fred A. (Rep.)			x		
Griswold, Dwight P. (Rep.)				x	
Bowring, Eva (Rep.)				x	
Reynolds, Sam W. (Rep.)				x	
Abel, Hazel (Rep.)				x	
Hruska, Roman L. (Rep.)					x
Curtis, Carl T. (Rep.)					x
Nevada					
McCarran, Pat (Dem.)	x	x	x	x	
Malone, George W. (Rep.)	x	x	x	x	x
Brown, Ernest S. (Rep.)				x	
Bible, Alan (Dem.)					x
New Hampshire					
Bridges, Styles (Rep.)	x	x	x	x	x
Tobey, Charles W. (Rep.)	x	x	x	x	
Upton, Robert W. (Rep.)				x	
Cotton, Norris (Rep.)					x
New Jersey					
Hawkes, Albert H. (Rep.)	x				
Smith, H. Alexander (Rep.)	x	x	x	x	x
Hendrickson, Robert C. (Rep.)		x	x	x	
Case, Clifford P. (Rep.)					x
New Mexico					
Chavez, Dennis (Dem.)	x	x	x	x	x
Hatch, Carl A. (Dem.)	x				
Anderson, Clinton P. (Dem.)		x	x		x
New York					
Wagner, Robert F. (Dem.)	x	x			
Ives, Irving M. (Rep.)	x	x	x	x	x
Dulles, John Foster (Rep.)		x			
Lehman, Herbert H. (Dem.)		x	x	x	x
North Carolina					
Hoey, Clyde R. (Dem.)	x	x	x	x	
Umstead, William B. (Dem.)	x				
Broughton, J. Melville (Dem.)		x			
Graham, Frank P. (Dem.)		x			
Smith, Willis (Dem.)			x	x	
Ervin, Sam J. (Dem.)				x	x
Lennon, Alton A. (Dem.)				x	
Scott, W. Kerr (Dem.)					x
North Dakota					
Langer, William (Rep.)	x	x	x	x	x
Young, Milton R. (Rep.)	x	x	x	x	x
Ohio					
Taft, Robert A. (Rep.)	x	x	x	x	

	Period of Service				
	80th Congress 1947-49	81st Congress 1949-51	82nd Congress 1951-53	83rd Congress 1953-55	84th Congress 1955-57
Bricker, John W. (Rep.)	x	x	x	x	x
Burke, Thomas A. (Dem.)				x	
Bender, George H. (Rep.)					x
Oklahoma					
Moore, E. H. (Rep.)	x				
Thomas, Elmer (Dem.)	x	x			
Kerr, Robert S. (Dem.)		x	x	x	x
Monrony, A. S. Mike (Dem.)			x	x	x
Oregon					
Morse, Wayne (Rep.-Ind.-Dem.)	x	x	x	x	x
Cordon, Guy (Rep.)	x	x	x	x	
Neuberger, Richard L. (Dem.)					x
Pennsylvania					
Myers, Francis J. (Dem.)	x	x			
Martin, Edward (Rep.)	x	x	x	x	x
Duff, James H. (Rep.)			x	x	x
Rhode Island					
Green, Theodore Francis (Dem.)	x	x	x	x	x
McGrath, J. Howard (Dem.)	x	x			
Leahy, Edward L. (Dem.)		x			
Pastore, John O. (Dem.)			x	x	x
South Carolina					
Maybank, Burnet R. (Dem.)	x	x	x	x	
Johnston, Olin D. (Dem.)	x	x	x	x	x
Daniel, Charles E. (Dem.)					x
Thurmond, Strom (Dem.)					x
Wofford, Thomas A. (Dem.)					x
South Dakota					
Bushfield, Harlan J. (Rep.)	x				
Gurney, Chan (Rep.)	x	x			
Mundt, Karl E. (Rep.)		x	x	x	x
Case, Francis (Rep.)			x	x	x
Tennessee					
McKellar, Kenneth (Dem.)	x	x	x		
Stewart, Tom (Dem.)	x				
Kefauver, Estes (Dem.)		x	x	x	x
Gore, Albert (Dem.)				x	x
Texas					
Connally, Tom (Dem.)	x	x	x		
O'Daniel, W. Lee (Dem.)	x				
Johnson, Lyndon B. (Dem.)		x	x	x	x
Daniel, Price (Dem.)				x	x
Utah					
Thomas, Elbert (Dem.)	x	x			
Watkins, Arthur V. (Rep.)	x	x	x	x	x
Bennett, Wallace F. (Rep.)			x	x	x

	80th Congress 1947-49	81st Congress 1949-51	82nd Congress 1951-53	83rd Congress 1953-55	84th Congress 1955-57
Vermont					
Aiken, George D. (Rep.)	x	x	x	x	x
Flanders, Ralph E. (Rep.)	x	x	x	x	x
Virginia					
Byrd, Harry Flood (Dem.)	x	x	x	x	x
Robertson, A. Willis (Dem.)	x	x	x	x	x
Washington					
Magnuson, Warren G. (Dem.)	x	x	x	x	x
Cain, Harry P. (Rep.)	x	x	x		
Jackson, Henry M. (Dem.)				x	x
West Virginia					
Kilgore, Harley M. (Dem.)	x	x	x	x	x
Revercomb, Chapman (Rep.)	x				
Neely, Matthew M. (Dem.)		x	x	x	x
Laird, William R., III (Dem.)					x
Wisconsin					
Wiley, Alexander (Rep.)	x	x	x	x	x
McCarthy, Joseph R. (Rep.)	x	x	x	x	x
Wyoming					
O'Mahoney, Joseph C. (Dem.)	x	x	x		x
Robertson, Edward V. (Rep.)	x				
Hunt, Lester C. (Dem.)		x	x	x	
Barrett, Frank A. (Rep.)				x	x
Crippa, Edward D. (Rep.)				x	

NOTES: The above does not distinguish between those who served for a part or an entire two-year Congress. It is therefore possible for more than two men to have served n the Senate during the same Congress.

Senators sworn in between the date of their election and the beginning of a new Congress the following January are shown as serving from the later date. This practice provides an excellent way for a senator to gain a seniority edge over other senators elected at the same time. Since the Senate is rarely in session between November and January, the "service" involved can safely be ignored for our purposes.

Vera Bushfield (Rep.) of South Dakota was appointed to fill the vacancy caused by her husband's death during the Eightieth Congress. She did not choose to serve and was never officially sworn. Thus she has been omitted. Theodore Bilbo (Dem.) of Mississippi presents a slightly different case. Re-elected to the Eightieth Congress, opposition to seating him was so strong that he was not immediately sworn. He died a few months later, before he was officially sworn. Since he had been sworn in as a United States Senator before, he was included.

Senator Morse of Oregon was a Republican during the Eightieth, Eighty-first, and Eighty-second Congresses, an Independent during the Eighty-third Congress, and a Democrat during the Eighty-fourth Congress.

SOURCES: *Congressional Directory* (Washington: Government Printing Office, 1947-57); *Senate Manual* (Washington: Government Printing Office, 1955), pp. 595-659.

APPENDIX B

Sources of Biographical Information

The *Congressional Directory* (Washington: Government Printing Office, 1809——); *The Biographical Directory of the American Congress, 1774-1949* (Washington: Government Printing Office, 1950); *Who's Who in America* (Chicago: A. N. Marquis, 1899——); the *National Cyclopaedia of American Biography* (New York: J. T. White, 1916-46); and *Current Biography* (New York: H. W. Wilson, 1940——) were consulted for biographical information on each of the 180 subjects. In some cases, all the biographical material needed was obtained from these five sources.

In most cases, however, a further search had to be made. Specialized biographical directories such as *Who's Who in United States Politics* (Chicago: Capitol House, 1950——); *Who Was Who in America* (Chicago: A. N. Marquis, 1943——); *Who's Who in Law* (New York: J. C. Schwarz, 1937——); *Poor's Register of Directors and Executives* (New York: Poor's, 1925——); *Who's Who in Commerce and Industry* (New York: Institute for Research in Biography, 1936——) were consulted next. (An excellent check list of these may be found in H. D. Lasswell, D. Lerner and C. E. Rothwell, *The Comparative Study of Elites* [Stanford: Hoover Institute Studies], Series B, Number 1, pp. 70-72.) While most libraries possess the well-known biographical directories, they vary widely in their holdings of those which are less famous and more specialized. At one time or another, the directory holdings of the libraries of Princeton University, Smith College, Columbia University, the New York Public Library, and Library of Congress were employed. The clipping files of the Legislative Reference Service, Library of Congress, proved of great value. (The biographical clippings of this organization are no longer open to scholars.) Biographical articles appearing in the popular press and in recent books were canvassed. They are indexed in the *Biography Index* (New York: Wilson, 1946——).

If all these sources failed to supply the requisite information—and unfortunately it was usually a matter of feast or famine—a personal letter to the editor of the newspaper in the senator's home town often uncovered the missing facts. [The names and addresses were obtained from *Ayer's Directory of Newspapers and Periodicals* (Philadelphia: N. W. Ayers, 1950).] The willingness of the press, especially in the smaller cities and towns, to answer such queries was one of the pleasant surprises connected with writing this book.

As a last resort, a letter was sent to the senator, or a visit was made to his office if he still lived in Washington.

Some of these sources suppress information considered to be unfavorable or politically embarrassing. Inconsistencies, both within individual sources and between the life-histories contained by different sources, were frequent enough to dictate caution in their use. In order to guard against possible error, all facts were checked by reference to several different sources. Greater weight was assigned to the contents of sources which were not determined by the senators themselves.

The data was entered on a separate biographical form for each senator. Once data collection was completed, this information was coded and transferred to five-by-eight-inch cards for hand sorting and analysis.

APPENDIX C

Interviewing Procedures

Most of the interviews used in this book were conducted in Washington between January and September of 1956. A few follow-up interviews were held during 1958.

In all, 109 formal interviews were held. Twenty-five of these were with senators, either incumbents or men who had served in the Senate during the 1947-57 period. Sixty-two interviews were held with Capitol Hill staff members, fourteen with lobbyists, and eight with journalists. The interviews varied in length from about twenty minutes to over four hours. Those with seated senators tended to be the shortest, averaging about forty minutes in length. The interviews with non-senators generally lasted about an hour to an hour and one-half. The longest interviews were held with former senators. They averaged about two hours in length.

Choice of Informants

A high level of rapport with a limited number of informants was deemed more desirable, given the exploratory nature of this study, than a highly "representative," but uncommunicative, group of respondents.

The author began by interviewing a handful of friends and contacts on various Capitol Hill staffs. These men in turn suggested other persons to be interviewed and often arranged an introduction. This grape-vine process was not permitted, however, to proceed without some guidance from the author. As the interviewing progressed, a strenuous and generally successful effort was made to interview a wide

variety of the senators, staff members, lobbyists, and journalists. A
word or two on how and why this was done is in order.

Political scientists tend to have easiest access to the "egg-heads" in
the Senate. Since they, and their staffs, are intelligent men who understand the academic mind, confining one's interviewing largely to this
group is certainly the easiest and most comfortable thing to do. In
some cases, it may even be the most profitable course. But these men
are hardly "typical" senators; they are mostly Democrats from Northern, industrial, two-party states. Often, for reasons explained in Chapter V, they do not quite "belong." Moreover, academic persons are
usually perceived on the Hill as "liberals" and "left-wingers" and treated
accordingly. To avoid possible isolation and the bias which would
result from it, special efforts were made to establish communications
with conservative Republicans and Southern Democrats during the
early stages of the interviewing program. This campaign met with
a fair degree of success. Of the twenty-five senator-interviews, ten
were with Republicans, and fifteen with Democrats. Of the Republicans interviewed, exactly half might be called "Taft Republicans,"
and half, "Eisenhower Republicans." Of the fifteen interviews with
Democratic senators, five were with Southern Democrats, and ten,
with Northerners and Westerners. Access was easiest to, and the
interviews most fruitful with, the relatively junior senators. The bias
thus introduced is at least partially compensated for by the high quality
of the interviews with former senators, most of whom had considerable
seniority before their defeat or retirement.

The largest number of interviews, sixty-two, were conducted with
Senate staff members. Forty-four of these were with members of the
senators' personal staffs, eleven with committee staff members (usually
the staff director or chief clerk), and six with members of the staffs
of the political parties. Approximately 60 per cent of these interviews
were with Democrats and 40 per cent with Republicans. The senators
were, with but one or two exceptions, approached for an interview
only after one or more members of their personal staffs had been interviewed at length. It was felt that this would save considerable time
in the necessarily short interviews with senators. It was also hoped
that this procedure might result in greater cooperation from the
senators.

The lobbyists interviewed were chosen for several different reasons.
First, an effort was made to talk with several representatives of groups
with wide-ranging legislative interests and several from groups with
very limited legislative objectives. A spread was also obtained between

groups active in different areas of policy, such as labor, business, agri-culture, and with different ideological positions. Finally, the lobbyists were also chosen because they either were attempting, or had recently attempted, to influence the actions of a senator or staff member already interviewed.

The interviews with newspapermen were divided about equally between full-time Capitol Hill reporters for large papers and press associations and the Washington correspondents for smaller papers who did much in addition to covering legislative news. Two reporters for news magazines and a radio-television commentator were also interviewed.

Thus we can see that, while the senators, staff members, lobbyists and journalists interviewed were in no sense "samples" of these groups, they were rough cross sections.

The Interviews

The interviews were of the "focused" type. No formal interview schedule or questionnaire was used. Instead, a standardized list of topics to be discussed with each type of informant was developed, committed to memory, and raised in each interview as time allowed.

The physical conditions for interviewing on Capitol Hill are not ideal. Only the senators and the lobbyists were interviewed in the privacy of their offices. It is a rare staff man, indeed, who does not share his office with several other people. Sometimes, if the senator was not in his private office, it was possible to conduct interviews with staff members there. Usually, however, the interviews with Senate staff members were held *sotto voce* in the questionable privacy of their offices, the Senate cafeteria, or the dining room. The interviews with journalists, almost all held in and around the Press Galleries, were equally lacking in privacy.

All interviews were, either explicitly or by implication, not for attribution. Notes were not taken during the course of the interview but were written up as nearly verbatim as possible immediately there-after. The raising of the same topics, usually in the same order and in nearly the same language, with each informant greatly facilitated recall.

Personal Observation and Informal Conversations

It would be a mistake to conclude that the author learned every-thing he knows about the inner workings of the Senate from these hundred-odd interviews. When not engaged in interviewing, the author sought to immerse himself completely in the world of Capitol

Hill, to see personally as much of the Senate in operation as it is possible for a single outsider to observe, and to see and feel these things as the senators did. As the author became a familiar fixture on the Hill and as the interviewing progressed, a wide acquaintanceship and a number of personal friendships were developed. Hundreds of highly informal but enlightening conversations were held with these people over lunch, a cup of coffee, during chance encounters in the corridors, and at evening social gatherings. The insights obtained in this fashion are hard to document, but they were considerable.

Nonetheless, it should be admitted that these procedures seem relatively subjective and unscientific when compared with the methods of present-day scientific survey research. But highly structured interviews with representative samples of respondents are most fruitful when variables are well identified and when all types of respondents are likely to be equally cooperative. Neither condition held in this case. This suggested that the less rigorous methods employed would be more profitable.

APPENDIX D

Statistical Indices

The major statistical indices used in this study are described below, in the order in which they are introduced in the text. Some of them have been widely used by social scientists in the past and are presented with a minimum of discussion. Others are original creations and require more extended and technical analysis.

The Index of Overrepresentation

This index was devised by students of social mobility.[1]

If senators were selected on a chance basis, we would expect their social characteristics to be the same as those possessed by the universe from which they were chosen, all Americans who meet the legal requirements for holding the office. The characteristics of this universe can be determined, with reasonable accuracy, from the United States Census and other sources. The ratio

$$\frac{\% \text{ of senators possessing attribute ``A''}}{\% \text{ of population possessing attribute ``A''}}$$

represents the index of overrepresentation. The index is also used in this book in studying the selection of Senate leaders. The same reasoning follows and the ratio then becomes:

$$\frac{\% \text{ of leaders possessing attribute ``A''}}{\% \text{ of all senators possessing attribute ``A''}}$$

1. See N. Rogoff, *Recent Trends in Occupational Mobility* (Glencoe, Illinois: Free Press, 1953).

An index smaller than 1.0 means that the attribute is underrepresented; an index of 1.0 means perfect representation; an index of 2.0 indicates twice the expected proportion, and so on.

The Index of Floor Speaking

The index of floor speaking was obtained simply by counting the number of speeches made by each senator during the Eighty-third and Eighty-fourth Congresses. The number of speeches given by senators serving during the entire four-year period ranged from 28 to 1,953. All senators who gave more than 500 speeches were ranked as high in floor speaking, those who gave from 250 to 499 speeches were ranked as medium, those giving fewer than 250 speeches were ranked as low. (Cutting points of 200 and 400 were used to distinguish between the low, medium, and high floor speakers in individual Congresses.)

Table D-1

LEVEL OF FLOOR SPEAKING AND OTHER FORMS OF FLOOR ACTIVITY
(83rd and 84th Congresses)

| Floor Speaking | Other Forms of Floor Activity* | | | | |
	1st Quartile	2nd Quartile	3rd Quartile	4th Quartile	
1st Quartile	11	8	1	0	= 20
2nd Quartile	8	6	5	1	= 20
3rd Quartile	1	6	8	5	= 20
4th Quartile	0	0	6	15	= 21
	20	20	20	21	81

* All insertions into the body or Appendix of the *Record*, motions and resolutions offered, and committee reports made by the senators.

This count includes all "remarks" listed in the index to the *Record*. Insertions in the Appendix, or editorials, letters, petitions, etc., inserted into the body of the *Record* without comment are not included. Other forms of floor activity, the offering of motions and resolutions, making of committee reports, etc., are excluded as well. It would not make a great deal of difference in the rankings if these other forms of floor activity were included. As can be seen in Table D-1, there is a high correlation between giving speeches and engaging in other activities on the floor. Since the Capitol Hill interviews suggested that actual speech-making was abhorred by the folkways more than other forms of floor activity, the less inclusive measure was used.

The limitations of this measure are obvious. It entirely ignores the length, content, and timing of speeches. A few dull, dreadfully long addresses given at inopportune moments may do more damage to a senator's intra-Senate reputation than more numerous but short and to-the-point speeches. All speeches good or bad, long or short, important or unimportant, are assigned equal weight.

The Index of Specialization

The index of specialization was computed from data in the *Congressional Quarterly Almanac* by determining the proportion of all public bills and resolutions introduced by each senator that were referred to the two committees receiving the largest number of the bills and resolutions he sponsored. (If, for example, a senator introduced fifteen bills or resolutions during the Eighty-third and Eighty-fourth Congresses and each was referred to a different committee, his score would be 2/15 or .13. If, however, seven of these bills were referred to Committee "A" and remaining eight to Committee "B," his score would be 15/15 or 1.0.) Co-sponsors were ignored, except in the case of bills and resolutions introduced jointly by two senators. The index numbers obtained ranged from .29 to .95 for the senators serving during the entire Eighty-third and Eighty-fourth Congresses. Senators with scores below .50 were considered to have low; those from .50 to .69, medium; and those above .70, high indices of specialization.

The "two highest committees" definition was adopted only after experimenting with a measure based on the proportion of bills and resolutions senators sponsored which were referred to the committees on which they served. This measure, which on the face of it seems more appropriate than the one finally decided upon, had the unfortunate characteristic of discriminating against members of the Appropriations Committee and had to be abandoned for that reason. In most cases the "two highest committees" are those on which the senator serves; thus the present index is, except, of course, for the members of the Appropriations Committee, much the same as one based upon committee membership.

This index is based on the arguable assumption that the bills and resolutions introduced by a senator adequately reflect the scope of his legislative interests. Moreover, the jurisdictions of Senate committees are sufficiently broad and overlapping that two bills on very different subjects may be referred to the same committee while two bills on similar subjects may be referred to different committees. By assigning equal weight to all bills and resolutions, the index overlooks the fact that some are more important than others.

The Index of Conservatism-Liberalism

The *New Republic* magazine publishes voting charts for each Congress in which it indicates approval or disapproval of every senator's and congressman's votes on selected roll calls. The index of conservatism-liberalism was constructed simply by dividing the total number of "liberal" votes (according to the editors of this magazine) a senator had cast by the number of the selected votes on which he took a position.[2] Pairs and announced positions were counted, issues on which the senators did not vote, pair, or announce a position were ignored. Roll call votes on foreign policy issues, while included in the *New Republic*'s ratings, were excluded from this analysis. This procedure yields a score which varies from .00 (the most "conservative" position) to 1.00 (the most "liberal" position). The details for each Congress are as follows:

Eightieth Congress (*New Republic,* September 27, 1948, p. 30)— The index was constructed on the basis of thirteen roll calls. The subjects of these votes were: the admission of Jewish displaced persons, portal-to-portal pay, Taft-Hartley Act veto, inflation, excess property tax, a general tax cut, exemption of railroads from anti-trust legislation, federal aid to education, rent control, public housing, social security, Tennessee Valley Authority, and school segregation. Senators with less than eight recorded votes were omitted.

Eighty-first Congress (*New Republic,* November 14, 1949, p. 25, and October 9, 1950, p. 15)—The index was constructed on the basis of twenty-one roll calls on the following subjects: anti-strike injunctions, Taft-Hartley Act extension, minimum wage, public power funds, aid to education, rent control (two votes), public housing (two votes), confirmation of Leland Olds, Senate cloture rule, natural-gas exemption from federal regulation, anti-trust legislation (two votes), control of Communists, Fair Employment Practices Commission, social security, increased funds for agricultural price supports, reorganization of the National Labor Relations Board, excess profits tax, price control, and racial segregation in the army. Senators with less than ten recorded votes were omitted.

Eighty-second Congress (*New Republic,* September 22, 1952, p. 17) —This index was based on ten roll calls on the following subjects:

2. For earlier uses of this index see B. R. Brimhall and A. S. Otis, "Consistency in Congressional Voting," *Journal of Applied Psychology,* XXXII (February, 1948), 1-15; N. L. Gage and B. Shimberg, "Measuring Senatorial 'Progressivism,'" *Journal of Abnormal and Social Psychology,* XXXIV (January, 1944), 112-17; S. P. Huntington, "A Revised Theory of American Politics," *American Political Science Review,* XXXXIV (September, 1950), 669-77.

meat price control, over-all price and wage controls, tax loopholes, public housing, school construction, use of federal income from off-shore oil leases for schools, reorganization of Internal Revenue Bureau, steel strike injunction, federal aid to medical schools, and a vote on the McCarran Act veto. Senators with less than six recorded votes were omitted.

Eighty-third Congress (*New Republic,* October 11, 1954, p. 20)—The index for this Congress is based on eight roll calls on the following subjects: The Saint Lawrence Seaway, farm prices, tidelands oil, Dixon-Yates controversy, public housing, tax revision, unemployment compensation, and internal communism. Senators with less than six recorded votes were omitted.

Eighty-fourth Congress (*New Republic,* October 15, 1956, p. 21)—The index was based on eight roll calls on the following subjects: an income tax cut, farm price supports, public housing, social security extension, natural-gas regulation, civilian atomic power, the censure of Senator McCarthy, and Hells Canyon dam. Senators with less than six recorded votes were omitted.

The index of conservatism-liberalism is obviously dependent upon the subjective judgment of the editors of the magazine. Both their selection of issues and their evaluation of one side as "liberal" and the other as "conservative" can, at times, be challenged. The magazine, however, is a widely acknowledged and responsible spokesman of the "liberal" point of view. It is the author's belief that the rankings obtained would have been much the same if they had been made by an organization of a different political persuasion.

Perhaps a more serious difficulty is that an index such as this one tends to be multi-dimensional.[3] A senator may be very "liberal" on some kinds of issues (i.e., labor relations) but quite "conservative" on others (i.e., race relations). By lumping the senators' votes on many different types of issues together, a great deal is lost. Foreign policy votes were excluded from the index in the hope that this would mitigate the common failing of indices such as this one. It seems likely that this maneuver did not entirely solve the problem. Certainly Guttman scaling would have resulted in purer measures than the technique adopted here.[4] For an exploratory study of this type, how-

3. D. MacRae, Jr., "Some Underlying Variables in Legislative Roll Calls," *Public Opinion Quarterly,* XVIII (Summer, 1954), 193 ff.

4. See D. MacRae, Jr., *Dimensions of Congressional Voting* (Berkeley and Los Angeles: University of California Press, 1958); G. M. Belknap, "A Study of Senatorial Voting by Scale Analysis" (Ph.D. dissertation, University of Chicago, 1951); H. D. Price, "Scale Analysis of Senate Voting Patterns, 1949-56" (Ph.D. dissertation, Harvard Uni-

ever, it seemed more desirable to use a single, relatively simple measure of the senators' ideological position than the numerous but more refined scales which the Guttman technique provides.

The index does not discriminate sharply at the ends of the ideological spectrum; a larger number of senators have scores of either .00 or 1.00 than is statistically desirable.

Finally, this index is expressed in cardinal numbers. A senator is not just a liberal, he is 86 per cent of a liberal. The assumptions underlying a cardinal index of this type are highly dubious.[5] These have been avoided as much as possible by converting the cardinal index numbers into broad categories. Thus senators with scores of .67 and above are considered liberals; those with scores between .34 and .66, moderates; and those with scores below .34, conservatives. With a single important exception discussed below, statistical manipulations requiring the use of cardinal numbers have been avoided.

The Index of Legislative Effectiveness

As was the case for the index of specialization, the data for the index of legislative effectiveness was obtained from the *Congressional Quarterly Almanac*. The index was obtained by dividing the number of bills and resolutions that a senator sponsored which passed in the Senate by the total number he introduced. Private bills were ignored, as were co-sponsorships (except in cases in which bills and resolutions were introduced jointly by two senators). The index numbers so obtained ranged from .00 to .49 for the senators who served during the entire period of the Eighty-third and Eighty-fourth Congresses. All senators with scores below .15 were considered low in effectiveness; those with scores from .15 to .34, medium; and those with scores of .35 and above were rated as high.

This measure is, of course, based on the assumption that a senator's bill-sponsoring "batting-average" is a fair index of his over-all "effectiveness" in the Senate. This assumption might be disputed on a number of grounds. First, a man might be highly "effective" in, say, his committee work but not be highly successful in shepherding his own bills through the legislative machinery. It is the author's impression that this is a rare occurrence. Second, by weighting all bills equally, the measure gives disproportionate weight to minor pieces of legislation. It is precisely on this kind of measure that a senator's standing with his colleagues is important in getting legislative results.

versity, 1958); C. D. Farris, "A Method for Determining Ideological Groupings in the Congress," *Journal of Politics*, XX (May, 1958), 308-38.

5. See Price, "Scale Analysis of Senate Voting Patterns, 1949-56," Ch. 1.

Third, the measure ignores the fact that many bills and resolutions are not expected to pass by the sponsors who take little if any action in their behalf. But senators who habitually introduce bills with no intention of their passing differ from those who introduce bills only when they intend to see them through. The first type of senator is concerned with the propaganda consequences of his actions outside the chamber. The latter's actions are directed toward direct legislative pay-offs. Legislative "effectiveness" as used in this study should not, therefore, be confused with over-all political influence. Some men with considerable influence on public opinion were quite ineffective as legislators, narrowly defined.

At this author's suggestion, Warren Hollinshead, "Influence Within the United States Senate" (A.B. thesis, Amherst College, 1957) checked the index of legislative effectiveness scores of members of the Eighty-third and Eighty-fourth Congresses against "influence" rankings obtained through interviews with a panel of legislative assistants to senators. The correlation between the two measures was very high.

The Index of Party Unity

This index is one of many measures of party unity and regularity that have been devised since A. Lawrence Lowell's, "The Influence of Party upon Legislation in England and America," *Annual Report of the American Historical Association for 1901* (Washington, 1902), I, 321-544. Party unity scores for individual senators have been figured by the *Congressional Quarterly Almanac* and are therein available for each session during the postwar decade. They show the proportion of the time, when he took a stand, that a senator voted with a majority of his party on roll calls in which a majority of the Republicans voted against a majority of the Democrats. Both actual votes and public announcements (including pairs and answers to the *CQ* poll) were counted during the Eightieth through Eighty-third Congresses. Unfortunately for our purposes, the *Congressional Quarterly Almanac* changed its definition of a party-unity vote during the Eighty-fourth Congress to include actual votes only. Because of inevitable absences, this results in a drop off in the senators' party-unity scores of several points and makes comparison between this Congress and the earlier ones impossible. Comparisons between the Republicans and Democrats during the Eighty-fourth Congress can, of course, still be made.

The index, by definition, tends to yield a distribution of scores skewed toward party regularity. It discriminates best at the low end of the scale while it lumps together a large number of party members

near the top without differentiating degrees of party loyalty between
them. This weakness is less noticeable for some other measures of
party unity, although most of these suffer from other statistical limitations. This measure was adopted in this study because of the ease
with which it is understood and its availability.

The Index of Party Effort

The index of party effort was computed in the following manner.
First, a scatter diagram was made for each Congress and each party,
plotting the senators' conservatism-liberalism scores along the "x" axis
and party-unity scores along the "y" axis. Then the equation of the
line of regression was computed. Since the senators' conservatism-
liberalism scores were known it was then a simple matter to determine
from the equation what their party-unity score would be if they were
normal partisans.[6] The difference between a senator's expected party
score and his actual score (the distance between his position on the
scatter diagram and the line of regression) is his index of party effort.
All senators whose actual party-unity scores were four points or more
higher than expected were classified as having high party-effort scores;
those whose actual party-unity scores were within three points of the
expected value were classified as having average indices of party effort;
those whose party-unity scores were four points or more below the
expected value were classified as having low party-effort scores.

This index can be no better than the measures of the two variables
involved—party unity and conservatism-liberalism. Both have their
limitations as we have already indicated.

Another difficulty is that in order to use this approach, the two variables must be measured by cardinal numbers. One cannot compute
a line of regression using rankings, ordinal numbers, or broad categories. We have already questioned the desirability of treating our
indices in this way. A more conservative statistical procedure would
have been merely to cross-tabulate conservatism-liberalism scores and
party-unity scores, dispensing with the scatter diagrams and lines of
regression altogether. The trouble with this approach is twofold: no
adequate measure of central tendency exists; and the very small number of cases requires the use of such gross categories in cross-tabulation
that they largely smother the variations of senators above and below
the party-unity norm.

6. See V. O. Key, *A Primer of Statistics for Political Scientists* (New York: Thomas Y.
Crowell Company, 1954), pp. 74 ff. for a more extended treatment of scatter-diagrams
and lines of regressions than it is possible to present here.

The Index of Administration Support

This index was also obtained from the *Congressional Quarterly Almanac* which publishes the percentage of the time individual senators vote in favor of the president's legislative requests. All those supporting 80 per cent or more of the president's proposals were considered high in administration support; those supporting from 60 to 79 per cent, medium; and those supporting the administration less than 60 per cent of the time were rated as low in administration support.

The Index of Cohesion

This index, originated by S. A. Rice, *Quantitative Methods in Politics* (New York: Alfred A. Knopf, 1928), pp. 208-9, has been very widely used by political scientists as a measure of the relative unity of legislative parties and other groups. Arithmetically, it is merely the difference, within a group, between the percentage voting for and percentage voting against a given motion. A fifty-fifty split (a total lack of agreement) is represented by an index of zero, and a unanimous group receives an index of one hundred.

The probability assumptions underlying this index have been challenged,[7] but it remains a conventional and generally accepted statistical measure.

Index Construction and Tests of Statistical Significance

As the above indicates, the author has no illusions that the statistical indices used in this study are perfect. At best, and this is true of all statistical indices and not just those used in this book, they are but approximate measures of the variables they seek to represent.

These distortions and limitations of indices cannot be overcome no matter how many tests for statistical significance are computed. Indeed such significance tests can be very misleading. It is possible, for example, for a researcher to find a statistically significant relationship between two indices, but, because of the crudities of these indices, this does not necessarily demonstrate such a relationship between the two variables which the indices purport to measure. Of course, the opposite is true as well. For this, as well as other reasons,[8] tests of significance have not been used in this study.

7. W. E. Miller, "A Study of Some Statistical Techniques for Investigating Legislative Voting Behavior" (Master's thesis, University of Oregon, 1950).

8. See S. M. Lipset *et al.*, *Union Democracy* (Glencoe, Illinois: Free Press, 1956), pp. 427-32, for an excellent discussion.

APPENDIX E

Supplementary Tables

This appendix contains tables of substantial interest to students of legislative behavior but inappropriate for inclusion in the text.

Table E-1

OCCUPATIONS, BY STAGE IN CAREER

	First Nonpolitical, Full-time Job after Completion of Schooling	Principal Nonpolitical Occupation	Occupation at First Election/ Appointment to Senate
Professional			
Political Official	...	...	102
Lawyer	88	97	38
Teacher	13	1	0
Journalist	12	6	2
Professor	5	7	4
Engineer	3	1	1
Civil Servant	3	1	1
Pharmacist	2	0	0
Missionary	1	0	0
Dentist	1	1	0
Proprietor and Official			
Merchant	6	11	6
Manufacturing Executive	5	9	5
Other Executive	4	4	1
Publisher	3	10	5
Insurance-Real Estate Agent	1	7	0
Construction Contractor	1	3	3
Oil-Gas Producer	1	5	4
Banker	0	4	3

	First Nonpolitical, Full-time Job after Completion of Schooling	Principal Nonpolitical Occupation	Occupation at First Election/ Appointment to Senate
Farmer	8	13	4
Low Salaried Worker			
Clerk	8	0	0
Salesman	4	0	0
Industrial Wage Earner			
Printer	3	0	0
Laborer	2	0	0
Electrician	1	0	0
Machinist	1	0	0
Pipefitter	1	0	0
Factory Worker	1	0	1
Servant	0	0	0
Farm Laborer	1	0	0
Unknown	1	0	0
TOTALS	180	180	180

Table E-2

ALL PUBLIC OFFICES HELD BEFORE ELECTION/APPOINTMENT

Type of Office	Democrats	Republicans	All
Governor	7%	11%	9%
U.S. Representative	12	9	11
State Legislator	15	18	17
Statewide Elective Office	3	3	3
Local Elective Office	7	11	9
Law-enforcement Office	32	20	26
Administrative Office	22	25	23
Congressional Staff	1	3	2
	100% (276)	100% (219)	100% (495)

Table E-3
CHARACTERISTICS OF DIFFERENT CAREER TYPES

	Professional Politicians (n-98)	Patrician Politicians (n-13)	Amateur Politicians (n-60)	Agitators (n-8)
Fathers' Occupational Class				
Professional	17%	85%	23%	25%
Proprietor & Official	31	15	51	12
Farmer	44	0	19	38
All lower classes	8	0	7	25
	100%	100%	100%	100%
Relatives in Politics				
Father	11%	54%	8%	50%
Other relative	9	46	17	0
None	80	0	75	50
	100%	100%	100%	100%
Principal Occupation				
Lawyer	64%	62%	33%	75%
Professor	1	0	10	0
Businessman	21	23	45	25
Farmer	10	0	5	0
Other professional	4	15	7	0
	100%	100%	100%	100%
Age at First Public Office				
20-29	59%	85%	17%	50%
30-39	36	15	25	25
40-49	5	0	31	25
50 and over	0	0	27	0
	100%	100%	100%	100%
First Public Office				
U.S. Senator	0%	0%	27%	12%
Governor	1	0	3	0
U.S. Representative	3	8	3	0
State Legislator	25	46	13	0
Statewide Elective Officer	2	0	0	0
Local Elective Officer	17	23	8	0
Law Enforcement Officer	38	8	17	63
Administrative Officer	10	8	27	25
Congressional Staff	3	8	2	0
Unclassified	1	0	0	0
	100%	100%	100%	100%

TABLE E-3 (cont.)

	Professional Politicians (98)	Patrician Politicians (13)	Amateur Politicians (60)	Agitators (8)
Age at Election to Senate				
30-39	6%	38%	7%	38%
40-49	39	38	27	25
50-59	44	23	37	25
60-69	10	0	27	12
70-79	1	0	3	0
	100%	100%	100%	100%
Last Public Office before Senator				
None	0%	0%	27%	12.5%
Governor	24	23	17	12.5
U.S. Representative	37	38	7	12.5
State Legislator	8	23	8	0
Statewide Elective Officer	2	0	0	0
Local Elective Officer	3	0	8	12.5
Law Enforcement Officer	19	8	8	38
Administrative Officer	7	8	23	12.5
Congressional Staff	0	0	2	0
	100%	100%	100%	100%
Manner in Which Senate Office Was Achieved				
Initially elected	84%	69%	67%	100%
Initially appointed	16	31	33	0
	100%	100%	100%	100%

Table E-4
PARTY AFFILIATION AND CAREER TYPES

Career Type	Northern and Western Democrats	Southern and Border Democrats	All Democrats	All Republicans	All Senators
Professionals	62%	65%	64%	45%	55%
Patricians	3	11	8	7	7
Amateurs	26	23	24	43	34
Agitators	9	2	4	5	4
	100%	100%	100%	100%	100%
	(34)	(57)	(91)	(88)	(179)

Table E-5

STATE PARTY SYSTEMS AND CAREER TYPES

Career Type	Two-Party	Modified One-Party (Senator Belongs to Stronger Party)	One-Party
Professionals	50%	69%	52%
Patricians	6	2	17
Amateurs	39	27	28
Agitators	5	2	3
	100% (97)	100% (48)	100% (29)

Table E-6

PARTY, STATE PARTY SYSTEMS, AND CAREER TYPES

Career Types	Two-Party		Modified One-Party (Senator Belongs to Stronger Party)		One-Party	
	Dem.	Repub.	Dem.	Repub.	Dem.	Repub.
Professionals	64%	40%	81%	61%	52%	50%
Patricians	5	7	0	4	18	0
Amateurs	26	48	19	31	26	50
Agitators	5	5	0	4	4	0
	100% (39)	100% (58)	100% (21)	100% (26)	100% (27)	100% (2)

Table E-7

(83rd and 84th Congresses)

	Index of Legislative Effectiveness				
	High	*Medium*	*Low*		
Last Public Office					
Governor	10%	70%	20%	100%	(20)
U.S. Representative	13%	62%	25%	100%	(24)
State Legislator	29%	43%	29%	100%	(7)
State Executive	0%	67%	33%	100%	(6)
Local Official	0%	67%	33%	100%	(6)
Judge	20%	20%	60%	100%	(5)
Federal Executive	11%	44%	44%	100%	(9)
None	0%	50%	50%	100%	(4)
Percentage Pre-Senate Adult Years in Public Office					
Under 40%	8%	51%	41%	100%	(39)
40%-60%	5%	67%	29%	100%	(21)
60% plus	24%	62%	14%	100%	(21)
Age at First Election or Appointment to Senate					
30-39	14%	64%	21%	100%	(14)
40-49	17%	48%	35%	100%	(29)
50-59	7%	63%	30%	100%	(30)
60 plus	0%	63%	37%	100%	(8)
*Political Ambitions**					
Presidential aspirants	0%	33%	67%	100%	(6)
Others	10%	62%	28%	100%	(73)
Party System in Senator's State					
Two-party	7%	59%	34%	100%	(44)
Modified one-party	6%	67%	28%	100%	(18)
One-party	26%	47%	26%	100%	(19)
Percentage Urban, Senator's State's Population (1950)					
80% plus	11%	67%	22%	100%	(9)
60%-79%	8%	44%	48%	100%	(25)
40%-59%	12%	67%	21%	100%	(33)
Less than 40%	14%	57%	29%	100%	(14)
Size of Senator's State's Population (1950)					
4 million plus	13%	53%	33%	100%	(15)
2-4 million	6%	60%	34%	100%	(35)
Less than 2 million	16%	58%	26%	100%	(31)
Ideology					
Liberals	3%	32%	65%	100%	(31)
Moderates	60%	0%	40%	100%	(10)
Conservatives	31%	40%	29%	100%	(45)

* Senators Johnson and Knowland omitted.

Table E-8

SECTIONAL DISTRIBUTION OF MEMBERS OF SENATE COMMITTEES
(80th through 84th Congresses)

Committee	New England and North Atlantic	Border	South	Great Plains	Great Lakes	Rocky Mountains	Pacific		
						Sections			
Foreign Relations	28%	10%	16%	19%	12%	10%	6%	= 100%	(38)
Appropriations	10%	12%	25%	20%	10%	15%	8%	= 100%	(31)
Finance	29%	7%	25%	11%	11%	18%	0%	= 100%	(28)
Agriculture & Forestry	8%	11%	31%	38%	4%	8%	0%	= 100%	(26)
Judiciary	10%	35%	19%	6%	10%	16%	3%	= 100%	(31)
Interstate & Foreign Commerce	31%	17%	20%	9%	9%	11%	3%	= 100%	(35)
Banking & Currency	34%	10%	14%	7%	17%	10%	7%	= 100%	(29)
Interior	7%	7%	10%	3%	55%	0%	17%	= 100%	(29)
Public Works	12%	29%	21%	9%	3%	12%	15%	= 100%	(34)
Labor & Public Welfare	25%	14%	11%	11%	18%	14%	7%	= 100%	(28)
Government Operations	21%	16%	16%	18%	18%	5%	5%	= 100%	(38)
Rules & Administration	26%	10%	10%	21%	14%	16%	2%	= 100%	(38)
Post Office & Civil Service	27%	18%	22%	16%	4%	11%	2%	= 100%	(45)
District of Columbia	25%	12%	19%	15%	4%	19%	6%	= 100%	(48)
ALL SENATORS	21%	13%	22%	14%	8%	16%	6%	= 100%	(167)

NOTE: Committee assignments of less than one year's duration omitted. The sections used here are taken from G. L. Grassmuck, *Sectional Biases in Congress on Foreign Policy* (Baltimore: Johns Hopkins University Press, 1951), Ch. 2.

Table E-9

URBAN-RURAL DISTRIBUTION OF MEMBERS OF SENATE COMMITTEES

(80th through 84th Congresses)

Committee	*Per Cent Urban, State Population in 1950*		
	80%+	*40%-79%*	*Under 40%*
Foreign Relations	16%	72%	12% = 100% (38)
Appropriations	7%	73%	20% = 100% (20)
Finance	7%	79%	14% = 100% (28)
Armed Services	10%	61%	29% = 100% (31)
Agriculture & Forestry	4%	61%	35% = 100% (26)
Judiciary	10%	55%	35% = 100% (31)
Interstate & Foreign Commerce	6%	80%	14% = 100% (35)
Banking & Currency	10%	83%	7% = 100% (29)
Interior	14%	79%	7% = 100% (29)
Public Works	6%	71%	23% = 100% (34)
Labor & Public Welfare	21%	65%	14% = 100% (28)
Government Operations	14%	65%	21% = 100% (28)
Rules & Administration	14%	72%	14% = 100% (38)
Post Office & Civil Service	9%	66%	25% = 100% (45)
District of Columbia	12%	67%	21% = 100% (48)
ALL SENATORS	11%	68%	21% = 100% (167)

NOTE: Committee assignments of less than one year's duration omitted.

Table E-10

(80th through 84th Congresses)

					Occupations		
Committees	_Lawyers_	_Business-men_	_Farmers_	_Professors_	_Other Professionals_		
Foreign Relations	59%	16%	6%	16%	4%	= 100%	(38)
Appropriations	55%	27%	12%	0%	5%	= 100%	(31)
Finance	46%	36%	11%	4%	4%	= 100%	(28)
Armed Services	55%	32%	6%	3%	3%	= 100%	(31)
Agriculture & Forestry	50%	19%	27%	4%	0%	= 100%	(26)
Judiciary	81%	6%	6%	6%	0%	= 100%	(31)
Interstate & Foreign Commerce	60%	29%	6%	0%	6%	= 100%	(35)
Banking & Currency	28%	55%	3%	10%	3%	= 100%	(29)
Interior	52%	27%	14%	0%	7%	= 100%	(29)
Public Works	50%	35%	6%	3%	6%	= 100%	(34)
Labor & Public Welfare	50%	25%	4%	14%	7%	= 100%	(28)
Government Operations	53%	26%	8%	3%	10%	= 100%	(38)
Rules & Administration	51%	29%	8%	3%	8%	= 100%	(38)
Post Office & Civil Service	56%	20%	13%	4%	7%	= 100%	(45)
District of Columbia	62%	27%	4%	2%	4%	= 100%	(48)
ALL SENATORS	54%	27%	7%	5%	7%	= 100%	(167)

NOTE: Committee assignments of less than one year's duration omitted.

Index